PRAISE FOR
TRANSFORMATIONS IN MOBILITY

T0292865

"A fascinating look at what is possible for the future of mobility when we balance innovation, travel and work trends and respect for the climate."
Martine Ferland, Chief Executive Officer, Mercer

"The mobility industry has experienced numerous disruptions in the past decades and is poised to face even more in the future. It is a pleasure to witness Gilles Roucolle sharing his invaluable insights on this sector and offering his strategic perspectives. He has a profound understanding of the global transportation industry thanks to his long-standing passion for the sector and extensive relationships network. *Transformations in Mobility* will prove to be beneficial for industry players, advisors and anyone with an interest in the field of transport and mobility."
Scott McDonald, Chief Executive, British Council

"The North American freight rail industry has been under siege lately. Gilles Roucolle presents a terrific counter to this in his exhaustive and illuminating look at the overall mobility sector. In drilling down into rail freight, he shows the importance of long-term planning and the ability to spend capital, in contrast to the stop-and-go nature that has characterized US passenger and especially potential high-speed rail. In reading this, perhaps a better future can be envisioned."
Anthony Hatch, Leading analyst of Class I Railroads in North America

"*Transformations in Mobility* delivers a remarkable and comprehensive exploration of mega-trends impacting the transport sector. While Gilles Roucolle rightfully emphasizes the significance of decarbonizing transport as a major growth opportunity for the rail industry, what truly distinguishes this book is not just his wealth of experience but also the insights and perspective provided by 30 of the most influential leaders in mobility. This combination makes it a must-read for anyone interested in this field."

Lilian Leroux, Chief Strategy and Sustainability Officer, Wabtec Corporation

"Globalization could be defined as the contraction of space and time. Therefore, transport is a key factor in the geopolitical challenges we are witnessing. Gilles Roucolle gives an insightful prospective on the challenges, including the geopolitical ones, facing the transport industry."

Pascale Boniface, Founder and Director, Institute of International and Strategic Relations (IRIS), and Professor, the Institute of European Studies at the University of Paris 8

Transformations in Mobility

Trends, disruptions and the future
of mobility and transportation

Gilles Roucolle

KoganPage

First published in Great Britain and the United States in 2024 by Kogan Page Limited

2nd Floor, 45 Gee Street
London
EC1V 3RS
United Kingdom

8 W 38th Street, Suite 902
New York, NY 10018
USA

www.koganpage.com

Kogan Page books are printed on paper from sustainable forests.

ISBNs

Hardback   978 1 3986 1587 8
Paperback   978 1 3986 1585 4
Ebook   978 1 3986 1586 1

British Library Cataloguing-in-Publication Data

A CIP record for this book is available from the British Library.

Library of Congress Control Number

2024932517

Typeset by Integra Software Services, Pondicherry
Print production managed by Jellyfish
Printed and bound by CPI Group (UK) Ltd, Croydon, CR0 4YY

*To my wife Shanar; and Thomas,
Matthieu, Nour and Nile*

CONTENTS

ABOUT THE AUTHOR

 Gilles Roucolle is Managing Partner and co-Head of the European region of Oliver Wyman, based in Paris, France, and a member of the firm's Global Leadership Team. Gilles is also a member of parent company Marsh McLennan International's Executive Committee.

For more than a decade, Gilles has been responsible for the firm's EMEA Transportation and Services practice and global Rail & Road Business. He previously served for eight years as the firm's Canada Market Leader.

He brings over 30 years' experience in high-stakes strategic and operational projects, spanning freight and passenger railways, airlines, logistics, postal and shipping, as well as rail and aerospace suppliers and financial institutions. Gilles sat for 15 years on the Business Advisory Committee of Northwestern University's Transportation Center.

He holds an MBA from INSEAD. He is also a chartered engineer with an MSc from École Centrale Paris and holds an economics degree from Paris-Sorbonne University.

FOREWORD

BY GWENDOLINE CAZENAVE, CHIEF EXECUTIVE OFFICER OF EUROSTAR GROUP

Imagine telling someone 30 years ago that in the future, taking a plane would be shameful, a long-distance train ticket would cost just €9.99 and the backbone of the Chinese transportation system would be a 40,000 km high-speed rail network. You might add that many people could live like digital nomads, doing their work from anywhere – and that those who chose to stay in the city could cross Paris in 30 minutes on an electric scooter. They likely wouldn't have believed you. But these have all come true.

Humans have always wanted to travel – but especially now. In a fragmented world, they want to connect with new people, study abroad and discover other cultures. This is a global trend, as true for Europeans (including the British, who culturally and geographically are a part of Europe) as for Americans, Asians and Africans. The vehicles and infrastructure that make mobility possible are today a major part of every landscape – urban, suburban and rural. Just as technological innovations have transformed mobility in recent decades, they will continue to do so in the future. The smartphone has become the remote control of everyday life, presenting consumers with an array of choices for different stages of their journeys and placing the traveller at the centre of the mobility industry.

However, the climate emergency means that we cannot simply continue to demand more speed and convenience without regard for the climate impact. Currently, mobility accounts for 20 per cent of carbon dioxide emissions. The challenge from now is to satisfy the innate human desire to move around, while also limiting – or eliminating – the emissions that come from travel.

Personally, I believe that rail travel can help achieve this goal in the coming decades. Rail was the technology of the industrial revolution and the growth of the American West. Since then, it has survived technological disruptions that threatened its relevance. Trains have become fast enough to make day trips possible between a growing number of major European cities, while new technology means they can frequently respond to travellers' demand for flexibility. However, rail travel will only fulfil its potential under certain conditions. To maximize its potential, in my capacity at the Eurostar Group, I believe transport ecosystems should be organized around rail travel and make it the central component of mobility. Short trips in and around cities can then be carried out by road or urban rail, and long journeys by air.

Another important step in this change is for rail to become truly international. Rail networks mostly evolved as national projects and their services are still largely domestic. But Eurostar Group is an exception, built out of two companies that pioneered international high-speed rail in the 1990s: Eurostar ran cross-Channel routes to and from London; Thalys served routes in France, Belgium, the Netherlands and Germany. In 2022 they merged to form the Eurostar Group, which is making history by building the backbone of sustainable travel in Northern Europe. Part of this vision includes enlarging stations so that they function as 'open hubs' to reach a variety of destinations. Partnerships with national railway operators will enable travellers to reach destinations all over Europe and partnerships with airline operators will facilitate long-haul trips.

While I can't speak for all modes of mobility, in my career in the railway sector it's been rewarding to see the developments that have swept through the industry. The visions I've seen are indicative of cross-modal transformational approaches taking place across the industry.

Designing and implementing this kind of ecosystem is not only a question of public policies and funds but also of inventing new ways for the public and private sectors to work together to create value. Imagination like this requires a network of mobility leaders – the kind of people who make the impossible possible and who will create a future of green mobility.

Gilles Roucolle has witnessed the coming of this new era in transportation in 30 years of work supporting the transport sector. He has always been willing to challenge the status quo and implement strategic disruptions in order to help companies forge ahead and transform their businesses. This book contains his vision of the future and the visions of more than 30 of the biggest names in mobility. They offer ideas and points of view based on their varied expertise, experiences and stories. The book is an original, cutting-edge initiative – and who better than Gilles to gather these voices in trust and confidence.

PREFACE AND ACKNOWLEDGEMENTS

This book provides a guide to the changes being unleashed and the long-term evolution of the mobility sector. Based on more than 30 interviews with a panel of global leaders and experts in a variety of transport businesses and complemented by secondary research from the Oliver Wyman Forum and select Oliver Wyman experts, it celebrates the 30th anniversary of my career as a transportation consultant.

I invited the panel to participate based on my own experience collaborating with these leaders or serving their organizations over the past three decades. Combined, they have more than 850 years of mobility-sector experience in all modes of transport. On a global basis, they have worked in all corners of the globe. They have managed or are still leading a combined €750 billion of mobility assets across more than 80 enterprises involved in the transportation industry, generating over €500 billion in combined revenues. Their current and past organizations employ close to 2 million employees.

A majority of them have changed company at least twice, and more than one third bring experience across different modes and segments of the mobility market space.

They range from working at 100-plus-year-old incumbent players to leading some of the most successful mobility start-ups. I hope these interviews add some unique colour and personal perspectives to the insights in the book. They include some unique 'from the cockpit' stories from landmark events that have forged the collective memory of the industry. Detailed biographies of the panel participants are enclosed in the Appendix.

Their willingness and enthusiasm to contribute to this project speaks volumes about their interest in continuing to shape an ever-evolving industry and their passion for their sector. I have been humbled by this personal research experience and this trip down memory lane. I cannot thank them enough for their generous time and privileged insights.

The in-person interview process started just before the Covid-19 crisis, slowed down during lockdowns and was completed at the end of 2022. The strategic conversations covered trends and disruptions in mobility over the past 30 years and took in lessons on demand trends and dynamics, regulation, strategic technology, governance and leadership. They also helped me to envision scenarios for the future of mobility.

I have, myself, been an avid traveller for leisure and even more for business over the past three decades. Our transportation clients and I have always sought to learn from best practices. Our industry is universal in that there is always a best practice available somewhere in the world.

After starting my career in Europe and subsequently spending 10 years of my life in Canada, I have witnessed first-hand the fascination of North Americans for Japanese and European high-speed train technology. And I have seen the envy of European freight railways over the length of haul and profitability of Class I railroads in North America. Likewise Southwest Airlines remains the universal low-cost airline business model on both sides of the Atlantic. Bringing cross-mode, cross-Atlantic and global insights and benchmarks has always proven critical to industry practitioners and will certainly continue to be so going forward.

Many thanks to Oliver Wyman colleagues Carole Bouchard, Alexandre Devevey, Emma Faivre, Leopold Fort, Sten Frenzel, Robin Perrot, Théophile Reffet and Adrien Slimani, who have actively contributed at key stages of the project, as well as Sebastian Moffett for his skilled support and advice.

DISCLAIMER

I have worked for Oliver Wyman for 28 years, during which time I have written numerous papers for the firm. This book is different. It contains views and opinions about the sector, as well as personal memories, that are my own or those of the business leaders and experts I interviewed. It should therefore not be considered representative of the positions or viewpoints of Oliver Wyman or its partners. Please bear this in mind when reading.

The great fragmentation 1

How new challenges are different from the old

- Where the fragmentation of the mobility value chain comes from.
- Why people and goods need to keep moving.
- How the new challenges are different from the old ones.

Mobility and transport executives might dream of running a simple but effective business. The operator would have a small number of regular customers ready to follow a scheduled service. These would be unlikely to switch provider, despite relatively high prices that guarantee a healthy profit margin. And the transport company would own its infrastructure from one end to the other, so capacity would not be misallocated and costs would be controllable.

Such businesses actually exist. Some of the world's most profitable transport operations operate in parts of the North American Class I freight railroad industry, which earn their cost of capital or more in an ecosystem that is regulated, competitive and yet oligopolistic. They re-invest billions of dollars annually in their networks and remain a vital component of trade and the economy in North America. While rail systems in most developed countries are unable to cover even their variable costs, the US and Canadian freight railroads need no taxpayer funding. 'We are a major and essential part of the American economy's circulatory system, obliged to constantly maintain and improve our 23,000 miles of track along with its ancillary bridges, tunnels, engines and cars,' wrote Warren E Buffett, Chairman of Berkshire Hathaway, the owner of BNSF, one of the largest US railroads. 'It is inconceivable that our country will realize anything close to its full economic potential without its possessing first-class electricity and railroad systems.'[1,2]

In 2010, BNSF carried each ton of freight 800 km (500 miles) on a gallon (3.8 litres) of diesel fuel, according to its owner, Berkshire Hathaway. That's three times more fuel-efficient than trucking and gives rail freight a big cost advantage. 'Our country gains because of reduced greenhouse emissions and a much smaller need for imported oil,' said Buffett at the time. 'When traffic travels by rail, society benefits.'

The six Class I railroads in the United States and Canada (defined as those with operating revenues of $490 million or more) make up a rail-freight industry worth nearly $80 billion a year. They run on almost 225,400 km (140,000 miles) of track, according to the US Department of Transportation, and are widely considered to be the largest, safest and most cost-efficient freight system in the world. They move 42 per cent of North America's intercity freight and provide more than 167,000 jobs. They reduce the cost of logistics for the industries they serve, and their ancillary benefits include reductions in road congestion, highway fatalities, fuel consumption and greenhouse gases. The freight railroads are privately owned and responsible for maintaining and improving the infrastructure they use. As shown in Figure 1.1, their shareholder value grows over time at or above the S&P 500 index and well above the airlines' stock composites.

The complex world

These independent railway operations are exceptions in today's transport and mobility industry – the result of unified standards that stretch thousands of kilometres over a continent with a relatively sparse base of shippers and receivers.

In contrast, most transportation today is intermodal and highly competitive. Customers are offered an array of choices of mode of transport, destination, time and service level. A commuter from Queens in New York travelling to work in Midtown Manhattan can use their own car or a combination of taxi, car-hailing and e-scooters, as well as traditional buses, commuter trains and the subway. The choices might change from day to day, and even mid-journey. An online shopper is offered a range of delivery options, perhaps through different transport services, taking hours, days or weeks.

Unprecedented personalization makes shipments and trips extremely complex to engineer and serve reliably and profitably. Some mass transit systems cope with millions of commuters, who value comfort to a greater or lesser extent and who may want to use specific routings or need to arrive or

Figure 1.1 Class 1 stock price performance, indexed

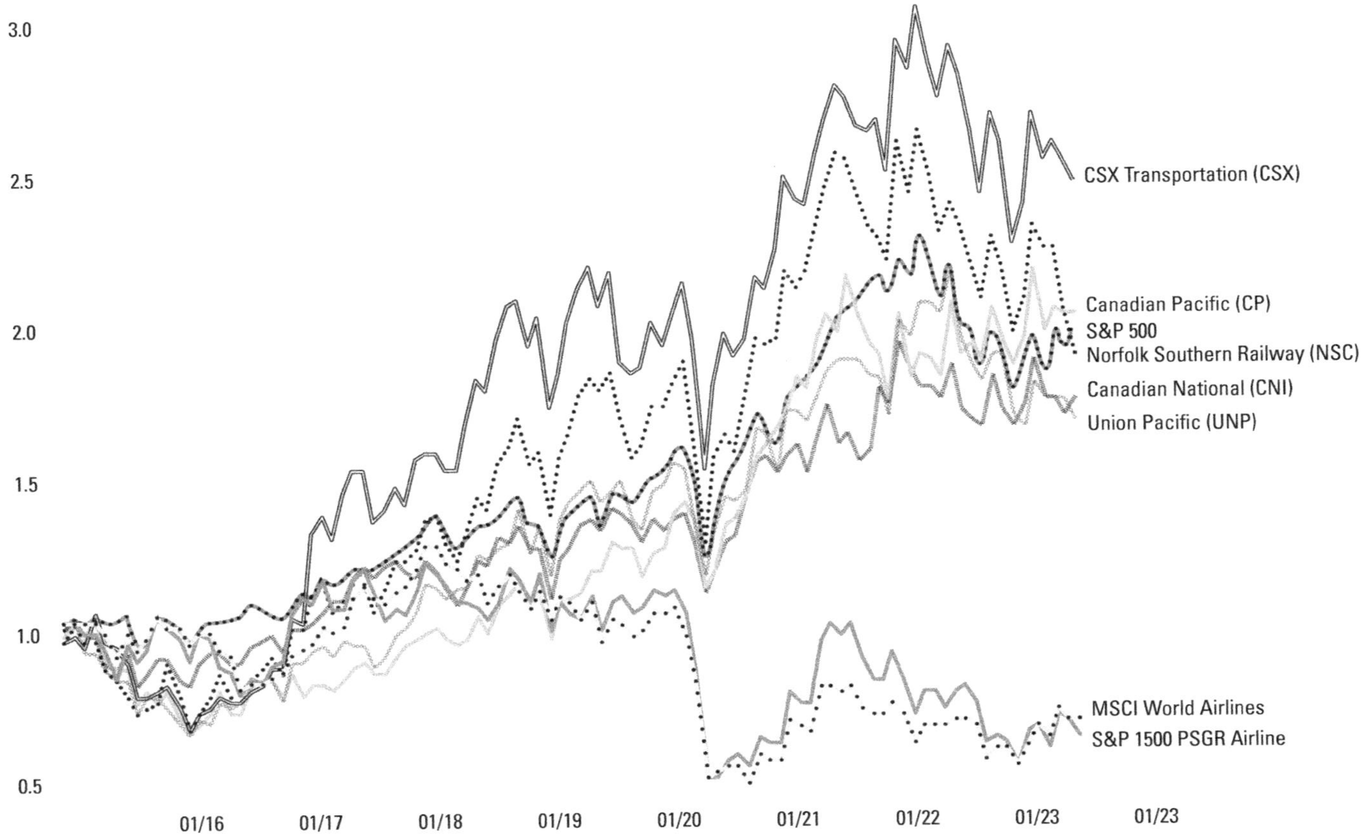

CSX Transportation (CSX)

Canadian Pacific (CP)
S&P 500
Norfolk Southern Railway (NSC)
Canadian National (CNI)
Union Pacific (UNP)

MSCI World Airlines
S&P 1500 PSGR Airline

3.0

2.5

2.0

1.5

1.0

0.5

01/16   01/17   01/18   01/19   01/20   01/21   01/22   01/23   01/23

SOURCE Publicly available stock price data and Oliver Wyman analysis

depart at certain times. As a result, the operators of the most complex mass transit systems, who are in direct competition with individual cars, have to cope with the entropy brought about by combinations of different routings, modes and connections – not to mention operating flaws as well as delays and cancellations and the related cascading network effects.

The fragmentation of journeys is the defining characteristic of mobility and transport today. In the past, the trips made by people and goods were decided by the available services: it was a supply-led value chain. New destinations were opened up by a train using a new railway, a new airport enabling flights, or a highway that cut road travel times and diverted traffic from smaller roads. Today, mobility value chains are converging around customer use cases. That can mean a daily commuter trip from the suburb of a small town to the centre of a big city, or a European family's holiday trip to Disneyland in Florida. In goods, a logistics operator might have to fulfil orders ranging from a consumer buying a special individual birthday present online to grouped deliveries of industrial components. Each case will use a variety of transportation modes, including rail, road, air and sea – and navigating the options has become one of the greatest challenges for transport businesses.

Mobility and transport are highly regulated and each leg of the trip might be regulated by a different authority. In Europe, for example, the European Union decides rules on air travellers' rights and on the kinds of road vehicles that can be sold. Member states may – or may not – charge lorries by the kilometre to travel on their roads, and most rail operators have a footprint of a single country, or perhaps just a region within a country. Large cities may operate a congestion charge or low-emissions zone, while parking restrictions can be decided at the level of individual boroughs. 'The fragmentation of mobility governance is a real challenge,' says Guillaume Thibault, an Oliver Wyman partner and leader of the Oliver Wyman Global Mobility Forum. 'Authorities differ according to geography – countries, regions, and cities – and according to modes of transport – air, rail, water, and road.'

"The fragmentation of mobility governance is a real challenge"
Guillaume Thibault

Moreover, city dwellers often expect to spend little on public transport, and very few of the world's public transit systems generate enough revenue from fares to cover operating expenses, let alone capital costs such as infrastructure investment. The profitability of a transit system is usually measured using the farebox recovery ratio, with a figure under 1 indicating that the system has to be subsidized. Many Asian transit systems have a high farebox recovery ratio because of dense urban populations that are accustomed to commuting by public transit. But North American and European transit systems have lower ratios – usually below 0.25 in car-dependent environments. That means most transit systems rely heavily on government subsidies, even in Europe, which is relatively public transit friendly.

New services for growing cities

More changes will come in the next 10 years than in the last 100, as technologies continue to progress and innovation accelerates. New payment systems mean that a visitor may need to apply online for a ticket to access public transport in a new city, or to gain access to a bike-share or e-scooter service. The expansion of artificial intelligence will lead to further innovations, as will the rise to dominance of Generation Z, who have different attitudes to mobility than their predecessors. One major user-driven shift already under way is many city dwellers' abandonment of car ownership for shared vehicles, whether they drive these themselves or hail a ride. 'The most noticeable trend is the decrease of car ownership among millennials and the decrease in the number of driver's licences in the US in particular,' says Alex Bayen, Director of the Institute of Transportation Studies (ITS) at the University of California, Berkeley. 'There will be a limit to it, but this is not going away.'

"The most noticeable trend is the decrease of car ownership among millennials"
Alex Bayen

These shifts disrupt incumbent operators and favour new mobility concepts and technologies, offering end-customers a wider range of options. A selection of 13 new mobility services will grow at an average of almost 10 per cent a year over the current decade to reach $660 billion in 2030, according to a study by the Oliver Wyman Forum and the ITS. That compares with growth of around 5 per cent for the overall mobility sector. The new offerings include cars-as-a-service – rental, sharing and subscription; micro-mobility, in the form of sharing services for bikes, mopeds and e-scooters; hailing services, such as carpooling, taxis and ride-hailing, bus-pooling and air taxis; and complementary services for battery charging, navigation and smart parking[3] (see Figure 1.2).

Setting up and running these services will require vast spending: mobility has the world's biggest need for economic infrastructure spending, accounting for about 40 per cent of investment, with the rest going mainly to power, water and telecommunications. But this spending will be different from that of the past. As well as traditional areas, such as highway networks and rail, airport and sea terminals, there will be more intermodal platforms, where numerous forms of mass transit will connect with a variety of rental, hailing and sharing services. Multimodal logistics hubs will proliferate, combining mechanized warehouses, specialized storage facilities and access for multiple forms of transport. Mobility start-ups will likely soon announce the first vertiports for electric aircraft that can taxi people over or between cities. Smart roads and vehicle-free zones will expand in dense urban areas and streets will be lined with sensors and electric charging infrastructure.

The burgeoning possibilities will further complicate the businesses of operators. They often have long-term fixed assets and now have to deal with a secular erosion of price levels in passenger transport driven by the emergence of low-cost players and economical shipping of goods due to the collapse of supply chain costs steered by the likes of Amazon. 'The big shifts in demand in all modes will be towards low-cost propositions: road with car sharing, rail with the likes of Ouigo and air with the continued push from Ryanair-type offerings,' says Marc Ivaldi, Professor at the Toulouse School of Economics and President of the International Transportation Economics Association.

Figure 1.2 Global value pool sizes for mobility services

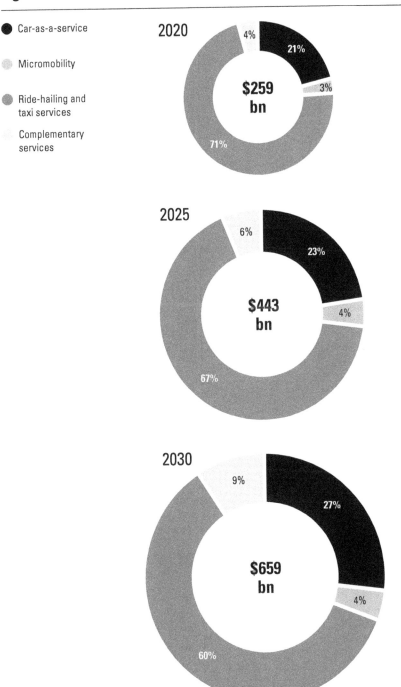

- Car-as-a-service
- Micromobility
- Ride-hailing and taxi services
- Complementary services

2020

$259 bn

21%
3%
71%
4%

2025

$443 bn

23%
4%
67%
6%

2030

$659 bn

27%
4%
60%
9%

SOURCE Oliver Wyman Forum Mobility Value Pool analysis

"The big shifts in demand in all modes will be towards low-cost propositions"
Marc Ivaldi

One thing that will remain constant is strong demand, driven by growth in the world's population and economic expansion. Human beings have a natural propensity to 'truck, barter, and exchange one thing for another,' Adam Smith observed in *The Wealth of Nations* in 1776.[4] Mobility and transportation have been essential elements of that activity, connecting merchants and customers, allowing commerce to flourish and helping raise living standards around the world. As the middle classes grow in Asia, Africa and South America, they will want to travel more: globally, the number of international tourist arrivals is forecast to increase 70 per cent between 2017 and 2030. The highest percentage growth in the mobility market will come from moving people (rather than freight), at 5.4 per cent a year, according to an Oliver Wyman analysis. 'Mobility adds value and generates economic growth,' says Xavier Huillard, Chief Executive Officer of VINCI. 'It supports daily home-to-job transit and helps human brains to connect and team up. It lets businesses export and multinationals operate efficiently.'

"Mobility adds value and generates economic growth"
Xavier Huillard

Much of the new demand will be urban. By 2030, 60 per cent of the world's population, or 5.2 billion people, will live in cities. As a result, urban mobility demand will rise 23 per cent over that period, which will be followed by a 35 per cent jump to 39 trillion passenger-kilometres in 2050[5] (see Figure 1.3). As these cities become denser, mass transit and micro-mobility systems will be needed to cope. But building these will be complex, as many developing countries still privilege road building to facilitate car use. 'There is a fundamental relationship between overall mobility and demographics,' says Pierre Lortie, retired President and COO of Bombardier Transportation. 'In some countries with a secular aging population, such as Japan, traffic volumes may erode over time.'

The volume of goods transported has grown over the centuries with global trade. But global logistics and logistics services outsourcing really began to expand in the 1980s, as global integrators such as UPS, FedEx and DHL helped technology manufacturers ship products around the world. Since then, other manufacturing sectors have adopted fast and reliable logistics to better integrate their supply chains. This enables them to provide end-customers with better service and to minimize inventories and working capital. Global trade expanded further in the 1990s, as Asian countries – in particular China – developed as global manufacturing centres. Multimodal logistics was needed to bring intermediate products to global manufacturers and final products to consumers, and increasingly sophisticated information technology helped make service providers more dependable and goods flows more reliable.

The increasing complexity presents a significant potential market for logistics specialists to provide services. The volume of global exports is forecast to increase 20 per cent between 2022 and 2030 to 215 trillion tonnes-kilometres[6] (see Figure 1.4), but only about $2.6 trillion of the

"There is a fundamental relationship between overall mobility and demographics"
Pierre Lortie

Figure 1.3   Global urban mobility demand, 2022–2050 (trillions passenger-km)

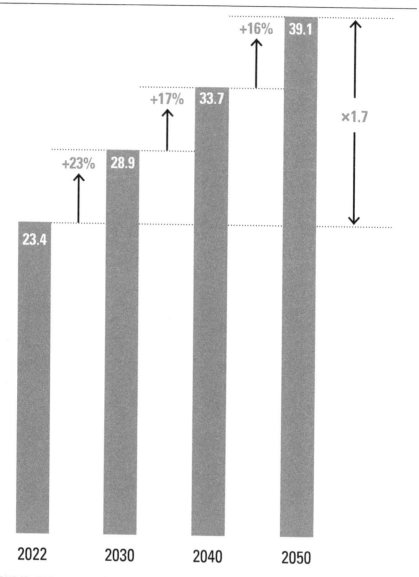

SOURCE ITF Transport Outlook 2023: Passenger travel demand 2022–50 as projected by the ITF Urban Passenger Model

world's $5.6 trillion spending on logistics is currently outsourced. The specialists can make use of four value creation levers, according to Marie-Christine Lombard, Chief Executive Officer of logistics provider GEODIS. One is process excellence and consistency. Another is service that is faster, cheaper and more reliable than that which the customer can achieve on its own. Third, they can offer an in-depth understanding of freight flows by combining industrial logic, information related to the manufacturing process, the nature of the demand and the type of customer. Finally, outsourcers can help their customers move towards carbon neutrality. 'The key to logistics services is the science and underlying logic of flows, from shipper to receiver,' she says. 'It is also the imperative to perform better than our customers would on their own, from the perspectives of time, cost and quality.'

The universal pressure to create value

Even the North American Class I railroads cannot avoid some degree of fragmentation, however the modern era's imperatives of efficiency and shareholder value have led them to focus on core business.

The Canadian Pacific Railway is a Canadian Class I railway incorporated in 1881 and a symbol of Canadian confederation. The railway was originally undertaken by Canada's first prime minister, John A Macdonald, after British Columbia insisted upon a land transport link to the east as a condition for joining the confederation. Today, it owns about 20,000 km of track and, like its railroad peers, carries heavy raw materials such as coal, fertilizer and potash, oil and ethanol on trains sometimes over 2 km long, a value proposition that road transporters cannot compete with. Canadian Pacific also ships forestry products such as lumber, panel, pulp and paper for

"The key to logistics services is the science and underlying logic of flows, from shipper to receiver"
Marie-Christine Lombard

Figure 1.4 Global freight transport volumes, 2022–2050 (trillions tonnes-km)

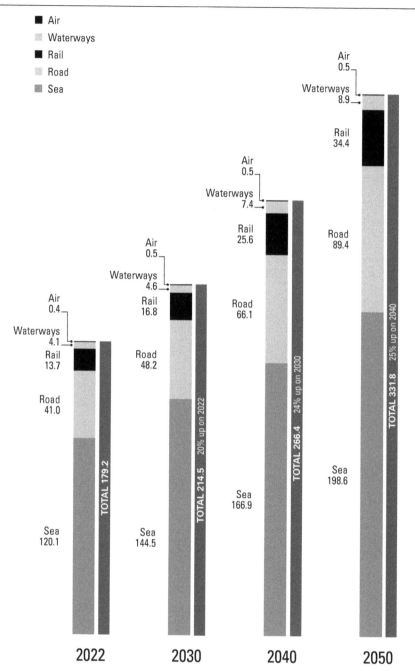

SOURCE ITF Transport Outlook 2023: Freight demand 2022–50 as projected by the ITF Domestic/International/Urban Freight Models

customers in all of the major production areas in Canada, including British Columbia, northern Alberta, northern Saskatchewan, Ontario and Quebec. It transports these over an integrated network that links with US and Mexican carriers, strengthened in the south by its hard-fought recent acquisition of Kansas City Southern, and provides access to its partners' trans-load facilities.[7]

Canadian Pacific also collaborates with the Port of Vancouver near the US border to take a leading role in growing trans-Pacific trade. Canada's largest and North America's most diversified port moves $550 million worth of cargo each day, ranging from automobiles and containerized finished goods to commodities such as forest products. It offers importers and exporters efficient and fast routes between key markets in Canada and the American Midwest towards trans-Pacific destinations. To do all this effectively and build scale, Canadian Pacific spent decades building synergies between an array of businesses: freight rail, natural resources, energy – but it also ventured in the not-so-distant past into adjacent markets, including passenger rail and hotels, initially positioned along the main rail lines.

In recent decades, however, Canadian Pacific has been divesting in order to focus on its core competence and become a pure logistics and freight rail business. In 1986, it sold its 53 per cent stake in Cominco, a significant mining company based in British Columbia. The company had bought Cominco shortly after it built the first rail line across Canada. Cominco was the second-largest mining group in Canada, producing zinc, lead, copper, silver and gold and had interests in chemicals and fertilizers.

Then in 1995, David O'Brien, a bilingual lawyer and native Montrealer, became the chairman, president and chief executive officer of holding company Canadian Pacific Ltd. He had made a name running oil-and-gas companies in Western Canada and was brought in to run one of Canada's biggest conglomerates, overseeing multiple sectors, including hotels, railroads, shipping, oil and gas, and mining.

But O'Brien focused on shareholder value management and launched a dynamic programme of strategic portfolio management. He moved the head office from Montreal to Calgary in 1996 and proceeded to sell some legacy operations and expand others, reshaping the company into a growing international presence. By the end of 1998, the company operated in five sectors: rail, shipping, coal, oil and gas, and a combination of hotels and real estate. Some level of vertical integration and collaboration existed across the portfolio. One example was the development of efficient coordination of a rail-port-ocean value chain spearheaded by CP Railway working with CP Ships and the Port of Montreal, making Montreal one of the leading container ports on the East Coast of North America.

By late 2000, however, strong performance by all five of the CP Ltd subsidiaries, as well as some perceived investor expectations related to the conglomerate discount, led O'Brien to conclude that the time had come to act. With such a diverse portfolio, Canadian Pacific was exposed to a range of business and market risks, including fluctuating energy prices, a falling Canadian dollar and changes in Asia's economic growth trajectory. Long regarded as a quintessentially Canadian corporation since its founding, 45 per cent of its shares were now owned by American investors and much of its business was taking place far beyond Canada's borders. Eventually, the intra-portfolio synergies were not sizeable enough to convince investors that they significantly exceeded the holding company discount and there was a growing belief that the sum of the company's parts would exceed its current market capitalization.

In 2001, the company announced that it would split into five publicly traded independent companies – CPR, CP Ships, PanCanadian Petroleum, Fording Canadian Coal Trust and Canadian Pacific Hotels. The demerger was completed in October 2001 and each new carved-out company gained listings on both the Toronto and New York stock exchanges. That led to a major unbundling of the group's activities.

In 2002, PanCanadian merged with the Alberta Energy Company to form EnCana, which at the time was the world's largest independent petroleum company. CP Ships had been one of the company's fastest-growing subsidiaries, with 1998 revenues of $675 million. It was based in London and its ships were registered in many countries around the world – but not in Canada. The business was sold in 2005 to German conglomerate TUI AG for US$2.0 billion in cash and was merged with TUI's Hapag-Lloyd shipping division.

The hotel division had previously diversified from its original Canadian rail line footprint and bought Canada's Delta Hotel chain and Princess Hotels, which operate in Bermuda, Barbados, Mexico and the United States. CP Hotels, the company's upscale flagship chain, spent millions upgrading its iconic properties, which include the Château Frontenac in Quebec City, the Banff Springs and Palliser hotels in Alberta, and the Hotel Vancouver and Château Whistler in British Columbia. In 1999, Canadian Pacific Hotels acquired a majority interest in US luxury chain Fairmont Hotels and adopted its stronger brand. But in 2006, Fairmont was acquired by Colony Capital and eventually in 2016 became a subsidiary of AccorHotels.

Canadian Pacific now operates purely as a freight railroad and logistics company. In 2023, Canadian Pacific made a US$31 billion acquisition of Kansas City Southern to create Canadian Pacific Kansas City (CPKC). The merger created the first single-line railway connecting Canada, the US and Mexico, and it gives both the original companies' customers new options and an expanded market reach. CPKC now has solid port access on coasts around the continent, from Vancouver to Atlantic Canada to the Gulf of Mexico to Lázaro Cárdenas on Mexico's Pacific coast. The new company employs close to 20,000 people. Full integration of CP and KCS was expected to take place over three years.

Close to 150 years after its founding, Canadian Pacific operates as an independent rail logistics pure play. After multiple moves to integrate its business further vertically, the company managed its portfolio towards a more attractive strategy based on the sum of its parts. Like its Class I peers, it was built as a greenfield project in the wilderness of a vast, sparsely populated continent. Such giant projects defined progress in transport and mobility for more than a century.

KEY TAKEAWAYS

- A vast array of new businesses and mobility services is being launched worldwide. Many are in micro-mobility; others are related to green sources of power.

- Fragmentation of demand is disrupting existing mobility patterns. This makes things very complicated for legacy providers, especially those, like rail companies, with high fixed infrastructure and costs.

- A very small number of transport businesses have been relatively immune to this trend so far. But even they are under pressure to answer to shareholder demands to create greater financial value.

- Despite all this turmoil, one thing that will not change is the underlying growth in demand for mobility. There is a fundamental need to move people and goods.

Notes

1 Socci, L. (2022) Learning from Buffett and Berkshire about investing in railroads: The BNSF case study, Seeking Alpha, 5 October. Available at: https://seekingalpha.com/article/4544724-buffett-investing-railroads-bnsf-case-study (archived at https://perma.cc/DRU2-7EMW)

2 Buffett, W. (2010) Berkshire Hathaway Inc. Shareholder Letter. Available at: www.berkshirehathaway.com/letters/2010ltr.pdf (archived at https://perma.cc/7NCZ-CUAE)

3 Nienhaus, A. et al (2022) How urban mobility will change by 2030, Oliver Wyman Forum. Available at: www.oliverwyman.com/content/dam/oliver-wyman/ow-forum/mobility/2022/Value%20Pool%20Report.pdf (archived at https://perma.cc/827V-L96A)

4 Smith, A. (1776) *The Wealth of Nations*

5 OECD (2023) ITF Transport Outlook 2023. Available at: www.oecd-ilibrary.org/transport/itf-transport-outlook-2023_5fc66b10-en (archived at https://perma.cc/9W5Q-KCYZ)

6 CPKC (2023) Transload. Available at: www.cpkcr.com/en/our-markets/transload

7 Canadian Pacific (2023) Transload & trucking. Available at: www.cpr.ca/en/choose-rail/transload-trucking (archived at https://perma.cc/FU76-CYYM)

The steel backbone

2

How infrastructure drove mobility growth in rail

- How rail infrastructure and operations drove mobility growth.
- Why China saw rail as an essential component of an advanced industrialized nation.
- Why networks and interoperability are essential to rail economics.

Before the first transcontinental railway in North America, travellers would have to risk an overland journey through hostile territory, sail round Cape Horn, or take a difficult short cut over the mountains of Panama. These options could take as little as a month if all went smoothly – or half a year if it did not.

In the middle of the nineteenth century, the country's leaders realized that the difficulty of travel between the coasts was a barrier to trade. It also left the west coast effectively as a colony of the eastern states, and they of all people were well aware that colonies might one day desire independence. So they set up the legal framework and helped to finance one of the world's greatest engineering projects – a railroad that was built westwards from Omaha, Nebraska and eastwards from Sacramento, California, meeting in the middle.

The first transcontinental railroad was completed in 1869. The journey from coast to coast now took just a week and its price for a single passenger fell from about $1,000 to about $100. The railroad cut the cost of sending suppliers to frontier outposts, enabled speedy communications thanks to the telegraph set up alongside and boosted the prices of the land that had now become accessible.[1] California – first through its farms, later through technology – was eventually transformed from a range of small, isolated towns into one of the world's economic powerhouses, with GDP in 2021 greater than that of the United Kingdom and France.

Major railways defined – and helped create – the modern world. Overland travel in the early nineteenth century had in many ways been similar to that during the Roman Empire. But in 1872, Phileas Fogg took just eight days by train to reach New York from San Francisco, as part of his successful attempt to go *Around the World in Eighty Days*, the title of the novel in which he appeared. While Fogg and his journey were fictions, the journey had become plausible thanks to engineering feats that inspired his creator, Jules Verne. Fogg took trains across America, Europe and India – after the 1870 completion of the Indian transcontinental railroad. The other legs of the journey were mainly completed by steamship, including a passage through the Suez Canal, which had been finished in 1869.

The great railway projects ended the era of exploration and welcomed that of tourism. They also made possible freight logistics of a speed and power never before achieved, triggering an explosion in global trade and an economic boom that ended only with World War I.

In France, a new rail network was begun from the end of the nineteenth century, leading to industrialization and urbanization. This threatened to leave rural areas behind, so in response, public works minister Charles de Freycinet launched an ambitious programme in 1878. This expanded rail and water transport networks and built up port infrastructure. The plan featured 16,000 km of railways, including 8,700 km of branch lines that connected small towns and villages to cities and local businesses. The network provided most of the French population with rail services and so opened up all regions to the era's booming economic development.

Nearly a century after these great advances, the next leap forward in rail travel was being developed: high-speed rail.

Japan had planned an early version of high-speed rail during World War II, but this was abandoned due to the war effort. However, as the country began its so-called economic miracle in the 1950s, the main line between Tokyo and Osaka was soon operating at full capacity. In 1958, the government approved a project to build a *shinkansen* – literally 'new main line', but better known in English as the bullet train. Construction of the first segment, between Tokyo and Osaka, began in 1959 and the trains went into service on 1 October 1964, just in time for the first Tokyo Olympics. The first *shinkansen* trains ran at up to 210 kph and the trip between the two cities took four hours, compared with six hours and 40 minutes for the regular train. This was reduced to three hours and 10 minutes by 1965 and the journey became progressively shorter as the trains became faster.

European rail after the World War II years was plagued by a number of problems. In particular, the rolling stock fleet was hugely diversified, making rail cars difficult and expensive to build and maintain. From 1966, French rail company SNCF worked with rail integrator Alstom on a TGV (*Train à Grande Vitesse* – high-speed train). This combined a long-term blueprint for a network, plus rolling stock that featured rigid consists, which significantly reduced the number of bogies per trainset. The result was greater stability and on-board comfort at considerably higher speeds. The first tests were carried out in 1972, using gas-powered turbine for the traction. But after the first oil crisis hit, the propulsion was switched to electricity and the project was approved in 1974. As President Valéry Giscard D'Estaing later promoted a national energy campaign, he celebrated such solutions with the words, 'In France, we have no oil, but we have ideas.'[2]

On 22 September 1981, the first service ran between Paris and Lyon, taking two hours and 40 minutes, down from four hours for the regular train. Europe had entered the age of high-speed rail.

The TGV gradually lured passengers away from air travel – before the boom in low-cost airlines – and from cars. It induced long-distance travel that otherwise would not have taken place because people either could not afford to fly or their journey lay outside the airlines' catchment areas. For business travellers, the TGV allowed many more professionals to connect with business partners via ground transport in less than a day, significantly improving productivity and opening long-distance business travel to a much larger volume of passengers. For leisure travellers, the trains opened up long-distance journeys to the wider middle classes. People going on holiday spent less time travelling and more at their destination, and high-speed rail was also safer than road travel, for which congestion was a growing problem, especially during the critical holiday periods.

Under Jean-Marie Metzler, who became head of SNCF's long-distance passenger division and oversaw the launch of the TGV, innovations developed by airlines were used, such as capacity and yield management and dynamic pricing, which were licensed from American Airlines. These helped to commercialize the product, maximize load factors and optimize margins for the business. This was a cultural shift for rail passengers (and somewhat controversial for the public), as people had been used to a less flexible and more transparent pricing structure. SNCF also designed a blueprint for expansion, which transformed mobility in France, bringing numerous large and medium-sized cities within a three-hour train ride of Paris.

How new track transforms regions

The TGV's success is an example of mobility driven by supply. A high-speed rail network is first designed with the right technology and capacity based on initial traffic forecasts and it is then put into operation. Over time, passenger traffic will follow and the network can shape the population distribution and affect the location of businesses along the line. It must of course fulfil certain conditions, such as a train fleet large enough to deliver a high-frequency service, which is essential to attract business travellers who require flexibility in their schedules, and a reduction in door-to-door transit time which is sizeable enough to outcompete the transit time performance of road travel and somewhat match that of air. 'The success of the TGV was supply-centric,' says Jean-Pierre Farandou, Chairman and CEO of SNCF Group, 'a technology which found its market and redefined long-distance travel with a new mode of transport.'

A high-speed rail connection boosts a region's economic growth, spurs the creation of new businesses and sends real estate prices higher along the new line. Some people were able to work in Paris but decided to live in a provincial town. Others found they could travel easily to second homes that were now only one or two hours away from Paris by train. After the Paris–Lyon line was extended south in 2001, 'TGV Méditerrannée' enabled people to reach Marseille in three hours from Paris. Real estate prices in France's third largest city rose by 143 per cent in 2007 from their 1999 levels, according to FNAIM, the national real estate federation. Parisians bought property as a second home, as an investment or for their retirement. When prices in the city rose too far for some locals to afford, they bid up prices in areas that had been less favoured, thereby lifting the overall real estate mar-

"A technology which found its market and redefined long-distance travel with a new mode of transport"
Jean-Pierre Farandou

ket. Tourist numbers rose too, from 2.7 million in 1996 to 4 million in 2010. A similar effect occurred after the Atlantic line started commercial operation in 2017 between Paris and Bordeaux on the west side of the country.[2,3]

Such an economic impact did not escape private sector investors and the latest extension of the South Europe Atlantic high-speed line is operated by VINCI Railways subsidiaries LISEA (line manager) and MESEA (maintenance). This is one of the largest transport infrastructure projects in Europe and it now represents a backbone for the Nouvelle-Aquitaine region. Unlike existing partnership contracts for other high-speed lines, the concession contract means that LISEA, in which VINCI Concessions has a 33.4 per cent stake, bears all the risks – financing, construction, traffic, maintenance, operation and safety – for the duration of the concession (50 years).

International high-speed

High-speed rail soon began to spread internationally too. In 1996, SNCF and Belgian operator SNCB launched Thalys, a link from Paris to Brussels and later to the Netherlands and beyond. It was set up as a joint venture in order to share costs and maximize market reach on both sides of the line. These rail services catered to a range of customer segments and travel needs: leisure, business travellers, as well as short trips for what industry jargon calls VFR, or 'visiting friends and relatives'.

But the most dramatic illustration of the geopolitical and economic impact of new rail came with the 1994 launch of train services through the Channel Tunnel – both the Eurostar and the Eurotunnel (now Getlink) shuttle trains carrying freight and passenger vehicles between the United Kingdom and the continent.

The idea for a tunnel between Britain and France goes back more than two centuries. In 1802, mining engineer Albert Mathieu presented Napoleon with a proposal for a tunnel for stagecoach travel, which would be ventilated by chimneys rising above the surface of the water. That was just the first of 27 proposals. In the 1880s, tunnelling began and reached over a mile from both sides. But the British worried that it could provide an invasion route and cancelled the project.

Though the defence concern faded over the years, there was still emotional opposition by Britons attached to the idea that they lived on an island, unconnected to the European continent. Money was also a concern. In 1975, after 10 years of study and 14 months of digging, the British government decided that it could not afford both Concorde and a tunnel and abandoned the latter. France in contrast has a long tradition of large infrastructure projects and the tunnel fitted the new TGV technology. Moreover, while the point of arrival in the UK is the relatively prosperous southeast of England, northeastern France was suffering from the decline of its coal, steel and textile industries. The new link was seen as a way to promote the economy of this area.[4]

Eventually, after both governments agreed to restart the project, 10 proposals were examined, including plans for drive-through road and rail tunnels and even one for a bridge. In 1986, a winner was selected, a rail-only proposal that would run three types of train: passenger trains, shuttle trains for cars and trucks, and container trains. After the signing of the bilateral treaty by Prime Minister Margaret Thatcher and President François Mitterrand, this soon became the Eurotunnel companies and was the largest privately financed engineering project in history. After several years of financial difficulties and schedule overruns – and the unexpected need to install an air-conditioning system to cope with the heat generated by trains – the tunnel opened in 1994. 'In the history of human enterprises, some satisfy the dreamer that is resident in each of us, and some fulfil a social and economic utility,' Mitterrand told the newspaper *La Voix Du Nord* in May 1994. 'They are rarely the same. What makes the Channel Tunnel exceptional and exemplary is that it fulfils both objectives at the same time.'[4]

Both Eurostar, the new rail service between Paris and London, and Le Shuttle, the car-train service, proved immediate hits. Surface travellers used to need around 12 hours to travel between London and Paris by rail and car or coach and ferry. From 2007, after a track upgrade on the British side and the inauguration of the St Pancras International terminal in London, the journey time from London to Paris was reduced to 2 hours 15 minutes and that from London to Brussels to just 1 hour 51 minutes. More than 19 million passengers boarded the Eurostar or Le Shuttle trains in the UK in 1998. From 2013 to 2019, the average was 20.9 million a year. In 1994, tourist numbers to the UK rose 8 per cent – but those for day visitors jumped 30 per cent. The shorter transit time even sparked new customer behaviour, with a surge of business travellers making day trips. Board the train at around 7 am in Paris and, thanks to the one-hour time difference, you arrive in the heart of London at 8.15 am local time, ready for a business meeting at 9 am in the City of London. Catch a 5 pm Eurostar at St Pancras and you get back home to Paris for a not-too-late dinner.[5,6,7]

In contrast, other modes declined – either a bit or significantly. In the years following the opening, the number of vehicles and their passengers travelling across the Dover Strait via the tunnel shot up, while those going by ferry declined slightly. The average number of flights per day between London and Paris was 100 when the Eurostar opened for business, but by 2019 was down to 46. In 1996, airlines offered capacity of 4.8 million seats annually between the two capitals, but 23 years later there were just 2.7 million seats.[8]

The Channel Tunnel also boosted business. It facilitated trade worth €138 billion in 2016, when it represented 26 per cent of total UK–EU trade. In particular, the tunnel became an integral part of just-in-time production: to boost competitiveness, many companies transport semi-finished products and components which will be used in the next stage of production in another country. The Channel Tunnel plays a key role in helping businesses build their operating model around an efficient and streamlined process. Most EU–UK trade facilitated by the tunnel is with the UK's near neighbours, such as France and Belgium, or countries that are linked to key trade routes from the tunnel, such as Germany. These three countries made up over half of all trade through the Channel Tunnel. That said, the tunnel also provides a trade route for countries in Northern Europe, such as Denmark, and Eastern Europe, such as Poland.[9]

TGV overall has been a success in part because the design is based on adaptable technology. The trains, developed by Alstom, initially consisted mostly of integrated systems of 8–12 passenger cars with a locomotive at each end. The popularity of high-speed services led to the development of double-deck versions to increase capacity on high-volume routes and at peak hours. Another way to increase capacity has been to combine two trainsets to form a multiple unit. These configurations are made possible by the increased power generated by modern AC motors.

Another way in which the trains are adaptable is that they can run not only on dedicated high-speed lines but also on conventional lines, albeit more slowly. As a result, France's so-called high-speed rail services are in fact a hybrid of full high-speed services and TGVs running on other lines at whatever speeds these allow, so the reach of the trains far exceeds the dedicated network.

This potential has not escaped French politicians, seemingly most of whom want a TGV to stop at a station in their electoral district, even if there is no sound economic case for a stop. That makes it extremely difficult to streamline the TGV footprint and improve fleet productivity by removing marginal stops from the system. 'You would receive a call from the local deputy, senator or mayor in the next day, or hours, if we decide to reduce a certain service,' a former SNCF executive told me once. 'Our TGV blue-print,' he added, 'has let the French population believe that most of the country owns the right to be transported by train to Paris in a maximum of three hours.'

This leads to a high penetration of the domestic travel market but also uses up a lot of the available high-speed trains on tracks that are not equipped to support full high-speed services. That means the trains – a highly capital-intensive technology – are not always used to maximum effect. One response might be to design the train timetable in a way that coordinates connections, a technique used in Switzerland. This makes it easy to change quickly and easily from a high-speed train on dedicated lines to a slower regional train on a conventional line. However, the designs and configurations of many large city stations in France make this more difficult. They also have a longer connecting time due to a 'dead-end' design that complicates train operations and passenger connections.

Speed trade-offs

Germany provides an example of how the fastest, newest trains are not always the financially optimal solution and of how sometimes it's easier to make a sound business case for a more modest technological advance. In the early 2000s, Deutsche Bahn's long-distance fleet was a mix of BR101 locomotives pulling passenger coaches at up to 200 kph and first-generation InterCity Express trains – ICE 1 and ICE 2 – at up to 250 kph. Much of the rolling stock was coming up for retirement between 2015 and 2025, so Deutsche Bahn (DB) needed to decide on a long-term replacement strategy.

One available technology was an upgrade of the technology used for the existing ICE 1 and ICE 2. Another was a new type of train, ICE 3, which would be followed by the ICE 4. The ICE 3 would be lighter and more powerful than the old trains, thanks to the distribution of 16 traction motors beneath the entire length of the train. This would make all the cars available for passenger seats, including the first. The trains would be designed to run at up to 330 kph, though they would have to keep to 300 kph, the maximum design speed of German high-speed lines. However, this technology and the lifecycle of the ICE 3 and ICE 4 would be much more costly than a new version of the ICE 1 and ICE 2.

Would the faster of the two options be worth the investment across the country? One argument to challenge the ICE 3 and ICE 4 options was

Germany's long-distance tracks, only about 20 per cent of which were then built for trains running at over 250 kph. Moreover, speeds much above 250 kph would not significantly cut journey times on routes between many of Germany's city pairs because they were just too close to each other: the trains would only be running at maximum speed for a relatively short time between acceleration after a stop and deceleration before the next stop (this was a key difference from the case in France, a larger country with a radial footprint and fewer mid-sized cities). Another consideration was the need to standardize the ICE product for branding purposes and to harmonize the traveller experience. Finally, the new trains would need to conform to a modular fleet platform in order to reduce operational complexity and lifecycle costs.

In the end, there was no commercial justification for full immediate ICE 3 and ICE 4 trains deployment and in the short term DB opted for the upgrade to the ICE 1 and ICE 2, very high-speed trains being focused on an upcoming limited number of high-volume city pairs.

China: The world's biggest high-speed network

China was aware of the importance of transport links for an economy and the government kept a close eye on the development of high-speed rail in Japan and in Europe. Nearly 30 years after the founding of the People's Republic in 1949, the Chinese Communist Party in 1978 launched a variety of economic reforms termed variously the 'socialist market economy' and 'reform and opening up'. The result was an unprecedented rapid economic expansion. Although investment and development in the transport sector were increased in the 1980s, the system was soon put under strain by the increase in the production and exchange of goods. Mobility requirements were also amplified by the growing demand for labour in industrial areas close to growing cities and ports – demand that would be met by people from inland rural areas.

In the early 2000s, the Ministry of Railways (MOR) drew up a multi-decade plan to develop a high-speed rail network. China is vastly larger than any country in Europe and the scale of its rail network would be correspondingly more ambitious. Though TGV technology was considered the segment leader, Bombardier Inc. of Canada won an initial contract, recalls André Navarri, who was then president and chief operating officer of the company. The contract was based on a platform its Europe-based engineers had built for Swedish railways and the company adapted it to the immediate demands of the Chinese plan. The first tracks in China allowed trains to run at up to 200 kph. This was subsequently updated with another Bombardier platform, Zefiro, that reached speeds of up to 350 kph. Andrew Lezala, then a member of Bombardier Transportation's executive committee and subsequently Managing Director and CEO of Metro Trains Australia, and subsequently Managing Director and CEO of Metro Trains Australia, adds: 'China is shaping the future of mobility and needs to be deeply understood. Producing rolling stock in the late 1990s from Europe, we thought we needed to be as Chinese in China as we were German in Germany.'

The first passenger service from China Railway High-speed (CRH) – the Beijing–Tianjin intercity service – opened in August 2008. China's network has since expanded dramatically and now covers 40,000 km, making up around 60 per cent of the world's total high-speed track (see Figure 2.1). Building on this technology acquired and transferred from Europe, China is now presenting itself as a provider of high-speed rail systems to export markets. Projects include the Jakarta–Bandung high-speed link in Indonesia, which began tests in 2022.

The Chinese government, as much as those in Europe, believes that rail drives economic growth. The rate of return of China's high-speed rail network is 8 per cent, according to a 2019 World Bank study, above the opportunity cost of capital in China for major, long-term infrastructure investments. Benefits include shortened travel times, the facilitation of tourism and labour, less highway congestion and fewer road accidents. High-speed rail is estimated to generate one-fiftieth of the CO_2 emissions of passenger road travel.

High-speed rail has also boosted the share of rail travel relative to air, which generates greenhouse-gas emissions 80 times higher, according to some estimates. One study found that high-speed rail services led to a

"China is shaping the future of mobility and needs to be deeply understood"
Andrew Lezala

Figure 2.1   Evolution of China's high-speed rail network

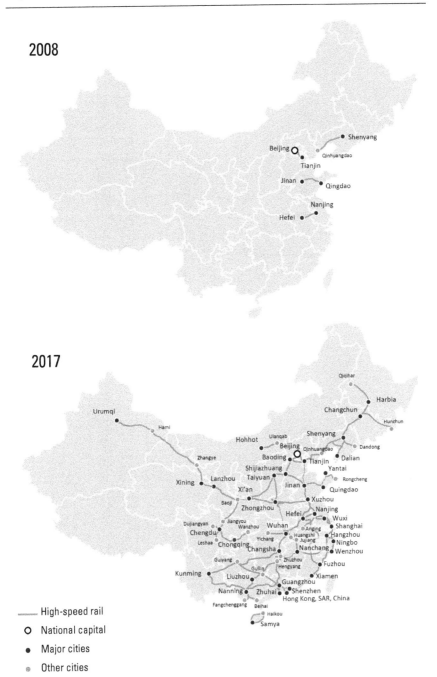

2008

2017

_____ High-speed rail

O   National capital

●   Major cities

◉   Other cities

SOURCE Lawrence, Martha, Richard Bullock, and Ziming Liu. 2019. China's High-Speed Rail Development. International Development in Focus. Washington, DC: World Bank. This is an adaptation of an original work by The World Bank. Views and opinions expressed in the adaptation are the sole responsibility of the author and are not endorsed by The World Bank.

decrease in air domestic passengers of 28.2 per cent, in flights of 24.6 per cent and in seat capacity of 27.9 per cent. The impact varied according to distance between destinations and was much stronger on routes between 500 km and 800 km. For example, air travel declined approximately 45 per cent after commencement of the high-speed line between Wuhan and Guangzhou, cities which are 833 km (518 miles) apart. But it fell only 34 per cent after the opening of the Beijing–Shanghai high-speed line: those cities are some 1,100 km (680 miles) apart.[10]

China also borrowed plans from abroad for urban metro systems. The first model was that of Moscow and a new Beijing subway system was proposed in 1953 by the city's planning committee with help from Russian experts. This used small trains bought from Moscow and powered by DC current provided through a third rail. After the end of the Korean War, Chinese leaders turned their attention to domestic reconstruction and were keen to expand the capital's mass transit capacity. But they also valued the subway system for its potential use in civil defence. The Moscow Metro had been used to protect civilians, move troops and serve as a military command headquarters during the Battle of Moscow in World War II and the Beijing subway system was designed for both civilian and military purposes.

Later, Hong Kong became the template for urban rail technology. The city of Shanghai drew up an initial blueprint for 15 metro lines using an overhead power supply and this was rolled out between 1994 and 2015. The urban planning that went into this blueprint was thorough and extensive and it responded as well as possible to the mobility needs of the city anticipated for the next decades. It detailed residency and business districts, anticipating future citizens' migration from rural areas to the metropolis. Shanghai is considered by many experts to be a best-practice model of city planning and a blueprint for urban growth supported by a mobility masterplan.

New challengers to rail

Despite the advances in speed, safety, comfort and software integration, much about rail technology has not changed dramatically in recent decades. However, there are at least two potential challengers.

One is magnetic levitation, or maglev. Instead of being held up by wheels in contact with steel rails, a maglev train floats several centimetres above a concrete guide using magnetic levitation. Magnets also propel the train, typically consisting of 10–16 cars. The lack of physical contact greatly reduces friction, so the trains can accelerate rapidly and maintain a high speed – potentially over 500 kph – using relatively little energy. They should also have lower lifecycle costs and produce less noise and vibration than with rail mainstream technologies.

The first commercial maglev train was operated in Birmingham, in the UK, as an airlink shuttle from 1984 to 1995. The best-known current commercial service has run since 2003 between Shanghai and Pudong International Airport at 430 kph (268 mph) and it remains the world's fastest electric train. Maglev has since been proposed in Germany and North America, but the most serious programme outside China is in Japan. Japan's current plan calls for a maglev line that will cover the 285 km (178 miles) distance between Tokyo and Nagoya at speeds of 500 kph, slashing the journey time from 1 hour 40 minutes for the bullet train to just 40 minutes. In 2015, a Japanese maglev train reached over 600 kph in a test run, setting a new world speed record.[11,12]

I have been involved in two Oliver Wyman maglev assessments and benchmarks against other types of high-speed rail service – one for a province in Canada and one for a rail equipment manufacturer. When working on these, the consulting team reviewed other comparative studies from Europe and the United States. The conclusions were, roughly, as follows: Maglev scores relatively high on aspects such as ride comfort, noise and the ability to climb steeper grades than high-speed rail trains. But the combined advantage of these factors does not make a significant, revenue-enhancing difference to people's propensity to travel (at the distances considered at the time), and the advantages were not great enough to outweigh the far higher investment needed for maglev. In Japan, for example, to bring Osaka within an hour of Tokyo by 2045, a maglev line would be built 80 per cent underground and would cost about $35 billion, according to JRailpass.com.

However, to enhance its competitiveness, high-speed rail has been getting faster thanks to dedicated high-grade tracks and technical improvements in all key components of the train system. The first TGVs had a top speed of 270 kph, but both the TGV and the German ICE ('InterCity Express') now reach above 350 kph, while Japan's shinkansen has a maximum cruising speed of 320 kph. This means that maglev, while faster at 500 kph or more, would have a relatively smaller time advantage for travel between two city pairs with the greatest number of passengers. Moreover, the advantages in travel time that come from higher speeds depend heavily on the length of the run between stations because of the time taken to accelerate to the top speed after a stop and the time to decelerate before the next station. Germany in particular has numerous cities, as mentioned above, that are fairly close to each other, meaning that maglev would not have a great advantage over high-speed trains (ICE).

For established railways complementing their other passenger services footprint, traditional, track-based rail also has an advantage in being more compatible with existing rail networks. That is, it is easier to connect high-speed rail with lower grades of track (such as those for the TGV) so passengers will be able to change trains more fluidly. In addition, while maglev operating cost details were still unknown at the times of the studies, energy consumption was assumed to be lower for high-speed rail. In general, the marginal cost of increases in maximum speed – due to system design, construction and operating costs – grows more than proportionally to speed.

Finally, the most common argument levelled against maglev has been initial capex investment, as the projects start from scratch and cannot be integrated into standard rail infrastructure. The line in Shanghai is reported to lose between $85 million and $100 million a year. 'The maglev constitutes not only an extraordinarily costly but also an abnormally energy-wasting project, consuming in operation between four and five times as much power as the Tokaido Shinkansen' (between Tokyo and Osaka), Japanese researchers Hidekazu Aoki and Nobuo Kawamiya wrote in a 2017 paper studying their country's project.[13]

My conclusion, and that of the rail experts I have been talking to, is that maglev could conceivably be viable but will most likely remain a niche product, serving areas of very high population density on a point-to-point basis over distances above 600 km and in markets commanding high price points.

Another potential high-speed surface technology to compete with rail is the hyperloop. Unlike maglev, this has not yet been commercialized and is still largely at the concept stage. The idea is to create a low-pressure environment – close to a vacuum – in a tube, so that pods can travel at high speed without air resistance. They would use magnetic levitation technology to glide smoothly without touching the tube walls, covering long distances at high speed – 1,000 kph or so – with little energy expenditure. The pods are coaches and kept at atmospheric pressure for the passengers inside.[14,15]

The technology made headlines in 2012 when it was championed by billionaire and serial entrepreneur Elon Musk, who said the pods would travel from downtown Los Angeles to downtown San Francisco in less than 30 minutes, compared with a six-hour drive, one-and-a-half-hour flight or the two hours 40 minutes that a proposed high-speed rail link would need. He added that solar panels could make it self-powering and even generate more electricity than it consumed. However, by 2023 this project had been slowed by cost and regulatory hurdles, while there is an ongoing attempt to construct a California high-speed rail connection – a technology that has been proven in several other countries.

In Europe, too, progress has been slow. Hyperloop Transportation Technologies installed a research and development (R&D) centre and test track in 2017 on a decommissioned military airfield near Toulouse, in south-west France's aerospace cluster. But activity at this centre never really took off. Its headcount never exceeded 10 and in 2021 the company decided to cancel construction of a second test track. The airfield owner then discontinued the lease, planning to replace the hyperloop centre with a cluster of green aviation start-ups.[16]

In Switzerland, the EuroTube project is planning a 3 km test track. This will eventually look at challenges such as switching vehicles from an environment at atmospheric pressure to a vacuum, and how to adapt the pods for freight, which is normally heavier than human passengers. Here too, however, the costs of infrastructure, development and certification are major hurdles. Mobility experts I talked to also question the ability of the hyperloop to serve high-density markets, given that pods used in concept models are quite small.[17]

Towards a pan-European rail network

Unlike these emerging technologies, high-speed rail has a record of safe, efficient operation in a variety of countries. That success suggests that the systems could be the basis for trunk transport connections that increase mobility around the world. However, even the early adopter Europe has a long way to go before it has a high-speed rail network that serves much of its population. In continental Europe, high-speed rail lines are now mainly concentrated in western and central Germany, France, Spain, Italy, Belgium and the Netherlands. Eastern Europe has relatively few lines.

The European Union approved an initial plan in 1996 for a Trans-European Transport Network (TEN-T), which includes a Trans-European high-speed rail network (TEN-R) with a target for completion of 2030. The TEN-R will add connections between the western European networks as well as a line through the Baltic states (see Figure 2.2). The scheme has been updated several times, most recently as part of EU plans to achieve climate

Figure 2.2 European high-speed network vision for 2050

.... Baseline (current HSR network)

━━━ 2030 scenario (TEN-T Core)

.... 2050 scenario (TEN-T extended core & comprehensive)

_____ 2050 scenario (study's ambition)

.... 2050 scenario EU accession candidates scenario

A detailed colour version of this figure is available at www.koganpage.com/TIM

SOURCE Europe's Rail Joint Undertaking

targets. The European Commission's 2020 'Sustainable and Smart Mobility Strategy' outlined a plan for sustainable mobility in the context of the European Green Deal. The strategy is supposed to guide the mobility sector to reduce carbon emissions by 90 per cent by 2050, and increased rail travel was given an important role. Notably, the Commission wanted high-speed rail traffic to double by 2030 and triple by 2050. And it targeted a doubling of rail freight traffic by 2050.[18,19,20]

Europe's Rail Joint Undertaking (EU-Rail), a group that connects the EU with major companies in the rail industry, commissioned a study on what would be needed to construct a more ambitious high-speed rail network – that is, one that connects European cities with more than 250,000 inhabitants. It concluded that the existing high-speed rail network would need to be at least tripled, at a cost of some €550 billion.[19]

After several decades of development and operations, there is ample evidence that high-speed ground transport boosts economic growth. The four decades the TGV has been running in France have been a period of almost continuous expansion. Jean-Pierre Farandou, Chairman and CEO of SNCF Group, puts this down to the widespread appeal of saving time during travel. In the UK, then-Prime Minister David Cameron told the Institute of Civil Engineering in 2012, 'Infrastructure matters because it is the magic ingredient in so much of modern life; it is not secondary to other more high-profile elements of economic strategy, it affects the competitiveness of every business in the country, it is the invisible thread that ties our prosperity together.' EU-Rail said that its plan would bring net positive benefits in the range of €750 billion by 2070 as high-speed rail became the dominant mode of travel with a 54 per cent share.

Still, tripling high-speed rail traffic over 30 years would imply compound annual growth of about 4 per cent, which is higher than the historical average, and it would therefore need rail to take market share from other forms of transport. There are several ways in which this could happen.

Traffic on existing lines, both domestic and cross-border, might be increased by more sophisticated, interoperable control capabilities, which could raise the frequency of service and therefore boost capacity. Faster, more reliable rolling stock would also increase capacity. 'The performance of rail lies in its ability to transport 1,000 passengers at a speed of 100 metres per second with only 10 square centimetres of friction surface per car,' according to Jean-Pierre Loubinoux, Honorary Director General of the International Union of Railways, the global rail industry association. 'That's why rail will remain a backbone of the mobility value chain.'

Demand might end up being further boosted by regulatory and reputational pressures to restrict or tax air travel, due to public concerns over climate change and the use of fossil fuels in aviation. In the past, fuel price increases have boosted demand for high-speed rail as it disproportionately affected the price levels of flights. And travellers could also be attracted by open access competition between rail operators on long-distance services, leading to higher frequencies and service levels and driving a better travel experience and lower prices.

However, the industry also faces challenges that might block or slow down its ambitions. The past decades have shown repeatedly that rail expansion is about more than just infrastructure building.

How much new rail will be needed? Population growth drives mobility demand, but Eurostat projects that the EU's population will peak at 453 million people in 2026 before decreasing to 420 million in 2100. While very large metropolises are expected to continue to grow, this might not be the case in secondary cities.[21]

Even where demand is sufficient, there are questions over the ability to finance new projects, with costs varying a lot depending on the project design and the market. A 2016 UK government assessment of 20 European high-speed rail networks ('High speed rail international benchmarking study') concluded that 'high speed rail lines can be delivered under certain circumstances at an average cost of £32M (€38M) per km'. A European Court of Auditors benchmarking report in 2018 put the average cost on continental Europe at £25 million per kilometre for dedicated high-speed rail lines. But in 2022, the British Institution of Civil Engineers estimated the cost of the UK's High Speed 2 project at as much as £200 million (€235 million) per kilometre. Much of the financing might be expected to come from governments, but average government debt in the European Union reached 84 per cent of GDP in 2022, which is well above the fiscal goal of 60 per cent outlined in the EU Treaties.

"The performance of rail lies in its ability to transport 1,000 passengers at a speed of 100 metres per second with only 10cm² of friction surface per car"

Jean-Pierre Loubinoux

Air transport, in contrast, requires relatively modest spending: just a simple runway is enough to launch thousands of planes that will eventually transport millions of travellers for thousands of air miles per flight, shared with me once one airport authority executive.[22]

Beyond funding, bottlenecks and delays often result from a lack of industrial capacity, value chain fragmentation and project planning.

Moreover, these plans will need to be developed and executed over a long period of time, so they will require sustained commitment from governments. But the period until 2050 will see six different European Commissions and Parliaments and their level of ambition might change. Member states, too, will experience a number of political changes and enthusiasm for high-speed rail tends to fluctuate. The Swedish government recently dropped plans for two high-speed rail lines because of a change in priorities. However, Poland, Czechia and the Baltic states signed a cooperation agreement in January 2023 to construct a high-speed link from Poland to Ukraine. While the war in Ukraine will of course affect timing, Poland in the meantime is developing almost 2,000 km of new railway lines, mainly high-speed. Czechia has plans for 700 km of new high-speed lines connecting to its neighbours.[23]

Above all, high-speed rail is essentially a greenfield project – one that works when there is enough space for new construction and business opportunities. As economies develop, transport infrastructure needs to take into account the cities and infrastructure that already exist, and building has to be carried out alongside, around or in place of them. Transport projects also need to be complemented by a range of connected services. These considerations can make them extremely complicated, as several recent examples show.

KEY TAKEAWAYS

- Railways helped shape the modern era. They allowed people to cross whole continents and travel on land at unprecedented speed. They helped to unite countries, opening up isolated regions and connecting them to growth and opportunities.

- High-speed rail services redefined the possibilities of travel for ordinary people, providing broad access to long-distance ground mobility.

- Other technologies have been challenging rail as a means of mass, high-speed mobility, but they have not yet succeeded commercially.

- However, it is very hard to develop cross-border train services. This is a significant challenge in comparison with air travel.
- China's high-speed rail system has become the foundation for the country's new role as a global mobility trendsetter.
- The network effect, whereby a good or service becomes more valuable when more people use it, is key to ensuring the viability of infrastructure investment. This is crucial for rail as it is capital-intensive and requires long-term planning.

Notes

1 Ambrose, S.E. (2005) *Nothing Like It in the World: The men who built the Transcontinental Railroad, 1863–1869*. New York: Simon & Schuster.

2 leparisien.fr. (2011) Les 30 ans de la révolution TGV. Available at: www.leparisien.fr/archives/les-30-ans-de-la-revolution-tgv-07-04-2011-1397176.php (archived at https://perma.cc/BPL6-DC5U)

3 Haddard, M.-P. (2011) Le TGV fait flamber l'immobilier à Marseille, BFMTV.com, 7 April. Available at: www.bfmtv.com/immobilier/prix-immobilier/le-tgv-fait-flamber-l-immobilier-a-marseille_AN-201104070165.html#:~:text=Entre%201999%20et%202007%2C%20le,de%20la%20ville%20au%20TGV (archived at https://perma.cc/MT9P-8XYZ)

4 Allen Veditz, L. (1993) The Channel Tunnel – a case study, Industrial College of the Armed Forces, National Defense University.

5 Eurostar (2023) About us: The whole story, from A to B and beyond. Available at: www.eurostar.com/be-en/about-eurostar (archived at https://perma.cc/2X9C-FZ9B)

6 UK Department of Transport (2023) Rail statistics. Available at: www.gov.uk/government/collections/rail-statistics (archived at https://perma.cc/J8EP-VFEG)

7 Sen, S. (2004) The Channel Tunnel and its impact on tourism in the United Kingdom, Department of Geography – University of Reading.

8 Rowland, B. (2019) High speed rail vs air: Eurostar at 25, the story so far, OAG, 28 November. Available at: www.oag.com/blog/high-speed-rail-vs-air-eurostar-at-25-the-story-so-far (archived at https://perma.cc/6A5P-ENHU)

9 Ernst & Young (2018) Economic footprint of the Channel Tunnel in the EU. Available at: www.getlinkgroup.com/content/uploads/2019/09/180604-EY-Channel-Tunnel-Footprint-Report.pdf (archived at https://perma.cc/P37E-4BV6)

10 Chen, Z. (2017) Impacts of high-speed rail on domestic air transportation in China. *Journal of Transport Geography*, 62, 184–96.

11 Davies, R. (2020) Magnetic pull: China and Japan battle it out for maglev train supremacy. *Railway Technology*. Available at: www.railway-technology. com/features/maglev-train/#catfish (archived at https://perma.cc/WL68-GMGM)

12 JRailPass (2019) Le Maglev japonais: le train à grande vitesse le plus rapide au monde, JRailPass. Available at: www.jrailpass.com/blog/fr/maglev-japonais (archived at https://perma.cc/LG4A-YKKB)

13 Hidekazu, A. and Nobuo, K. (2017) End game for Japan's construction state – the linear (Maglev) Shinkansen and Abenomics. *The Asia-Pacific Journal | Japan Focus*, 15. Available at: https://apjjf.org/-Kawamiya-Nobuo--Aoki-Hidekazu/5050/article.pdf (archived at https://perma.cc/C8UV-6CR6)

14 EuroTube (n.d.) Hyperloop: A new mode of transport. Available at: https://eurotube.org/hyperloop/ (archived at https://perma.cc/EX5X-2DT7)

15 Raimondi, M. (2022) Swiss EuroTube to experiment with hyperloop tech for moving goods, RailTech.com, 19 October. Available at: www.railtech.com/ innovation/2022/10/19/swiss-eurotube-to-experiment-with-hyperloop-tech-for-moving-goods (archived at https://perma.cc/F5XH-PT4Y)

16 Lynley, M. (2012) Elon Musk wants to invent a fifth mode of transportation called 'Hyperloop', Business Insider, 13 July. Available at: www.businessinsider. com/elon-musk-is-kicking-around-an-idea-that-would-send-you-from-san-francisco-to-los-angeles-in-30-minutes-2012-7?r=US&IR=T (archived at https://perma.cc/3XYQ-PUAP)

17 Yao, D. (2023) SXSW '23: Whatever happened to the Hyperloop?, AI Business. com, 17 March. Available at: https://aibusiness.com/verticals/sxsw-23-whatever-happened-to-the-hyperloop-

18 Chebara, S. (2020) New European mobility strategy aims to triple high-speed rail traffic, Railtech.com, 10 December. Available at: www.railtech.com/ policy/2020/12/10/new-european-mobility-strategy-aims-to-triple-high-speed-rail-traffic/?gdpr=accept (archived at https://perma.cc/A8YF-ZXDB)

19 Ernst & Young (2023) Smart and affordable rail services in the EU: A socio-economic and environmental study for high-speed in 2030 and 2050. Available at: https://rail-research.europa.eu/wp-content/uploads/2023/01/HSR_Technical_Report_1_Final_220123_v1_update.pdf (archived at https://perma. cc/MX9X-56SX)

20 transport.ec.europa.eu (n.d.) TEN-T revision. Available at: https://transport. ec.europa.eu/transport-themes/infrastructure-and-investment/trans-european-transport-network-ten-t/ten-t-revision_en (archived at https://perma.cc/ RHK2-74C7)

21   Eurostat (2023) EU's population projected to drop by 6% by 2100. Available at: https://ec.europa.eu/eurostat/web/products-eurostat-news/w/DDN-20230330-1 (archived at https://perma.cc/4ZK9-4GED)

22   Gauret, F. (2023) Europe's fiscal rules review – what does it mean?, Euronews. next, 7 June. Available at: www.euronews.com/next/2023/06/07/europe-fiscal-rules-review-what-does-it-mean (archived at https://perma.cc/EV85-Q425)

23   Geerts, E. (2023) A high-speed rail network from the Baltics to Central Europe is one step closer, Railtech.com, 19 January. Available at: www.railtech.com/infrastructure/2023/01/19/a-high-speed-rail-network-from-the-baltics-to-central-europe-is-one-step-closer/ (archived at https://perma.cc/G95L-VVJV)

Designing futures　　　　　　　3

Why long-term planning is needed and is increasingly difficult

- Why long-term planning is needed – and increasingly difficult in some regions.
- How transport planners cope with the trade-offs between economic and political agendas.
- Which governance systems may best support the long-term building of fixed infrastructure.

Giant mobility projects can have great positive impacts for economies, nations and societies. But their scale means they need to be planned and financed over years or decades and it is difficult to anticipate the changes – from demand or technology to politics – that will occur over such a period of time. One example where evolving reality did not match a grand plan was in Montreal, Canada.

The city's Mirabel Airport seemed destined for great success. Canada's second biggest city was booming in the 1960s. Its first Metro line was inaugurated in 1966 and the following year it hosted the 1967 International and Universal Exposition. The city was also bidding to host the 1976 Olympic Games, and new highways, a performing arts centre and a sizable underground shopping mall were being planned or under construction. It seemed that Montreal would soon rival Toronto as the country's main economic and social centre.

For a city on the up and up, its main air link was becoming too small. Opened in 1941, 19 km (12 miles) from downtown, Dorval Airport handled 3 million passengers in 1965, but Canada's Department of Transport forecast the number of passengers per annum would reach 30 million by 1990. Moreover, Montreal needed an airport that could handle new types of aircraft: some were especially large, such as the Boeing 747, which went into service in 1970; others were especially noisy, such as the Concorde, which would start commercial flights in 1976. But expanding Dorval Airport would have required land purchase orders and local residents were already complaining about Dorval's noise. In 1968, the Canadian government decided to build a new airport.

The federal government's preferred site was in the county of Vaudreuil-Dorion, about 40 km (25 miles) west of central Montreal – and also just 129 km (80 miles) from Canada's capital Ottawa. The site had good rail and road links and could serve both cities if complemented by a high-speed rail connection. However, this proposed site was also close to the border between Quebec and Ontario. That raised the possibility that airport workers might move to Ontario in order to pay its lower taxes and Quebec Premier Robert Bourassa opposed the idea. He preferred Drummondville, 113 km (70 miles) east of Montreal. In March 1969, a compromise was found, that is Sainte-Scholastique, 48 km (30 miles) northwest of downtown Montreal.

Named Mirabel, after a nineteenth-century farm on the new airport site, this location suffered from a lack of surface transport connections: to make the airport function well, at least two new highways and a direct rail link would be needed. Still, these could be built. A new highway, Quebec Autoroute 50, would serve the airport, while passengers could reach Montreal in around 25 minutes via a high-speed train called TRRAMM (Transport Rapide Régional Aéroportuaire Montréal–Mirabel), which would run at up to 120 kph (75 mph).

To suit the projected increase in demand, Mirabel was designed along the lines of Dallas-Fort Worth Airport in Texas, which was then under construction. This had an open plan apron design – that is, terminals lined a central spine road and it could easily be expanded or extended. The layout provided enough space for high-priority wide-bodied aeroplanes to manoeuver to the terminal buildings without causing traffic jams on the taxiways or apron. A train station would go in the basement, while a road tunnel under the runways would take drivers right to the international terminal. Passengers would be transported to aeroplanes with newly designed transfer vehicles, which cost C$400,000 each.

The airport was allocated 6,890 hectares (17,000 acres), with enough space to eventually host six long runways, plus a shorter seventh to handle regional turboprops and short take-off and landing (STOL) flights to and from nearby destinations. With a buffer zone of 32,400 hectares (80,000 acres) included to host a new industrial park, the airport would cover 38,800 hectares (96,000 acres), approximately 80 per cent the size of Montreal Island itself. This would make Mirabel the largest airport in the world in terms of property area at the time. In the final layout, the total capacity would be 60 million passengers, expected to be attained by 2025. The initial cost: $500 million, equivalent of $2.6 billion in 2020. As features and capacity were added over the years, the cost would end up at around $1 billion.[1,2,3]

Montréal–Mirabel International Airport opened on 4 October 1975, 10 months before the start of the Olympic Games. All international flights from Dorval were transferred to Mirabel. After all domestic services were transferred to Mirabel by 1982, Dorval's facility would be sold off for other developments. 'Through the ingenuity of its progress, through its extreme technical refinement, though its tremendous size, Mirabel in effect announces the year 2000,' said Pierre Trudeau, Canada's then prime minister, at the opening. 'What we see will be multiplied by six over the next 50 years.'[4]

Once the Olympics had finished in August 1976, Montreal's fortunes took a downturn, as its economy slowed in the wake of the 1973 oil crisis. Another reason was the election of separatist provincial governments in Quebec, which held two referendums on independence and introduced strict language laws. Some 200,000 anglophone Montrealers left, as did the corporate headquarters of several major banks and industrial giants, and during the 1970s and 1980s Montreal fell out of favour relative to Toronto as a business centre. 'In the Sixties, Montreal was the metropolis of Canada,' Aéroports de Montréal's operations director Normand Boivin told *The Guardian* in 2003. 'Banks, international organisations, commercial activity – everyone wanted to be here. It was booming.' But in 1976, a year after Mirabel opened, 'a separatist government was elected in Quebec and commerce started running away'.[5]

Another blow came from the evolution of aircraft. Early jet airliners, such as the Boeing 707, needed to refuel on journeys between Europe and the western United States and Canada, and Montreal had become an important fuel stop and connection point. But improved airlines had longer range and did not need to make fuel stopovers any more.

Due to the oil crisis, air fares rose, the growth in air traffic slowed and Mirabel's passenger traffic failed to grow as expected. The proposed TRRAMM rapid transit service – originally intended for opening in 1980 – was abandoned. Instead, a bus service connected the city with the airport, taking about an hour in fluid traffic or two during the rush hour. With no suitable ground transfer between Mirabel and downtown Montreal, the Quebec government shelved the original plan to move domestic flights to Mirabel from Dorval. This decision was supported by Air Canada, the national flag carrier, as its maintenance base was in Dorval. But that meant connections between domestic and international flights at Montreal required an hour-long bus ride. As a result, most foreign airlines preferred to schedule international trips with transfers at Toronto or Vancouver rather than Montreal. Despite the forecasts of 50–60 million passengers per year, Mirabel never attracted more than 2.8 million.

The final blow came in 1997 when Dorval was allowed to host international flights once again. Noise had become less of a concern as the relatively quiet Boeing 747 came to dominate international travel and Air Canada had cancelled its initial order for Concorde in 1972. As a result, residents around Dorval lobbied to expand the airport. It was renamed Montréal–Trudeau International Airport and expanded at a cost of C$716 million, which meant it could accommodate up to 20 million passengers a year.

Mirabel, which the Quebec taxpayer was subsidizing by C$20 million a year, now served only a few daily charter flights run by holiday companies, as well as some cargo carriers. It was also used for exterior shots in *The Terminal*, a 2004 comedy starring Tom Hanks about a man stuck in an airport terminal because he is denied entry to the United States but is unable to return to his native country after a military coup. The final passenger flight took off on 31 October 2004, an Air Transat service to Paris.

Infrastructure to serve passenger flights was dismantled during the 2000s and 2010s, including the Chateau Aeroport-Mirabel, a 354-room hotel located opposite the main terminal, which had opened in 1977 and closed in 2002. The terminal and gates were demolished between 2014 and 2016. However, cargo operations are still carried out at the airport and a base for aircraft manufacturers has been opened. 'When the decision was taken to build the airport there, I think it was an error,' James Cherry, CEO of Aéroports de Montréal, told Canadian broadcaster CBC/Radio-Canada in 2014, while pointing out that he had been only 14 years old at the time. 'All the premises on which the reasoning to build Mirabel were based – the growth and evolution of traffic, the type of aircraft – none of these hypotheses came about. That means the whole basis of the project was false.'[6]

Political compromises and sub-optimal decisions

The fate of projects such as Mirabel International Airport highlights one of the greatest challenges for the design and economics of the mobility and transport sector. These types of projects can have great positive impacts for society, so they are often planned and financed over several decades. But it's hard – very hard – to foresee how they will evolve over this time-scale.

More than most other industries, mobility is based on long-lived assets. Fixed infrastructure such as highways and rail lines can last 50 years or more. The US Congress first funded motorways in 1916 and by 2020 the Interstate Highway System had a total length of 78,465 km (48,755 miles). Europe now has about 75,000 km of motorway and China 130,000 km. Aircraft and rail rolling-stock may have 30- or 50-year lifecycles. The ideal framework calls for stable long-range planning horizon accompanied by large-scale investment.

However, history in most territories tells us that these needs are routinely upset by changes in demand, the economy and governments' political and infrastructure priorities. Future demand for mobility can be forecasted from an array of parameters. But these all carry some degree of volatility. Technological development leads to new services, including shifts within a single mode of transport, while energy prices have already resulted in huge shifts over the past half century. The spread of cars slowed after the 1970s' oil shock, for example, but cheaper oil in the 1990s later encouraged a boom in SUVs and pickup trucks.

Changes in population and in lifestyle shift people's preferences for where they live and work – and how they move between their homes and their workplaces. The location of workplaces will depend on shifts in the flow and production of goods. Mirabel is a salutary reminder for policymakers not to get carried away with an industry's optimistic forecasts of growth. But in the time since its opening, demand has grown even more sophisti-cated and diverse.

Mobility infrastructure needs to be integrated with surrounding cities and the industrial landscape, and for an airport this can require still further infrastructure in the form of new ground transport links, such as metro lines and roads. Mature methodologies can be used to assess the economic im-pact on a region of a new port, the urban development that new high-speed rail lines will generate, or the business and tourism connections from new bridges, trains and highways. But this is highly complex. In the case of Mirabel, the design of a successful airport will depend on airline network and fleet planning decisions, so extensive dialogue is required among the participants in an ecosystem. Airlines say that a major problem at Mirabel was that it split Montreal's air hub into two.

As a result, large, long-term projects – while necessary for effective transportation networks – may turn out not to be attractive returns in a reasonable future as economic and technological changes occur. This is a major reason why governments and businesses have become increasingly hesitant to invest in them. This is also complicated by the fact that different modes of transport are often governed by different jurisdictions and regulators – or by different levels of government, such as city, regional and national. 'Long-range planning is required to build a functioning mobility system,' says Xavier Huillard, Chief Executive Officer of VINCI. 'It starts with infrastructure that generates economic value and requires a well-defined, holistic governance. Eventually, a multi-party, cross-mode mobility ecosystem can be organized to harmonize and optimize the outcome.'

Rail and urban development

Rail, with its need for dedicated infrastructure covering hundreds of kilometres, is a prime example of a mode that is easiest to build as a greenfield project – that is, one that is carried out on undeveloped land lacking constraints imposed by prior work. Today, a variety of infrastructure modes is increasingly intertwined, creating demand for connections between air and rail and between roads and mass transit systems in big cities. Climate and sustainability imperatives complicate networks further, due to the necessity of providing sources of renewable energy for green vehicles. This too requires long-term planning – as well as financing and economic models that have not yet fully emerged.

Andrew Lezala, former Managing Director and CEO at Metro Trains Australia, stresses, 'Mobility requires a long-term masterplan. All cities should look up to Shanghai and its impressive 1994–2015 programme of urban and transport planning. The blueprint was a best practice and the system now has 19 metro lines.'

....

"Long-range planning is required to build a functioning mobility system"
Xavier Huillard

....

"Mobility requires a long-term masterplan. All cities should look up to Shanghai and its impressive 1994–2015 programme of urban and transport planning"
Andrew Lezala

New urban developments need to integrate mobility infrastructure, which implies designing it in the early phases of the planning. Mobility options define the distribution of living space and commercial areas, which in turn orient other kinds of urban infrastructure. For instance, the newly developed Lusail City, Qatari Diar's flagship project, has been conceived as a self-contained sustainable and comprehensively planned city. A $45 billion project, Lusail is being developed in an area that until recently was desert. It will host more than 250,000 residents, with 170,000 people expected to work in the city's different districts and 80,000 expected to visit its recreation, retail and hospitality facilities. The transport network was designed early on to respond to the modelled future demand. To reduce vehicle emissions and save energy, it includes a light-rail system with 38 km of rail that connect 38 stations in the city's 19 districts. Underground car parks are intended to encourage people to leave their cars at stations and use the rail system to travel within the city. The rail network is also connected to both the national and international rail networks. Transport infrastructure forms a fundamental part of the city concept. 'Major projects, such as the Suez Canal, France's TGV and the Swiss interconnected commuter network, are driven by big political agendas,' says Joris D'Incà, Partner at Oliver Wyman, Global Head of the Logistics Sector and Market Leader of Switzerland. 'Governments today may still be in a position to play critical roles in shaping mobility infrastructure and solutions.'[7]

"Major projects – such as the Suez Canal, France's TGV and the Swiss interconnected commuter network – are driven by big political agendas"
Joris D'Incà

France, too, has developed new cities in the twentieth century. The *villes nouvelles* of the 1960s were designed as brand-new urban systems that would function as relatively autonomous areas – a contrast to suburbs that acted as residential areas for city commuters. Cities such as Cergy Pontoise to the north of Paris, Evry to the south and Saint-Quentin-en-Yvelines to the west have a balance between housing and employment in order to fix populations locally and reduce the concentration in big cities. As well as internal transport connections, they are linked to Paris and nearby towns through the regional express train network, the *Réseau Express Régional*, or RER.

André Navarri, former President and Chief Operating Officer at Bombardier Transportation, proposes that large urban areas gather relevant stakeholders – including government, urban architects, mobility providers and business representatives – to take a holistic approach to an ambitious, long-term, multi-modal transport policy. They could then structure and time the most important decisions and manage interdependencies. 'Better demand anticipation – and shaping – can help create a more holistic 20- to 30-year multi-modal end-to-end mobility blueprint,' he says.

However, Europe's dense cities and transport networks mean that most new projects are 'brownfield': they are constructed on top of, or around, existing structures. That is a far greater engineering challenge than building from scratch because the projects have to take account of the complexities of current and legacy infrastructure, making them complex to design and execute. These projects can lead to multi-year disruptions to legacy systems, as experienced with the 'Grand Paris' programme or Toronto's GO Expansion project in Canada. The route of London's Crossrail, which opened in 2022, had to be drawn around sewers, the foundations of high-rise buildings and other underground tunnels. And work on a new Brussels metro line came to a halt in 2023 due to the difficulty and extra cost of

"Better demand anticipation can help create a more holistic mobility blueprint"
André Navarri

constructing a tunnel under the Palais de Midi, a nineteenth-century commercial building with historic value.[8,9,10,11]

There are some exceptions, especially in East Asia, where countries such as Japan, South Korea and Singapore have managed to design modern transport systems in old, established cities. But these cities sometimes face criticism that they go too far with redevelopment. In 2023, the Tokyo Metropolitan Government approved a $2 billion plan to redevelop a 28-hectare area near the outer garden of the famous Meiji Shrine, triggering protests that this will destroy an important piece of the city's cultural heritage.

In general, however, the design of transport infrastructure lags behind cities' development and evolution and the result is often a patchwork of systems that are not well aligned with urban development needs. Reliability and service levels may become stressed, leading to customer dissatisfaction and overlapping modal offerings. The cost to serve is higher and operators' margins are thin.

Planning under political cycles

A major reason for the difficulty of large-scale transport infrastructure projects is growing political challenges, making execution difficult, leading to stop-and-go planning and significant waste in capital employed. Big projects work best with stable, long-term government support and financing. This is typically more easily available under a long-reigning consensus that the benefits are worth the huge costs.

But only a few countries in modern times have the long-term planning horizons and consistency required for such planning. In general, this is easier under authoritarian governments – or, at least, in countries with little political alternation and highly centralized governments that implement long-term decisions from the top down. Saudi Arabia, for example, is planning Neom, a futuristic city in the desert that will be made up of a number of regions and is planned for completion by 2030. It will feature a floating industrial complex, global trade hub, tourist resorts and a linear city – all powered exclusively by renewable energy sources.

China in particular has a highly centralized planning framework, which has enabled it to expand considerably its mobility capabilities, performance and innovation. Beijing set out a top-down integrated mobility strategy in the 1980s by drawing up a blueprint for mobility in megacities – both existing and prospective. One pillar of the strategy was consistent standardization across a range of infrastructure of systems ranging from telecommunications to signalling and control. A second was to import technologies developed overseas and then localize them. Overseas providers – rail is an example – had to come to China to install their capabilities and then further develop their competencies in the country. Third, China then developed its own industry around this nucleus of capabilities. The fourth pillar was to integrate the supply chain so that capabilities would be developed at every stage along it. Unlike countries with substantial legacy transport systems, where incumbents resist new standards, transport in China was a blank slate and could be built with a disciplined approach spanning decades. In rail, for example, consistent vehicle design standards have been maintained for metro lines, followed by suburban, regional and high-speed rail, as well as light transit.

Western democracies tend to have shorter governance cycles, often leading to changing transport priorities, policies and regulations. Mobility is a key ingredient of people's quality of life, a core component of economic prosperity and a factor in homeland security. It is therefore subordinated to priorities, policies and funding decisions of elected governments. The democratic world today is beset by competing visions of how the world – cities, in particular – should be: all-car versus low-car, for example, or pro-aviation versus low-aviation. Many cities set up temporary cycling infrastructure and pedestrian zones during the Covid-19 pandemic to improve people's quality of life during lockdowns. Nearly 70 per cent of respondents to a 2020 survey said they wanted to see restrictions on car use maintained after the pandemic.[12] Later, however, these restrictions provoked a backlash from motorists, as did low-emissions zones designed to improve air quality.

In Berlin, a new, conservative city government took office in 2023 and rolled back some bike-friendly measures, suspending bike infrastructure projects that threatened existing car lanes or parking spaces and freezing a plan to add thousands of kilometres to the city's cycling network. The British Conservative Party, trailing the opposition in opinion polls in 2023, spotted a chance to gain popularity with motorists who opposed the roll-out of low-emission zones, especially in London. Prime Minister Rishi Sunak claimed that the United Kingdom was a 'nation of drivers', pledged to end 'anti-car measures' and laid out ideas to prioritize the needs of motorists.[13,14,15]

When the transcontinental railroad was being planned in the United States, its proponents set up a lobbying operation in Washington DC, which eventually yielded a special legal act and government subsidies. The railroad required mass land purchases and appropriations, which led to constant wars with native people. Today, compulsory land purchases still form part of the legal complications of high-speed rail projects, and existing infrastructure needs to be integrated into a new project, built around or simply demolished. In any of these cases, the existing infrastructure will come with existing interests, which have to be dealt with somehow. Environmental considerations include the carbon emission resulting from construction and the potential of a railway to disrupt natural habitats and reduce biodiversity.

Typically, a number of groups come out in opposition: political opponents claim the investment is unaffordable; competing modes lobby to halt the development; and environmentalists and property owners point to the damage the construction will lead to. As a result, those governments find it hard to plan transport infrastructure over a very long period. That has an impact on transport operators, as many are subsidized by governments and their planning needs official sponsorship. The outside pressure on politicians therefore pushes them to adapt to changing opinions. As a result, they find it hard to make decisions that are consistent with the long-term success of projects and they are often forced to make trade-offs. Most senior transport practitioners interviewed during research for this book said this is at the core of their strategy and leadership challenge.

High-speed rail at snail's pace

The United States' struggles with high-speed rail are a case in point. Though the technology exists and the idea of high-speed rail has its advocates, the plans have been held up by a combination of factors that loom large in democracies in a way that they do not in authoritarian systems of government. Local politicians insist that plans are changed in a way that benefits their municipality. At federal level, politicians who oppose passenger rail refuse to fund it, while even its proponents cause difficulties through domestic procurement rules. And at the individual level, citizens can make use of various laws that enable them to protest against plans that might have a negative impact on their property.

As a result, high-speed rail has hardly penetrated the US market to date. The Northeast Corridor between Washington DC and Boston has a fast rail service using rolling stock derived from European systems. But it does not use fully dedicated tracks: it runs on the legacy Amtrak Northeast Corridor infrastructure and average speeds are far slower than those of the latest TGV or ICE.

In 2002, Oliver Wyman presented the US Congress with an initial blue-print scenario for high-speed rail, the role that national railway Amtrak might play, and what private sector involvement might be and under what framework. A lot of the analysis was based on benchmarks from Europe and overseas, as passenger rail was undergoing a revival in many parts of the world in the early 2000s, prompted by privatization and investment in high-speed lines. The growth in ridership was helping to reduce road and air traffic congestion, and high-speed lines had gained significant share from air: short-haul air services were often reduced, freeing up scarce airport slots and air traffic capacity for long-haul.

In Europe, 3,050 km of new or upgraded high-speed lines had been built over the past 20 years and another 3,200 km were expected to open in the following five years or so, by 2007. The French TGV had a share of over 90 per cent on the Paris–Lyons route and Eurostar had already reached a 60 per cent share of the Paris–London route. On the Paris–Brussels route, a high-speed rail service had quickly gained a 95 per cent share and point-to-point air services had been completely withdrawn. Japan already had an extensive, privately operated high-speed rail network, which had largely re-placed air service on several medium-distance routes. A new high-speed line was being constructed in Taiwan and one was planned for South Africa.

The success of high-speed rail services meant that an increasing number of passenger rail services were profitable on a stand-alone basis and did not need massive government subsidy. However, the development of low-cost airlines had led to the sustained challenge to regular long-distance train ser-vices. In Australia and Canada, long-distance services were operated essen-tially for tourists and some had been concessioned to private operators.

Investments were proposed in two areas. One was middle-distance, high-density routes – primarily city-to-city pairs of between 160 km and 640 km, where rail can be competitive with car and air travel. The other was urban commuter and light-rail, which had the potential to relieve road congestion. For rural areas, where rail is not competitive with cars, and long-distance routes (over 1,200 km, where air has a big advantage) the study generally proposed the minimum investment required to keep them in operation.

Importantly, Amtrak itself was projecting for growth service a total capi-tal requirement over the following 20 years of $97.2 billion. Most of the incremental growth service capital requested (61.3 per cent) was for planned high-speed rail offerings. The proposed high-speed rail corridors were ar-rayed in eight separate networks serving the largest American population centres (see Figure 3.1).

Figure 3.1 US high-speed rail potential assessed in 2002

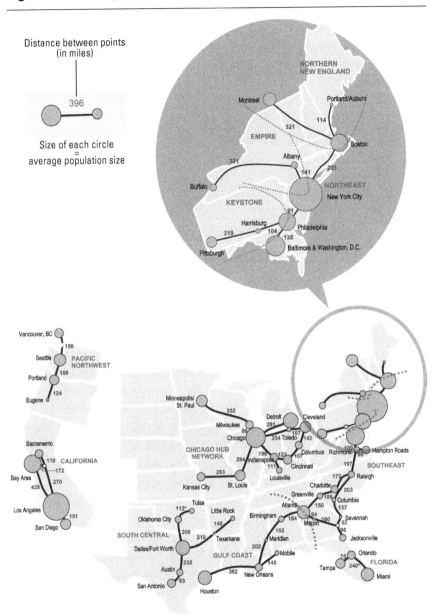

SOURCE US Department of Transportation, OW analysis
NOTE US Map modified for better visibility

Against this background, we reviewed the US travel market and screened every route based on a set of criteria: local population and population densities; the quality of connections and proximity to other modes such as airports and subway; the location of stations in urban centres and of airports relative to urban centres; and collateral public benefits such as the potential reduction in airport congestion. Taking into account the nature and intensity of modal competition, in particular low-cost airlines, we then modelled the optimal frequency of service and the resulting trade-offs in time, distance and speed. We also came up with propositions for the quality and type of onboard services required. Based upon markets and operating statistics, the best conditions to achieve operating self-sufficiency appeared to exist in the Northeast, Florida, Keystone, portions of the Chicago Hub network and California. However, progress has been slow. A detailed look at one of the proposed routes highlights why high-speed rail has had so much difficulty in the United States.

High-speed rail challenges in California

The route between San Francisco and Los Angeles is one of the most promising for high-speed rail in the United States. The journey takes less than an hour by plane, but that does not include time spent in two busy airports. By car, the trip is at least six hours. That means a high-speed rail connection at a bit over 2.5 hours is a sensible proposition. In the early 2000s, the California High-Speed Rail Authority considered various routes. The most obvious one went up the I-5 highway, a fairly direct route that connects the big cities on the West Coast. But it wasn't that simple.[16,17]

Politicians in Palmdale, in the north of Los Angeles County, wanted the train – and its riders and business opportunities – to head north from central LA to their district rather than immediately going northwest along the I-5. Therefore, the Los Angeles County Board of Supervisors insisted that Palmdale be added as a stop, lengthening the route by about 60 km (40 miles) and increasing the project's costs by 16 per cent. At the northern end, instead of following the I-5 along the west of the Central Valley, it would stop in cities further east – again to ensure support from the politicians there and again making the route slower and more expensive. Eventually, it was decided to build an initial phase 800 km (500 miles) long connecting San Francisco and Anaheim. In a second phase, the route would be extended north to Sacramento and south to San Diego, for a total of 1,300 km (800 miles).[18]

That was not the end to disputes over the route. Individuals began to sue the project, based on a law called the California Environmental Quality Act (CEQA). This requires the government to study the environmental impact of its projects and report on the findings. Some farmers in the Central Valley were concerned that the railroad might damage their land, irrigation systems and crops. But others just wanted to stop building in their neighbourhood. The lawsuits added time and costs to the project.

Financing threw up more hurdles. In 2008, California voters approved Proposition 1A, authorizing the state to raise $9 billion in bonds to contribute to a cost for the rail system then estimated at $33 billion. It was estimated that the line would be completed in 2020. Much of the rest would come from the federal government, which spends tens of billions of dollars a year on transportation infrastructure. However, policy towards rail is divided and only about $20 billion goes towards mass transit and rail, around the same amount as for aviation and less than half of the spending on highways. By 2010, the Democrat-controlled Congress had allocated just over $3 billion for the project.

But the Democrats then lost control of Congress to the Republicans, who opposed the project and made it difficult for more federal money to reach it. A business plan in early 2018 indicated the cost could rise to nearly $100 billion. By 2019, the opening date for services between Los Angeles and San Francisco had been delayed to 2033. That year, under the administration of then-President Donald Trump, the Federal Railroad Administration cancelled a federal grant of nearly $929 million. As of 2022, construction was under way on part of a 274 km (171 miles) line between several cities in California's Central Valley. This was scheduled for completion in 2030, though it was widely expected to miss that date. The California High-Speed Rail Authority's plan for the whole route estimated the new cost at $113 billion, but no source of funding had been identified to bring the line to Los Angeles and San Francisco.[19,20,21,22]

Another political complication, according to US high-speed rail advocates, may come from the country's 'Buy America' policy, a decades-old requirement to buy US products, including rail cars, in projects receiving federal funding. The administration of President Joe Biden said in 2022 that it would fund high-speed rail as a major technology to help achieve net-zero carbon emissions. And the head of the Federal Railroad Administration, which funds rail projects, said it was committed to delivering high-speed passenger rail.

But high-speed rail tracks have to be much stronger than standard tracks for slower passenger trains and freight. Specialized rail cars and signalling systems are also essential. Today only one domestic factory is capable of building this equipment, which it does based on designs developed in Europe. That means local engineering capability and experience are missing too. Siemens, for example, manufactures rail cars in Sacramento, California, but not for high-speed use. These considerations can have an impact on whether or not a plan goes ahead. When a project called DesertXpress wanted to build a high-speed rail line between Los Angeles and Las Vegas while President Barack Obama was in office, it asked for a $5.5 billion federal railway loan. According to Politico, the Federal Railroad Administration rejected the application because it failed to satisfy 'Buy America' conditions.

Of course, US manufacturers have engineering teams and manufacturing facilities that might manage to make products sufficient for high-speed rail that also comply with the regulation. But this is a complex endeavour that requires significant investment and time. The government could waive the 'Buy America' requirements. But Biden vowed strict adherence to the provisions: five days after taking office, he issued an executive order to establish a new Made in America Office.

Still, there are concrete signs the project is going ahead, even if slowly and not along an optimal route. In 2022, the California High-Speed Rail Authority selected a consortium to provide programme management support over four years in a contract valued at up to $400 million. In 2023, the Authority began to procure six electric trainsets capable of operating at 355 kph (220 mph) – two for delivery in 2028 for testing and trial running, plus another four for delivery by 2030 to support the start of revenue operations on the 275 km (170 miles) Initial Operating Section between Merced and Bakersfield.[23]

The current state of US rail

Overall, however, passenger rail continues to struggle in the United States. Freight is often prioritized over passenger services as freight railroads own most of the nation's rail tracks, passenger trains and facilities are often outdated, distances are much longer than Europe's and there is limited passenger service between cities. Amtrak says it runs 300 trains with about 87,000 passengers per day. As of 2022, the Acela passenger service in the Northeast Corridor is the closest to high-speed rail that operates in the United States. But Acela doesn't operate on dedicated high-grade tracks, instead using Amtrak's own Northeast Corridor infrastructure, which limits its speed and comfort. In the 2022 fiscal year, Amtrak served 22.9 million passengers, down from 33 million in 2019. In contrast, the Transportation Security Administration (TSA) screened some 736 million US air passengers in 2022, as airline travel returned to near pre-pandemic levels. The attachment of Americans to air travel and their individual cars is also a major factor in the slow progress of high-speed rail.

When travel to and from an airport is included, high-speed trains can get passengers door to door as fast as planes on certain routes, such as Beijing to Shanghai and London to Brussels. This also applies to Amtrak's Acela along the Boston to Washington DC route, even though it averages just 111 kph (68 mph), compared to European and Asian trains capable of 320 kph (200 mph).

If Amtrak ran a faster, more reliable service between Los Angeles and San Diego, it would have the potential to take thousands of cars off the road. It would also be an ideal way for tourists to visit Santa Barbara, Los Angeles and San Diego without a car or guided tour bus. But at the moment there's just the Pacific Surfliner, which runs at a maximum 145 kph (90 mph) and uses a single track for long stretches, requiring switches (points) that limit service. It is plagued by delays and service outages. Surfliner cars are comfortable and spacious, but for periods of 2022 and 2023, portions of the single track along the coast were closed due to the threat of landslides.[24]

Amtrak is planning to renew its Acela fleet with a new technology developed by Alstom in Europe under the programme name Avelia Liberty, which will be capable of higher speeds, up to 256 kph (160 mph). Prior to the improvements in New Jersey, existing Acela equipment was limited to slower travel on most of the line, except for short 240 kph (150 mph) segments in Massachusetts and Rhode Island.

Still, despite long-time evidence of a true potential for high-speed rail in the United States target corridors, the US train service has never developed to resemble that of leading countries such as France, Germany and Japan. A poll run in March 2022 by the Rail Passengers Association advocacy group showed that 78 per cent of Americans want increased investments in passenger rail.[25] However, many Americans prefer to drive and fly and there is no strong evidence that they are ready to switch.

Many more billions of dollars would be needed for true high-speed services. The 2019 Green New Deal called for the US to 'build out high-speed rail at a scale where air travel stops becoming necessary', as trains generate lower carbon emissions per passenger than airliners. And Amtrak was allotted $66 billion in the bipartisan Infrastructure Bill of November 2021 to deal with issues such as the network's frequent delays, especially along the East Coast, where many commuters depend on the trains. This 'represented the largest investment of its kind since Amtrak was founded in 1971', Amtrak CEO William Flynn noted. He said $44 billion would go to the Federal Railroad Administration for state grants and rail projects, with $22 billion for fleet acquisitions and various improvements. But $66 billion will hardly address the demand from green activists for more trains, fewer planes.

Stop-go all over the world

Despite Europe's growing high-speed rail networks, it is also not short of stop-go projects, which are held up by financing, city planning and environmental concerns. In France, the CDG Express rail link between central Paris and Charles de Gaulle Airport was initiated through public consultations in 2003. Construction was supposed to start in 2008, with rail services following between 2012 and 2015. But the selected bidder pulled out of the project in 2011 amid a lack of funding and governance challenges. The project was reignited by the Ile de France regional authority in 2014, as Paris prepared its (eventually successful) bid to host the 2024 Summer Olympics. The new project was also following a new route. However, delays and changes in governance mean the CDG Express might start services only in 2026 or later, thereby missing the 2024 Olympics. In the meantime, CDG airport will be served by the RER (a commuter rail).

On occasions, it's mere technical oversight that hurts brownfield projects. The rail network in northern Spain was built in the nineteenth century and has tunnels under the mountains of different dimensions to standard modern tunnels. In 2020, Renfe, Spain's national passenger railway company, ordered new commuter trains for nearly €260 million, but the following year manufacturer CAF realized that the dimensions it had been given were inaccurate. The trains it was building would be too big for the tunnels and it stopped construction.

The mistake means the trains will be delivered in 2026, two years late, and the region of Cantabria has demanded compensation for what the region's President Miguel Ángel Revilla called 'an unspeakable botch'. In February 2023, Spain's transport ministry fired a Renfe manager over the blunder, as well as the head of track technology at rail infrastructure manager ADIF. Later, the head of Renfe and the Secretary of State for Transport left their roles.[26,27] The incident shows the imperative of having common standards that everyone can work to.

KEY TAKEAWAYS

- Mobility depends in the long term on developments in economics, politics and technology. It is very hard to predict how some of these variables will evolve, which makes long-term planning complex. It requires scenario planning that takes into account future risks and uncertainties.

- Plans for fixed infrastructure require some level of consistency over time and the avoidance of stop-go decision making. Politics is a big driver of the development of large projects, given their impact on populations and economies.

- It is hard to build new transport infrastructure around and on top of existing cities and networks in response to population growth – so-called brownfield development. Politics is a bigger factor than normally considered in the development of large projects.

- The relative attractiveness of different modes of transport varies according to nations, cultures and geographies.

Notes

1 Krauss, C. (2004) End of era near in Montreal for white-elephant airport, *The New York Times*, 3 October. Available at: www.nytimes.com/2004/10/03/world/americas/end-of-era-near-in-montreal-for-whiteelephant-airport.html (archived at https://perma.cc/UF65-7DGX)

2 YouTube (n.d.) Airport stories – Montreal Mirabel. Available at: www.youtube.com/watch?v=b2BmQErIUUc (archived at https://perma.cc/6FEU-UTWU)

3 Clark, A. (2003) Lesson of Canadian airport in terminal decline, *The Guardian*, 23 September. Available at: www.theguardian.com/business/2003/sep/23/theairlineindustry.politics (archived at https://perma.cc/4S3G-JT6R)

4 YouTube (n.d.) Mirabel: autopsie d'un échec. Available at: www.youtube.com/watch?v=0VPz0ZXOVZE (archived at https://perma.cc/S8PR-SA2G)

5 Clark, A. (2003) Lesson of Canadian airport in terminal decline, *The Guardian*, 23 September. Available at: www.theguardian.com/business/2003/sep/23/theairlineindustry.politics (archived at https://perma.cc/4S3G-JT6R)

6 YouTube (n.d.) Mirabel: autopsie d'un échec. Available at: www.youtube.com/watch?v=0VPz0ZXOVZE (archived at https://perma.cc/S8PR-SA2G)

7   Foxman, S. and Nair, A. (2022) What Qatar built for the most expensive World Cup, Bloomberg, 18 November. Available at: www.bloomberg.com/graphics/2022-what-qatar-built-for-the-world-cup/ (archived at https://perma.cc/7GUA-4X4S)

8   Moore, R. (2022) A megalopolis of engineering: The verdict on London's $18bn new Elizabeth line, *The Guardian*, 13 March. Available at: www.theguardian.com/uk-news/2022/mar/13/elizabeth-line-crossrail-opening-london (archived at https://perma.cc/HJM3-9WLV)

9   (2023) Métro 3: l'éventuel démontage du Palais du Midi inquiète la Commission Royale des Monuments et des Sites', BX1, 24 February. Available at: https://bx1.be/categories/news/metro-3-leventuel-demontage-du-palais-du-midi-inquiete-la-commission-royale-des-monuments-et-des-sites/ (archived at https://perma.cc/863W-M26E)

10   Buckley, P. (2014) Royal Woolwich Arsenal – Crossrail box sewer diversion, ICE Publishing. Available at: https://learninglegacy.crossrail.co.uk/documents/royal-woolwich-arsenal-crossrail-box-sewer-diversion/ (archived at https://perma.cc/8LLW-NWFC)

11   Chini, M. (2023) Brussels to go ahead with fast track dismantling of iconic Palais du Midi, *Brussels Times*, 30 September. Available at: www.brusselstimes.com/715166/brussels-to-go-ahead-with-fast-track-dismantling-of-iconic-palais-du-midi (archived at https://perma.cc/7RW9-K3QL)

12   Jozuka, E. et al (2023) 'Like building skyscrapers in Central Park': Tokyo redevelopment plan sparks protests', CNN, 3 October. Available at: https://edition.cnn.com/style/tokyo-jingu-gaien-redevelopment-project-hnk-intl/index.html (archived at https://perma.cc/A5L9-PDD8)

13   *The Economist* (2021) The rise of dirty politics in Europe, *The Economist*, 20 February. Available at: www.economist.com/europe/2021/02/20/the-rise-of-dirty-politics-in-europe (archived at https://perma.cc/ZAY3-Q5SC)

14   Hernandez-Morales, A. and Wilke, P. (2023) Bikeless in Berlin: Europe's cycle backlash has begun, Politico, 12 October. Available at: www.politico.eu/article/europe-bikes-cycling-backlash-berlin-germany-cycling-cars-emissions/ (archived at https://perma.cc/R9RS-VSW7)

15   Walker, P. (2023) Sunak 'backs drivers' with curbs on 20mph limits and bus lanes, *The Guardian*, 29 September. Available at: www.theguardian.com/politics/2023/sep/29/rishi-sunak-plan-for-motorists-would-limit-travel-choices-campaigners-say (archived at https://perma.cc/H2JY-NWXP)

16   Ellis, S. (2022) This high-speed rail project is a warning for the US, Vox, 29 July. Available at: www.vox.com/videos/2022/7/29/23283654/california-high-speed-rail-palmdale-warning (archived at https://perma.cc/Y2NQ-3TDV)

17   Vartabedian, R. (2022) How California's Bullet Train went off the rails, *The New York Times*, 9 October. Available at: www.nytimes.com/2022/10/09/us/california-high-speed-rail-politics.html (archived at https://perma.cc/T52P-GUZ5)

18 California High Speed Rail (n.d.) Project sections. Available at: https://hsr. ca.gov/high-speed-rail-in-california/project-sections/ (archived at https://perma. cc/9CA5-HU5X)

19 Vartabedian, R. (2022) How California's Bullet Train went off the rails, *The New York Times*, 9 October. Available at: www.nytimes.com/2022/10/09/us/ california-high-speed-rail-politics.html (archived at https://perma.cc/T52P-GUZ5)

20 Daniels, J. (2019) California governor proposes 'new data dividend' that could call on Facebook and Google to pay users', CNBC, 12 February. Available at: www.cnbc.com/2019/02/12/california-gov-newsom-calls-for-new-data-dividend-for-consumers.html (archived at https://perma.cc/V7WS-VCSU)

21 Daniels, J. (2019) Trump administration pulls $929 million in funding for California high-speed rail, CNBC, 16 May. Available at: www.cnbc. com/2019/05/16/trump-administration-pulls-california-high-speed-rail-funding.html (archived at https://perma.cc/M864-43PC)

22 Kim, M. (2023) How 'Buy America' could delay high-speed trains, Politico. com, 28 May. Available at: www.politico.com/news/2023/05/28/buy-america-high-speed-trains-00097776 (archived at https://perma.cc/T978-7C8Q)

23 Railway Gazette International (n.d.) California high speed railway project news. Available at: www.railwaygazette.com/news/projects/california-high-speed-rail-project-news (archived at https://perma.cc/C9V4-LGUH)

24 Nguyen, A. (2023) Passenger rail reopens just in time for Comic-Con, kpbs, 17 July. Available at: www.kpbs.org/news/local/2023/07/17/passenger-rail-reopens-months-closure-san-diego (archived at https://perma.cc/R7PH-QPTH)

25 The Rail Passengers Association (2022). Majority Of Americans Want More Investments in Passenger Rail. Available at: https://railpassengers.org/ happening-now/news/releases/new-poll-78-of-americans-want-increased-investments-in-passenger-rail-in-the-u.s

26 Spender, T. (2023) Spain officials quit over trains that were too wide for tunnels, BBC, 21 February. Available at: www.bbc.co.uk/news/world-europe-64717605 (archived at https://perma.cc/WX8S-LKZW)

27 Symons, A. (2023) 'Unspeakable botch': Spain spends €258 million on trains that are too big for its tunnels, Euronews.travel, 21 February. Available at: www.euronews.com/travel/2023/02/21/unspeakable-botch-spain-spends-258-million-on-trains-that-are-too-big-for-its-tunnels (archived at https://perma.cc/ G3LM-8HQH)

Two keys to growth

4

Standardization and liberalization

- Why standards and norms are needed to unite networks.
- How liberalized markets create sustained growth.
- How other deregulated industries provide insights in the keys for growth.
- What happens when rail attempts to follow airlines' expansion.

Standardization

The container revolution

Loading a cargo ship was once like packing a suitcase. When a ship was moored in dock, hordes of longshoremen tried to fit cargo as efficiently as possible into the hold. Typical ships had curved sides and the longshoremen had to know how to fill the gaps so as not to waste space, which would also waste money. Cargo for the first port of call had to be loaded last so it could be removed without rummaging under items that were staying on board for distant ports. These were stored lower down. Items had to be stowed tightly so that they would not shift due to the ship's movement in heavy seas: if a load shifted on the ocean, it could be damaged and even cause a capsize. Unloading, too, was a lengthy task and carpenters were needed to repair broken crates and barrels. As a result, it could take a week or more to move a shipload of mixed cargo out of a port so that it could proceed to further destinations.

A study in 1954 for the Maritime Cargo Transportation Conference of the National Research Council quoted in Marc Levinson's book *The Box* showed the work involved in getting a shipload of cargo from Brooklyn, New York to Bremerhaven in Germany. The Warrior had a typical mix of cargo – 5,015 long tons (5100 tonnes), mainly food merchandise, household goods, mail and machine and vehicle parts, packed as 194,582 individual items ('cases', 'cartons', 'bags' and 'boxes'). This came from 151 US cities in 1,156 separate shipments, with the first arriving at the docks more than a month before the vessel sailed. Items were placed on pallets, which were then lowered into the ship's hold. The items were then removed and tied or fixed in place with $5,031.69 worth of lumber and rope. The longshoremen worked at this for six days.[1]

The journey across the Atlantic took 10.5 days, after which it took four days to unload the ship in Germany. That meant half the duration of the voyage was spent in dock. The total cost of moving the goods came to $237,577: of that, the sea voyage accounted for only 11.5 per cent, while cargo handling at both ends accounted for 36.8 per cent. (Shipping executives at the time often cited the proportion at 50 per cent, but this figure was reduced because of the relatively low wages of German longshoremen in the years after World War II.)

Then came a revolution that propelled maritime transport and logistics into the modern era.

In 1956, Malcolm McLean, an American trucking magnate, thought of a lower-cost alternative to move cargo. He thought that big savings could be had by packing goods in uniform containers that could easily be moved between trucks, railcars and ships. He loaded several trailer bodies onto a vintage tanker, the *Ideal-X*. This marked the start of containerization and it changed everything in the transportation of goods.

McLean worked out the costs of this first journey of a prototype container ship in 1956 and found that they came in at just $0.16 per tonne to load – compared with $5.83 per tonne for loose cargo on a standard ship. All of a sudden, the cost of shipping products to another destination was no longer prohibitively expensive.[2]

Over the next few years, further innovations speeded up loading and unloading. A new trailer chassis had sloped edges so that a container being lowered by crane would be guided into place automatically. A new locking system allowed a longshoreman to secure or release the container by raising or lowering a handle at each corner of the chassis, doing away with the labour-intensive routines of using iron chains to prevent the box from slipping off the truck. Later, automatic twist locks made the process of locking and unlocking even faster.

Port labour productivity rose from 1.7 tonnes per hour in 1965 to 30 tonnes per hour in 1970. The value of goods in transit halved, indicating that it was now economical to transport lower-value items such as consumer packaged goods. Insurance costs per tonne fell to a sixth of their 1965 level. And the average size of a ship more than doubled. Instead of nearly a week, it now usually takes between 24 and 48 hours for a port to deal with loading and unloading the largest vessels. Recent UN figures put the median time that a ship stays in port at 20.1 hours. The crew takes little part in the operation and most of the work is done by machines.[3,4,5]

Containerization quickly conquered the world: between 1966 and 1983 the share of countries with container ports rose from about 1 per cent to nearly 90 per cent, coinciding with a take-off in global trade. With container terminals built on shores and in ports all around the world, the container industry has evolved into a sophisticated global transportation system with a 2020 volume exceeding 800 million 20-foot equivalent units (TEUs) of containerized cargo annually. This was moved in more than 19 million vessel slots, as well as transit on roads, railways and waterways around the world.

According to one study, the impact of the container on global trade has been greater than that of free trade agreements. In a set of 22 industrialized countries, containerization explains a 320 per cent rise in bilateral trade over the first five years after adoption and 790 per cent over 20 years. By comparison, a bilateral free trade agreement raises trade by 45 per cent over 20 years and GATT (General Agreement on Tariffs and Trade) membership adds 285 per cent.[6]

The benefits of containerization were intimately linked to another major breakthrough for the global rail industry and trade: intermodal rail transport. This consists of the long-haul transport of shipping containers and truck trailers by rail, combined with stages by truck or water at one or both ends.

Containers were designed not only to be stacked on top of one another on a ship, they could also fit on trains and trucks. Containers thus became the basis for highly efficient rail–sea and road–sea interfaces at container terminals and allow for seamless and progressively highly automated handling of loads. After advances in crane technology, it takes only between one and three business days to unload an ocean vessel carrying more than 10,000 containers. A full container shipment can be available in the container yard of the arrival port. Intermodal rail became even more efficient and competitive with the invention of double-stack rail transport in the United States in 1984. This involves railcars carrying two layers of intermodal containers and is now being used for nearly 70 per cent of US intermodal shipments. 'The development of intermodal technology and double stack rail transport was a major breakthrough,' says Hugh Randall, formerly Managing Partner of the Global Transportation practice at Oliver Wyman. 'By combining the strengths of both modes, it allowed rail to stay competitive not against but with trucks in many more commodities.'

Container terminals have become a key component of logistics infrastructures allowing fast, cost-effective transfer of containers from sea to inland transportation. Take the Port of Halifax in Nova Scotia, Canada, where I have worked on multiple assignments in the mid-2000s. Halifax offers the fastest ocean transit time from Northern Europe to the East Coast of North America, at 11.3 days via the great-circle route. The water depth at the dock is a minimum of 16.8 metres (55 feet) along the entire length of the berth. The terminal has four gantry cranes, including three super post-Panamax cranes, which can load and unload containers from a container ship too wide to pass through the Panama Canal and which have especially long outreach and powerful lifting capacity. Canadian National Railway (CN) has direct access to the container terminal and containers can be offloaded from the vessel onto a double-stack intermodal train. The CN line offers direct access to Chicago, in the US heartland, in less than three days. Intermodal rail has great potential to make more efficient use of urban land in the future – something that is essential given how cities are becoming increasingly crowded.[7]

Why standards matter so much

The containerization revolution is a standout example of standardization. Broadly speaking, standardization is a precondition for any form of cultural or economic integration – locally, regionally, nationally or internationally. To function effectively, human communities need common languages, sign

"The development of intermodal technology and double-stack rail transport was a major breakthrough"
Hugh Randall

systems and agreed-upon rules of living together – that is, a basic set of shared standards and norms. One of the most systematic attempts at standardization was the metric system, which was taken up around the world as trade and commerce internationalized: comparable weights and measures were a precondition for a system of commerce and trade that depended on reliable common bases for exchange.

Another kind of standardization – industry standardization – helps generate efficiencies inside and between companies. Efficiencies facilitate economies of scale in manufacturing and promote interoperability between complementary products and systems, as well as customers and suppliers. When industry standards are not promulgated by a government body, they often emerge from a voluntary consensus.[8]

More broadly, common standards were essential for the EU single market. Launched in 1993 to facilitate trade between EU member states, it aimed to make it easier for European businesses to function and provide products to consumers on a wider scale.

That implies that businesses and consumers should be able to recognize the same products whatever country they were made in, so they need to be made according to the same standards. Products and services thus become interoperable and they can be slotted into value chains, creating a level playing field and boosting competition among suppliers. In this way, standardization promotes cost efficiencies and the ease of doing business. In many sectors, especially transport and mobility, standards help to improve safety as they harmonize rules and behaviour, and they remove cross-mode and cross-border friction. Because of these benefits, the EU has an active standardization policy that promotes standards to better regulate and enhance the competitiveness of European industries.

The European single market has special significance for transport and mobility because of its emphasis on free movement – of goods, services, capital and people. A goal of EU transport policy was therefore to ensure the smooth, efficient, safe and free movement of people and goods throughout the EU. This implies integrated networks of various transport modes – on road, rail and water, as well as in the air.

The economic benefits of common standards have proven especially clear in telecommunications, to give one example. In the 1990s, US mobile telephony had no common standard and poor interoperability. That made it awkward to use and increased the cost of equipment. Then 3G technology was introduced with the ultimate goal of bringing the internet and multimedia services to mobile users. 3G had higher spectrum efficiency and larger bandwidth for high-speed data communications – and different 3G standards were also more compatible with each other. As a result, the United States' telecommunications grid became more integrated.

At around the same time in Europe, the Telecommunications Standards Institute (ETSI) developed the Global System for Mobile Communications (GSM) for digital cellular networks. By the mid-2010s, this had become a global standard for mobile communications, achieving a market share of over 90 per cent and operating in more than 193 countries and territories. The GSM standard reduced costs because equipment could be mass produced for a global market at a greater economy of scale. Mobile telecoms then grew rapidly.

The creation of a unified mobile telecoms standard was fairly easy because it was a relatively young industry, giving it the characteristics of a greenfield project. In contrast, transportation, especially rail, has to work with legacy norms and systems. 'Europe's telecom liberalization in the 1990s was based on a harmonized adoption of the greenfield GSM standard,' says Bernard Amory, Partner at global law firm Jones Day and Co-Head of its Global Anti-trust Group. 'This made the decisions easier and the roll-out faster. But the European Commission realized that legacy rail infrastructure and states' national interests would make transport liberalization more complex and therefore slower.'

Rail as national project

In contrast, Europe's railway network has been fragmented into national markets, making its potential hard to unlock. 'Similar to the telecom industry until GSM, the major challenge of the rail industry is still its fragmentation,' says Josef Doppelbauer, Executive Director at the European Union

"Europe's telecom liberalization in the 90s was based on a harmonized adoption of the greenfield GSM standard. This made the decisions easier and the roll-out faster"
Bernard Amory

Agency for Railways. 'In Europe, the multiple country-based standards reduce volumes and the return on investment of infrastructure and rolling stock programmes. Innovation in rail is less flexible because the only way to develop new products in existing railway systems is to build them on top of the legacy infrastructure we've already got.'

One reason is that European countries initially each developed their own rail infrastructure. One concern was national security, as rail transport has been a key asset in defence logistics: different standards make it harder for an invader to use a country's rail network in the event of war.

Since the American Civil War, railways had been used to move troops and materials rapidly. This was especially notable in World War I, as railways dominated land transport at the turn of the twentieth century. Motor vehicles were only relevant for local traffic, while aviation was at an embryonic stage. Plans to mobilize and support armies, therefore, were built primarily around railways. Each nation developed sophisticated schedules for concentrating troops and equipment at key depots and then dispatching the forces rapidly to designated positions on their frontiers.

Germany's 'Schlieffen Plan', for instance, provided for concentrating forces by rail rapidly along both the Eastern and Western Fronts. The strategy was to sweep rapidly through Belgium and Luxembourg, invade northern France and encircle the north and west of Paris. Subsequently the forces could then rapidly face the Russian army on the Eastern front.[9]

But the plan ran into problems on both fronts. As the German army advanced in the west, it took control of many Belgian and French railways. But the single-track bridges were not accessible to German locomotives and the sidings were not long enough for the German trains. So the Germans had to reduce the axle size of their own trains. When the Germans attacked on the

"Similar to the telecom industry until GSM, the major challenge of the rail industry is still its fragmentation"
Josef Doppelbauer

Eastern Front, retreating Russian armies took their rolling stock with them. The Germans brought their own but could use these only after converting the broad-gauge tracks to standard gauge.[10,11]

Different standards have also historically protected national markets. Rail was originally vertically integrated: a national railway company was largely supplied by national rail integrators and component manufacturers. A local cluster thus developed its own technical standards, which made it difficult for outside providers to enter the market. Such standards are found in multiple elements of a railway system, including the gauge for track and rolling stock, the electrical current voltage, safety standards and homologation bodies. The resulting market fragmentation for decades has been a barrier to the development of a large, efficient market for railway equipment and components. More recently, however, especially thanks to mergers of rail integrators (for example, Bombardier with Adtranz; later, Alstom with Bombardier; and most recently the proposed merger of Thales and Hitachi signalling businesses), common technology standards have increasingly been developed.

These national standards also made it hard for operators to provide cross-border services – a goal at the heart of the EU single-market project. Unable to expand outside their own countries, operators could not increase their volumes as they might otherwise have been able to, limiting the potential return on their investments in their rail systems and rolling stock. This is another aspect of brownfield development, in which new systems have to take into account legacy norms and standards. This is still a reality European rail operators have to cope with as they expand their cross-border services.

One example of the legacy of different standards is the operational changes needed when a train from Munich, Germany travels to Verona, Italy via Austria. At the border between Austria and Italy, the driver has to be changed: while German and Austrian laws require only one German-speaking driver, Italy requires two licensed Italian-speaking drivers. (Unlike in air transport, which uses one working language – English – rail does not have such a convention.) Indeed, while Italy has moved towards the one-driver model since 2011, legal actions have required Trenitalia to return to two drivers for long-distance freight and non-high-speed passenger services. Moreover, Italy does not accept technical checks undertaken by the German railway authority and carries out its own at the border. A goods train is only required to have a reflective board at the back in Germany and Austria, but Italy demands tail lights. As a result, passenger trains must stop for at least 14 minutes and goods trains are delayed for 45 minutes.

Cross-border friction thus remains a major hindrance to reliability and punctuality and it holds back productivity of rail freight relative to road transport.[12]

The biggest interoperability challenge comes in signalling systems, which enable safe railway operation by connecting trains with ground infrastructure and regulating their movements. Signalling can enable more efficient exploitation of track capacity by controlling the passage of the trains that use it. But today's signalling systems are a patchwork of around 30 legacy systems on the European continent and they are not interoperable for the most part. That means trains crossing borders may need to be equipped with several onboard signalling systems to interact with local control standards, making international services less reliable and more expensive and slowing progress towards the goal of a competitive single EU rail market.

In the past, one-off fixes were used for international rail freight. In the late 1990s, the Community of European Railways (CER) developed the concept of freight freeways. On these, the interfaces of EU member states – sometimes as many as five or seven – were coordinated to make international through services possible. One example of such a corridor was Stockholm, Sweden to Bologna, Italy – a 7,000 km journey that crosses four national borders. A series of capacity upgrades and operational 'handshakes' was implemented, along with a one-stop shop of all infrastructure managers – an organizational construct to ensure timely coordination and standardized ad-hoc ways of working. I participated in the setting up of such a scheme in 1997. It was a huge, multi-party planning effort that required an initial study and plan, followed by regular meetings of steering committees to ensure proper implementation. An end-to-end pricing scheme was introduced at a more competitive rate than the sum of the applicable national tariffs, as these would have increased the shippers' costs too much and made the service uncompetitive.

Towards a solution for European rail

To get over the national barriers and make European railway systems interoperable (without the cumbersome collaboration scheme described above), the EU launched ERTMS, the European Rail Traffic Management System, in the late 1990s. This a single European standard for command-and-control systems and for automatic train protection (ATP) systems, which are currently installed trackside and partly on trains and check that a train is keeping to the speed limit and stopping automatically when needed. By replacing national equipment and procedures with a Europe-wide standard, the ERTMS thus aims to help create a system in which it is easier to operate trains between different European countries, making services safer and more efficient.

The European Commission has a target for deployment of the equipment over 67,000 km of main rail corridors and a total of 123,000 km of track by 2050. To speed progress, the EU Agency for Railways (ERA) was set up in 2004 to maintain, manage and control stable standards, and one of its main tasks is to implement the ERTMS. But progress has been slow. By the end of 2017 only 8 per cent of the Core Network Corridor (CNC) routes and 10 per cent of the train fleets had been fitted out, according to the European Court of Auditors (ECA). By 2030, a total of 57,170 km of CNC lines were scheduled to be equipped with the European Train Control System (ETCS), which is the signalling and control component of ERTMS. But by September 2021, the ETCS had been deployed on just 14 per cent of these lines (see Figures 4.1 and 4.2).

Why is it taking so long? One reason is that the ERTMS implementation costs are very high and require significant upfront investment. In a 2019 report, Oliver Wyman estimated (based on ECA estimates) the total costs for trackside and train upgrades over the next 12 years across nine European CNCs at nearly €100 billion.

This would be a heavy additional burden of capital expenditure for cash-strapped infrastructure managers, asset owners and operators. But the benefits of the ERTMS will accrue only in the future. To provide support, the EU budget allocated approximately €1.2 billion between 2007 and 2013 and another €2.7 billion for the 2014–2020 period. But this EU funding can only cover a limited portion of the overall cost and many national infrastructure managers lack an individual business case to invest in the equipment as they see no immediate net domestic financial benefit.

Another reason is that the ERTMS was conceived as a toolbox that each rail infrastructure organization could use. However, even when they achieved technical interoperability, the railways did not harmonize their operating rules and cross-border frictions remained.[13,14,15]

In contrast to rail, the airline industry has had an international mission right from the start. To connect countries and continents, it needed a structure that would achieve consistency around the globe. The industry therefore set up the International Air Transport Association (IATA) in 1945 as a vehicle for inter-airline cooperation to promote air services that would be safe, reliable and economical. The international scheduled air transport

Figure 4.1   Deployment of the European Rail Traffic Management System (ETCS) standard as of June 2022

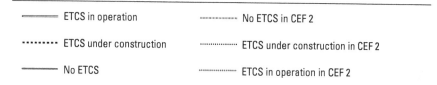

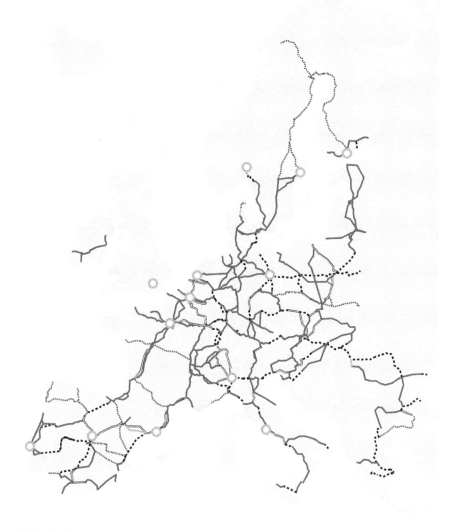

SOURCE Directorate General for Mobility and Transport – European Commission

Figure 4.2 European Rail Traffic Management System (ETCS) deployment per country as of June 2022 (ETCS in operation (km) as percentage of length to be equipped by 2030 (km))

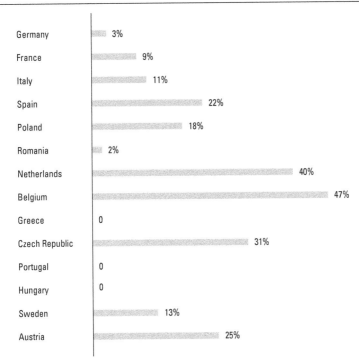

Germany 3%
France 9%
Italy 11%
Spain 22%
Poland 18%
Romania 2%
Netherlands 40%
Belgium 47%
Greece 0
Czech Republic 31%
Portugal 0
Hungary 0
Sweden 13%
Austria 25%

SOURCE Directorate General for Mobility and Transport – European Commission

industry is now more than 100 times larger than it was at the time of IATA's founding and it now has some 300 members in 120 nations, which carry 83 per cent of the world's air traffic.

IATA acts, first, as an advocate for the interests of airlines – it includes the world's leading passenger and cargo airlines – in front of regulators, governments, businesses and the broader public. The association has also developed global commercial and operational standards. By doing this, it aims to assist airlines by simplifying processes and increasing passenger convenience, while reducing costs and improving efficiency. It produces standards, guidelines and best practices across a wide range of areas in air transport, including dangerous goods, cargo, ground operations, finance, retailing, security, airports, flight and technical operations, sustainability and passenger experience. Few industries can match IATA's consistency of standards, practices and procedures.

Specifically, IATA developed and maintains a finance portfolio called the Interline Tariffs & Passenger Standards Publications. These guide the settlement and billing process between airlines, including pricing, auditing, reservations management and ticketing. In practice, if a traveller books an itinerary at a travel agent that consists of three connecting flights on three distinct airlines, first the travel agent collects the payment. The agent then subtracts commission and IATA organizes the distribution of the remaining revenue among the three carriers based upon pre-agreed quotas.

IATA's Flight and Technical Operations portfolio provides practical guidance and best practices for airline operations based on the regulatory standards for flights and technical areas. For example, a pilot crew approaching an airport for landing can, upon request, receive standardized information from air traffic controllers over the frequency with which to obtain automated weather data. It can also receive normalized information from the airport's control tower on which runway to align with. In contrast to the rail industry, such information enables airlines to operate in a similar manner in different continents.

Liberalization

Standards and norms developed for single markets for air carriers have also enabled the liberalization of those markets. They allow multiple competitors to use the same systems and facilities – ranging from reservation systems and revenue accounting methods to airport gates and boarding software – and they thus establish an environment of fair competition.

Aviation was a natural mobility segment to liberalize. When rival train operators want to use the same high-speed rail track, complex arrangements are required to manage them. Rolling stock has to be compatible with the installed signalling base and only a limited number of services can operate. Aviation, in contrast, does not need major infrastructure between the points of departure and arrival, making it easier to liberalize (although slots at popular airports remain highly contested). There are no major difficulties in allowing different airline operators to fly between two cities and operators can also fly to different airports near to a large city. Liberalization has thus had a rapid, large-scale impact on the airline industry.

Air liberalization started in the United States. In the past, the government regulated virtually every aspect of the airline business. Airlines would have to apply to change their fares, routes or ownership and then wait for administrative and judicial reviews that could take months – and sometimes years. Economists argued that this regulatory environment limited competition and resulted in high prices for end-customers. In 1977, air cargo rates and services were deregulated, and the next year the Airline Deregulation Act liberalized passenger aviation fares and services. The deregulation transformed the airline industry and changed it from a protected business environment into a vigorously competitive marketplace.[16]

Unbundling and new business models

One early move came from American Airlines, which introduced yield management to better control capacity utilization and maximize revenues. In the 1960s, American Airlines developed the first online reservation system, which it called Sabre (Semi-automated Business Research Environment). Sabre centralized and controlled reservations and by the time airlines were deregulated, the system was full of priceless data from more than 10 years of bookings.

As competition then intensified, CEO Robert Crandall set out to devise a way to vary dynamically the proportion of discount and full-fare seats on a day-by-day, departure-by-departure basis. Using the Sabre system, American Airlines monitored the rate of actual bookings in various fare categories and compared these to the predicted rates on which fares for a flight had been based. The airline then adjusted the fares on the remaining seats accordingly. Crandall later named this process 'yield management'. As this tool became increasingly sophisticated, American – and, eventually, almost every other airline – could price seats, even for the same class of travel, on the same flight at different levels. Today, most airlines consider yield management to be a basic – and critical – capability.

At this stage in the aviation industry development, the hub and spoke system was thriving. Huge airport platforms such as Chicago O'Hare or Atlanta Hartsfield-Jackson were connecting America to the world. In that context and in the wake of the North American Free Trade Agreement (NAFTA) starting in 1994, one specific aircraft product found its market as a regional feeder to these airports: the Canadair Regional Jet (CRJ) family of aircraft developed by Bombardier. Launched in 1992, this aircraft also started developing in Europe, with first customer Lufthansa of Germany, to connect Central and Eastern Europe secondary airports to the Frankfurt Hub and therefore support the newly created freedom of movement in the EU as well as connecting a broader set of European airports to the world. As

Pierre Lortie, former President of Bombardier Commercial Aircraft, under-scores: 'Even though its unit costs were higher, the commercial regional jet aircraft created a breakthrough in the 1990s and 2000s. It found its market in point-to-point regional city pairs and in feeders across North America and Central Europe. By offering mid-size capacity, it allowed greater fre-quency, making it much more convenient for business travellers, and made these trips profitable for the carriers.'

Some airlines introduced new tactics that ended up part of the main-stream airline business model. Among the most significant of these was the unbundling of the flight offer – that is, the introduction of ancillary fees in addition to and separate from the price of an airline ticket. Air travellers tend to buy tickets based on lowest ticket price, ignoring the additional fees associated with such things as checking a bag or selecting a seat, so unbun-dling makes travel appear somewhat cheaper than it is. This tactic has been used in a sophisticated manner by low-cost carriers to provide consumers with a perception of ultra-low fares when in fact a major portion of what they pay consists of ancillary fees for things like baggage and in-flight food and drink, which traditional airlines included in their headline ticket price.

Competition increased almost immediately with the arrival of start-ups, driving overall fares down, and some carriers either went into bankruptcy or were taken over, especially from the late 1980s.

Nearly all the new start-ups focused on a low-fare business model pio-neered by the standout airline of this era, Southwest Airlines.

Before deregulation, Southwest had grown rapidly by offering low fares in the unregulated intrastate Texas market. This was cited early on as an example of how deregulation on a national level might benefit consumers by

"The commercial regional jet found its market in point-to-point regional city pairs"
Pierre Lortie

unleashing new airlines with different prices and services. Instead of air-miles loyalty schemes, Southwest attracted customers through constant cost reduction and a unique culture towards customer service and experience. Check-in was simplified and the only class was economy, making boarding easier and faster. There was no pre-assigned seating, so passengers boarded like on a bus.

Southwest used a single type of aircraft, the Boeing 737, which meant that its maintenance and component inventory costs were lower than those of its peers. Utilization of aircraft was high: it flew short routes, often to markets that were underserved, as many times in a day as possible. Southwest turned around the aircraft quickly, usually in under 30 minutes, as against typically 90 minutes for other airlines. Founder Herb Kelleher used to say, 'You're only making money when you're in the sky.'

There were just two attendants rather than five on a 130-seater aircraft and they served no meals and told people to pick up their own rubbish. This saved on cleaning costs and helped with the fast aircraft turnaround, increasing the number of flights per day. Until the Covid-19 pandemic in 2020, Southwest never recorded an annual loss.

Nearly half a century after deregulation in the US, it appears to have been a success from most points of view. Fares are lower, which has boosted passenger volumes, both domestically and internationally. In 1971, air travel was considered a luxury experience rather than a commodity and only 49 per cent of Americans had ever flown, according to a long-running survey by the industry group Airlines for America. In 2022, this proportion had risen to 87 per cent.[17]

The low-cost revolution spreads to Europe

More than a decade later, Southwest became part of the story of European airlines too. In Europe, national markets were protected up to the end of the 1980s. Airlines, often government-funded national carriers, could keep flying despite inefficiency and massive losses. But in 1992, the single European aviation market was created, allowing any EU air carrier to operate freely on any route inside the EU.

All airlines, as long as they obtained the relevant landing slots, could now fly to a greater number of destinations across the EU without needing permission from individual states to fly into their airspace or land at their airports, ending protections for national legacy air carriers. A single EU air passenger market was created, in which airlines could set their own fares without regulatory approval and fly as many times a day as they wanted. Competition rules were introduced to stop bigger airlines from using predatory pricing to keep new airlines out of the market. And conditions were imposed on cash injections from governments to support state-owned airlines.

Deregulation allowed a handful of commercially aggressive airlines to thrive. Both Michael O'Leary, who had become CFO of Ryanair in 1988 and CEO in 1994, and easyJet founder Sir Stelios Haji-Ioannou have dubbed Herb Kelleher their role model for the way he eliminated anything superfluous to a safe, cheap and reliable flight. 'At their inception, European low-cost airlines borrowed from the success of Southwest Airlines in the US,' says Mike Cooper, Chief Executive Officer of public transport operator Arriva and a former easyJet commercial executive. 'They focused on the simplicity and scalability of the business model and easyJet focused more specifically on safety, point-to-point flights and frequency of service.'

Ryanair's O'Leary went to meet Herb Kelleher at Southwest when he was 26 years old and became a disciple. Launching a Dublin–Luton route in 1992, Ryanair had borrowed the lowest fare at Southwest ($29 from Dallas to Houston) and applied it: the cost of the flights started at £29 each way, followed by rises of £10, as the lowest-price tickets were bought up and the dates of the flights became closer.

O'Leary took cost cutting to extremes. First, like Southwest, Ryanair has centred its fleet on Boeing 737s to save costs on maintenance and on crew and pilot training. One new order of Boeing 737-800s specified no reclining seats, window blinds, headrest covers or seat pockets: passengers might put rubbish in the latter, creating extra work for the flight attendants. O'Leary told cabin crew to buy their own pens or to take them from hotels or wher-

"At their inception, European low-cost airlines borrowed from the success of Southwest Airlines in the US"
Mike Cooper

ever they were given away free. He banned sticky notes and forbade staff from charging their mobile phones in the office because it would constitute theft of the company's electricity. For passengers, items like bags and food and drink became extras that had to be paid for. Revenues from such ancillary sales – which flight attendants were charged with boosting – eventually became highly significant.

These moves generated plenty of publicity that to most people looked bad, as well as legal actions from employee groups and labour unions, which said Ryanair was flouting social protection rules in some jurisdictions. But O'Leary was pleased when these stories got out, as it told people that the airline was cheap – including the fares. 'People get what they paid for, a cheap seat, and they are not disappointed,' wrote Matt Cooper in 2018's *Michael O'Leary: Turbulent times for the man who made Ryanair*.[18] 'Ryanair under-promises and over-delivers, so the brand experience is positive. Traditional airlines promise high standards in adverts and then disappoint.' In 2012, O'Leary's obsession with cost cutting led him to apply to run test flights with standing berths, handrails and straps, the 'same as on the London Underground', according to *The Guardian*.[19] This application was rejected by the regulator.

At first, Ryanair operated just a few low-cost services in Ireland and the UK, but deregulation was the cue for the airline to expand throughout Europe. To do this, it borrowed another tactic from Southwest: seek out secondary airports some way away from a destination city. For example, Frankfurt–Hahn Airport, which Ryanair started using in 2001, is about 120 km from Frankfurt. One secondary airport in France is Beauvais-Tillé, 85 km north of Paris, and called Paris-Beauvais Airport. It could be argued that the secondary airports saved time because the passengers were away from busy runways and departure and arrival lounges. These airfields cost much less than primary airports and they were willing to offer Ryanair discounts on landing and handling charges. The additional passengers brought in more retail sales for the airfields.

Air travel surged. From 1995 to 2014, while the total number of passenger-kilometres in the EU increased 23 per cent for all modes of transportation, the figure for air travel jumped by 74 per cent. Aviation's share of total passenger transport increased from 6.5 per cent to 9.2 per cent. Much of the new business was grabbed by easyJet, Ryanair and other new low-cost airlines. Between 2005 and 2022, Ryanair's share quintupled to more than 160 million passengers and easyJet's more than doubled to 70 million passengers 'Low-cost carriers showed the world that you can make a profit in the airline industry,' says Alexandre de Juniac, formerly President and CEO of Air France KLM and a former Director General of IATA.

In Europe, many incumbents, which had previously operated as oligopolies or national monopolies, have since gone out of business, including Sabena, Swissair and Alitalia. The industry subsequently restructured into a few big, powerful groups: Air France merged with KLM, while Lufthansa Group now owns Austrian Airlines, Swiss International Air Lines, Brussels Airlines and Eurowings.

The low-cost airlines had a huge impact on leisure travel, in the same way that rail has transformed commuting. However, the impact has not come from technology: the runways and aircraft are basically the same and the reservation process is similar. Rather, the change comes from new business models – the ways that airlines devise to transport large numbers of people to distant vacation destinations.

Liberalization beyond airlines

Liberalization has mostly been less dramatic in other modes, but has it been positive? In France, the long-distance motorcoach sector was liberalized in August 2015 by the so-called 'Loi Macron', when Emmanuel Macron – later France's president – was Minister of Economy and Industry. New operators launched services, and the buses attracted 5.2 million passengers a year, 900 000 of whom would not otherwise have travelled, according to regulator Arafer. The buses also provided competition for railways, in particular long-distance services. Carriers that took advantage of the opportunity included Germany's FlixBus, SNCF's subsidiary Ouibus, which was later acquired by BlaBlaCar, and three companies that were eventually bought by FlixBus after they ran into financial troubles – Eurolines, Isilines and Megabus.

....

"Low-cost carriers showed the world that you can make a profit in the airline industry"
Alexandre de Juniac

....

Rail liberalization is far trickier to assess and there is still debate over the optimum model. Many railway systems developed originally as privately owned companies operating regional networks. But in the twentieth century, the typical model in Europe was a nationalized rail company running a countrywide system and generally having a monopoly over long-distance, regional and commuter services. These national companies were vertically integrated and it was difficult or impossible for private or regional enterprises to run their own trains on the national networks, or to compete in other EU countries' railway systems.

Rail began to decline and the EU thought a big reason was the lack of competition within the segment, a contrast with the free market for road and air services. This had made rail uncompetitive against other modes and the malaise was considered a factor in growing road congestion and the accompanying lack of safety. (The environmental benefits of rail were thought of later and they reinforced EU support for rail liberalization.) In 1991, the European Union issued the first of a series of directives and reforms designed to promote competition in member states' rail sectors and apply the principles of the new EU single market to rail. The guiding principle: to promote transparent access to and efficient utilization of existing rail infrastructure.

As Bernard Amory, Senior Partner at Jones Day and Co-Head of the Global Competition and Antitrust practice in Belgium, states: 'The European Commission – at the levels of both DG COMP and DG MOVE (the Directorates-General for Competition and for Mobility and Transport) – is well aware of the evolution of the transport market and of the need to liberalize. The regulator also welcomes digitalization as an enabler of end-to-end mobility connectivity for the benefit of the end-consumer.'

The first major directive was 91/440/EEC on the vertical separation of infrastructure and operations. One level was the separation of operations

"The European Commission is well aware of the evolution of the transport market and of the need to liberalize"
Bernard Amory

accounts and infrastructure accounts. The second was to have independent units within a larger organization. And the third was complete separation of the companies. The directive required at least a separation in terms of accounting. Other aspects of the business were deregulated later, including international and long-distance operations for passenger, freight and maintenance services. Rail infrastructure managers would be unbundled from rail operators and independent companies would be allowed to apply for track access, though they would of course have to pay for it: 'the future development and efficient operation of the railway system may be made easier if a distinction is made between the provision of transport services and the operation of infrastructure,' ran the preamble; 'given this situation, it is necessary for these two activities to be separately managed and have separate accounts.'[20,21,22] The most extreme example of liberalization was in the UK, then still in the EU. The Conservative government of Margaret Thatcher (1979–1990) had begun to privatize major industries. Just in transport-related industries, British Aerospace, Rolls-Royce, British Airways, National Express, British Telecom, British Leyland and the British Airports Authority were sold off to the private sector. But Thatcher did not touch the railways. Trains in many rural areas operated at a loss and privatizing the industry might result in the disappearance of these services – and the resulting disappearance of votes for her Conservative Party. Moreover, railways appeared too complex to run effectively while aiming to generate a profit.[23,24]

However, rail usage was in decline and public dissatisfaction was growing, so her successor as prime minister, John Major, decided to make a change. In 1992, his government embarked on a radical programme to break up of the formerly unitary system into dozens of parts and then to privatize them. Privatization, the government said, would lead to cheaper fares and a more efficient railway, requiring less taxpayer subsidy.

From 1994, a range of private companies was born. One was Railtrack, which owned the UK's tracks, stations, signalling, tunnels, bridges and level crossings. Trains were owned by three rolling stock companies (ROSCOs). Six new companies would operate freight services.

Passenger services were more complicated because the public had come to expect and rely on inherently loss-making rail operations: rush-hour trains between big cities tended to generate a profit, but not those between small towns at off-peak times. So the new system had to be designed to protect these non-profitable routes. Passenger services were divided into 25 train operating companies (TOCs) – seven running long-distance trains, 10 primarily running commuter services in and around London, and eight more running services in the rest of the country. Run by the government at first, these were later franchised to private companies.[25]

But the new franchise system trapped train operators between detailed service requirements and the need to make a profit. Companies competed to win the right to run rail services and the government would earn as much as possible from the franchise payments. But to maintain service quality, franchisees were bound by conditions. For example, the agreement issued in 2014 for the InterCity East Coast line, which runs from London to Edinburgh, runs to 619 pages. It details the process for altering the timetable, which requires consultation with the government and other stakeholders. It specifies that capacity should be sufficient for passengers to be able to find a seat upon boarding an off-peak train and after 20 minutes of boarding a peak service. It contains tables for acceptable levels of service cancellation and the payments that must be made for failure to keep to these. And it states that operators should allow folding bikes on all its services and full-size bikes when practical. By certain dates, it said, 'The Franchise Operator shall… install bean-to-cup coffee machines' on specific trains and 'ensure that… it offers a freshly cooked breakfast'. With the fares, operations and facilities bound by contract, potential franchisees were left to bid based on the profit they expected to make according to projections of future passenger numbers – which would lead to payments to the government. Consequently, the bidders tended to be over-optimistic.[26]

The InterCity East Coast line was initially operated by Sea Containers under the GNER brand. However, amid an unexpected fall in passenger numbers and rise in energy prices, the company in 2006 became incapable of meeting the terms of the franchise, which involved paying hundreds of millions of pounds to the government. In 2007, the franchise was awarded to National Express. But by 2009 this company was under increasing financial pressure due to rising fuel prices and the economic downturn and the franchise was renationalized in 2009. The franchise was then awarded to Stagecoach/Virgin in 2014, but this lost money too. In 2017 the government announced that this franchise would be terminated three years ahead of schedule. In 2018, Transport Secretary Chris Grayling said, 'The problem is that Stagecoach got its numbers wrong. It overbid and is now paying a price.'[27,28,29,30]

Then Covid struck, effectively stopping most train travel. In March 2020, the government announced that all rail franchisees would immediately be shifted to a concession model for six months, under which the government would pay all their costs, plus a small management fee. However, this shift was later extended, effectively bringing the UK's rail franchising system to an end. The new transport secretary, Grant Shapps, said, 'The model of privatization adopted 25 years ago has seen significant rises in passenger numbers, but this pandemic has proven that it is no longer working.'[31,32]

Despite the troubles of the operator franchising model, at least two parts of the liberalization of the UK rail industry have produced positive results and shareholder value. One is Trainline, the reservation platform for British train operating companies, which helps millions of travellers find and book the best-value tickets from a range of carriers, fares and journey options. It is available through a highly rated mobile app, a website and B2B partner channels. While Trainline was set up in the UK, it has expanded internationally and now works with more than 270 rail and coach companies in more than 40 countries. Net ticket sales rose 72 per cent to £4.3 billion in the fiscal year to 28 February 2023, while EBITDA rose to £86 million, up from £39 million.[33]

Rolling stock company ROSCO Eversholt belongs to another successful category of stakeholders. It was set up in 1994 as a subsidiary of British Rail ahead of privatization and then bought by its management for £580 million. Since then, it has played an integral role in the growth and modernization of the UK rail sector by introducing new rolling stock, technologies and manufacturers, including Japanese train manufacturer Hitachi. Twenty years later, after changing hands several times, it was bought by a consortium of CK Hutchison Holdings and Cheung Kong Infrastructure Holdings for €3.3 billion.[34]

A verdict on rail privatization?

Ridership had indeed increased. Journeys had more than doubled since the mid-1990s, from 700 million in 1994–95 to 1.7 billion in 2019–20. However, the UK also ended up with fares that were perceived to be high and with low passenger satisfaction. One report in 2017, by a group called Action for Rail, found that commuters travelling between Luton and London St Pancras spent 14 per cent of an average wage on a £387 monthly pass. In France, a monthly pass for a route of a similar length costs £61 (or 2.4 per cent of the French average monthly wage), while in Italy it cost £62 (equivalent to 3.1 per cent of the average monthly wage). Even European countries where monthly rail passes cost commuters more than the equivalent of £200, the cost still made up less than 8 per cent of the average worker's monthly earnings. In freight, the modal share for rail decreased from 11.3 per cent in 2005 to 9.1 per cent in 2019, a greater drop than the EU average, of 17.9 per cent to 17.0 per cent.[35,36,37]

The condition of the network improved, albeit with support from government grants. However, it was also argued that four major train accidents in the first decade of privatization – Southall in 1997, Ladbroke Grove in 1999, Hatfield in 2000 and Potters Bar in 2002 – could be traced to insufficient regard for safety during the industry breakup. Amid criticisms over safety, Railtrack went bankrupt in 2001 when the High Court agreed to place it into administration with debts of more than £3.3 billion. In 2002, most of its operations were transferred to the state-controlled non-profit company Network Rail. 'While successive governments have sought to balance the cost of the railways between taxpayers and farepayers,' reads a 2021 government report, 'government funding still made up nearly a third of the industry's income in 2019/20, and fares have risen by 48 per cent since 1997 in real terms. The model put in place at privatization has not done enough to deliver a more cost-efficient sector and many costs have consistently risen faster than inflation, with taxpayers and customers having to foot the bill.'[38,39,40]

The public increasingly favoured a return to public ownership of Britain's railways. Of 1,500 adults polled in June 2018, 64 per cent said they would support renationalizing the railways. Just 19 per cent said they would oppose it.[41]

Another approach to privatization

However, a glance at the other side of the world suggests that privatization may not be the sole culprit. Japan also had a nationalized rail network in the past, Japanese National Railways. Known around the world for its development of the world's first high-speed rail service, the shinkansen, it was known within Japan for losing money – unlike the private railways.

As in the UK, Japan was going through a wave of privatization in the 1980s under Prime Minister Yasuhiro Nakasone. This took in Nippon Telegraph and Telephone Public Corporation (NTT), Japan Tobacco & Salt Public Corporation and – in 1987 – Japanese National Railways (JNR). The company was privatized and divided into seven companies, known as the JRs – six passenger and one freight. Four of the passenger companies are listed on the stock exchange and three of these – JR East, JR Tokai (Central) and JR West – have been consistently profitable, with exceptions during the Covid pandemic.[42,43]

One reason for the success is the highly profitable shinkansen (bullet train) and express services, which subsidize other smaller, unprofitable lines. The shinkansen have had to become extremely efficient in order to compete with air services. The 550 km Tokyo–Osaka trip takes 2 hours and 22 minutes on the shinkansen or 2 hours and 40 minutes on a plane, when travel time to and from the airports is included. This line is very successful: each day, it runs 336 services, carrying a total of 229,000 passengers between the two megacities. The trains run on dedicated tracks at a maximum speed of 285 kph. In bad years, the average delay is 54 seconds; in good years, it is just 12 seconds. Safety and security measures are excellent: In nearly 60 years of operations, the service has never had an accident resulting in fatalities or injuries. Stations are crammed with amenities to make the journey as pleasant as possible.[44]

Capital expenditure requirements have been limited by high maintenance levels for tracks and signals and fast operations: the 12-minute turnaround at Tokyo Station means the company requires fewer platforms and fewer trains. The JRs therefore need little or no subsidy from central government. Mass-transit researcher Rei Sato estimates JR Central's farebox recovery ratio at more than 245 per cent.

Another key contributor to the JRs' finances has been their commercial and real estate businesses. Non-transportation revenues make up roughly a third of JR East's revenues and nearly 60 per cent at JR Kyushu. JR East operates shopping centres, restaurants and hotels. Other large railways in Western countries own and manage large real estate portfolios, but for the most part they do not directly operate businesses in the buildings they own.

A crucial aspect of the privatization was the long-term vision on which it was based, according to a 2019 report for the Asian Development Bank Institute by Chul Ju Kim and Michael C Huang. One feature was the basis provided for rapid technological development: privatization led to more freedom and incentives for research and development activities, especially in high-speed rail. As of 2019, five of the passenger companies – JR Tokai (Central), JR West, JR East, JR Kyushu and JR Hokkaido – maintain shinkansen capacity. This includes safety devices, ever-higher speeds, the development of track and trains that are resilient in the country's variety of weather conditions, and even artistic design. In addition, the JR companies introduced a prepaid card system in the 2000s, which has since spread all over Japan, contributing to efficient commuting and cashless payment.[45,46]

The UK privatization was characterized by short-term franchises and a split between track and service operations. In Japan, the former Japanese National Railways was split up by region and then all aspects of the business were sold together, so the companies own tracks, trains and stations. A long-term vision requires long-term contractual arrangements between the government and the rail company, according to Kenichi Shoji, a professor at Kobe University. He suggests these should last at least 30 years. 'Long-term relationships should be used to create an environment in which railways not only provide transportation but are also able to effectively design and improve their services,' he wrote in a 2001 paper.[47]

Today the JR companies define themselves as 'social infrastructure companies' that are close to local communities and their mobility needs.

First, the organizations and investments centre on punctuality and safety. Platforms are designed so that passengers can navigate them easily, with indications of where to board, guard railings and safe storage places for luggage in the train cars.

Second, the trains are focused on the convenience and comfort of customers. Well-trained, diligent personnel aim to reduce hassle and make the journey as smooth as possible. For example, the composition of the trains is always the same, making it easy for passengers to find their seats, which are functional and comfortable. Noise levels and vibrations are low and the air conditioning has been optimized.

Third, the JR companies run a range of differentiated, innovative trains. As well as the shinkansen, there are other train services on long-distance routes with names such as Firebird and Thunderbird. Overall, collaboration between different regions and rail companies results in a vast proposition of rail travel experiences. Finally, stations are attractive and provide holistic capacity management and multimodal offerings.

On the freight side, Canadian National Railway (CN) is another successful rail privatization, documented in Harry Bruce's *The Pig That Flew: The battle to privatize Canadian National*.[48] CN was originally a crown corporation, a Canadian term for an organization wholly owned by the federal or a provincial government but structured like a private-sector company. Crown corporations typically have a mixture of commercial and public policy objectives, and CN had a relatively weak commercial focus. Revenues were mostly derived from freight rail and CN was competing with private railroads such as Canadian Pacific Railway and the US freight railroads.

Though it had a strong traffic base, volumes were declining and it was losing market share to other railroads as well as to trucking competition. Operating costs were between 20 per cent and 25 per cent higher than those of other North American railroads and the company was plagued with excess labour and middle management. Debt levels were high and a significant part of the company's capital was deployed in non-core activities, including real estate, hotels, and oil and gas exploration.

The aim of privatization was to improve service and market responsiveness by making the required capital investments as soon as possible, including the redeployment of government assets. In this way, CN could eventually attract high-quality private investors and new talent. In 1992, the company started to prepare for the privatization by taking on new leaders from the Canadian public sector, including Paul Tellier as Chief Executive Officer and Michael Sabia as Chief Financial Officer. They started by restructuring internally in the period from 1992 to 1994, and in November 1995 CN was privatized. The initial public offering was the largest and most successful IPO in Canada up to that time.

CN then began to expand. In 1999, it acquired US-based Illinois Central, gaining north–south access to the US and bringing on board Hunter Harrison, who later became the company's CEO. CN also bought Wisconsin Central, thereby gaining density in the strategic US Midwest. Harrison pioneered the concept of precision-scheduled railroading (PSR), which is based on several tenets. Instead of running trains on demand, a freight railroad should run scheduled trains to maximize asset utilization and minimize costs. The railroad should take on only high-margin business and avoid low-margin or loss-making business. And the organization should incentivize each employee to do what is right for the entire network rather than what is right just for their immediate terminal, railyard or department.

PSR has since become the best practice in North American freight railroad and the principles have turned CN into a top performer in the industry for the past two decades. It has a best-in-class operating ratio of below 60 per cent (the ratio of total costs to revenues, the reference for railroad productivity), while adjusted EBITDA in 2022 was $6.6 billion, from $13.0 billion in revenues.

Europe's variety of rail systems

In Europe, most successful railway systems are still owned by governments. Switzerland in recent years has been the European country whose inhabitants travel most by train – an average of 2,526 km per citizen by train in 2019 (the year before passenger numbers declined because of the Covid pandemic). That was over 60 per cent more than second-placed Austria, where an average citizen travelled 1,507 km, and third-placed France at 1,442 km.[49,50]

Why is SBB, Swiss Federal Railways, so attractive for travellers? It runs one of the most densely used mixed-traffic railway networks in the world, transporting more than 1.2 million people and 210,000 ton-kilometres of freight every day on more than 10,000 trains. And it does this while achieving world-leading punctuality. The average utilization of SBB infrastructure (in number of trains per kilometre of track) is second to none and traffic is expected to increase still further. The major reason is unsurpassed levels of intermodality, promoted by financial incentives to use infrastructure as much as possible. The constituent parts of the Swiss public transport network have been linked and service frequency is the highest in the world – above even Japan, explained Christian Desmaris, of Lyon (France) University, in a 2010 article.[51,52]

Though Swiss Federal Railways was excluded from federal administration in 1999 – so the government no longer ran the railways – it remained a fully state-owned limited company regulated by public law. Local authorities are increasingly implicated in decision-making and the Swiss cantons have full responsibility over decisions on services. Local services are also funded by local public funds.

SBB corporate governance has introduced clear, demanding strategic objectives, combined with strict financial constraints. The company's explicit aims are to limit operating and production costs and to seek new revenues wherever possible. These have laid the basis for considerable productivity gains and sweeping innovations in organization. Unlike with many other European railways, efficiency gains have been based more on an increase in passenger and freight traffic and less on staff reductions.[53]

In other parts of Europe, competition is being emphasized as the way to improve rail services, through the elimination of monopolies and liberalization of transport markets to unleash untapped growth. To further these aims, the EU has been harmonizing norms and standards to secure cross-network interoperability.

But there is a long way to go before markets become open and competitive on high-speed lines. Unlike in the telecommunications sector, where the greenfield nature of the market made harmonization relatively fast and easy, the harmonization of transport norms is complex and slower, especially in rail. So far, only a handful of countries has introduced effective competition on high-speed tracks. One is Austria, where WESTbahn entered the market in 2011. This provided competition for the incumbent train operator and boosted passenger numbers, including for the incumbent, ERA staff say.

In Italy, competition was introduced in 2012 on the Italian Turin–Salerno high-speed line and this highlighted the importance of a regulator that is not only independent but also perceived to be independent. Italian railway infrastructure manager Rete Ferroviaria Italiana (RFI) and the country's primary train operator, Trenitalia, are owned by the same state-owned holding company, Ferrovie dello Stato Italiane (FSI). After the new private sector entrant NTV (*Nuovo Trasporto Viaggiatori*) applied to run services, it had to wait one year to obtain a railway licence from the Ministry for Transportation. To obtain authorization to operate the new trains from the National Railways Safety Agency (ANSF) required nearly three years of assessment. NTV perceived this period to be excessively long and a barrier to entry and it appealed to the antitrust authority several times. However, the authority found no evidence of abuse of the incumbent's dominant position. There are now more trains to choose from in Italy and ticket prices have fallen by at least 24 per cent in just a few years thanks to the competition.[54]

Spain inaugurated high-speed rail travel in 1992, with a service between Madrid and Seville, and has since built Europe's biggest high-speed network. It stretches over 4,000 km to make it the world's second largest after China's, and the latest corridor was inaugurated on 19 December 2022, linking Madrid with Murcia in southeast Spain. These high-speed lines have cost more than €55.89 billion, with €14.09 billion funded by the European Union and another €15.86 billion by debt issued by infrastructure manager ADIF AV, the Administrador de Infraestructuras Ferroviarias.

To increase use of the track, the Spanish government decided to open up services to competition and in 2019 ADIF launched a call for tenders. This approach was different from the UK privatization: rather than dismantling the existing system, Spain kept its incumbent track and service operator, Renfe, but allowed other operators to provide services too. The first railway operator to compete with incumbent Renfe in high-speed train services was Ouigo Spain, the low-cost brand of France's SNCF. It has been taking travellers to popular destinations at competitive prices and is the only high-speed operator in Spain to use double-decker trains. Now it also competes with Renfe's low-cost company, Avlo, as well as the market's new entrant, Iryo, which is owned by Italian operator Trenitalia, Spanish airline Air Nostrum and infrastructure giant Globalvia. Iryo began to operate services on the Madrid–Barcelona route, which attracts a business clientele, making it Spain's busiest and most profitable high-speed line, with 25 per cent of the country's high-speed traffic. Iryo also runs trains in two other corridors, which are dominated by tourist passengers: Madrid to Valencia and, from spring 2023, Madrid to Andalusia.

The competition appears to have lowered prices. Since the end of Renfe's monopoly in 2020, the average price of a Madrid–Barcelona ticket has fallen from €81 to €46, according to ticketing website Trainline. Iryo offers some tickets for just €18 as part of an effort to capture 30 per cent of the market on the lines where it operates. Many of the low-cost trains are packed and passenger numbers per kilometre on high-speed lines increased by 34.5 per cent in one year (from November 2021 to November 2022), according to ADIF figures. In May 2022, a year after its launch, Ouigo Spain boasted 2 million passengers and an average load factor of over 97 per cent.[55]

Liberalization has made it possible to 'democratize the high-speed train, which thus loses its elitist character', declared Raquel Sánchez, Minister of Transport at the time of Iryo's inaugural trip. 'Competition gives passengers more choice at more competitive prices. And all this promotes the development of decarbonized transport.' She said they would expand the experiment, particularly in northwestern Spain.

In France, Trenitalia in December 2021 launched two daily high-speed round trips between Milan and Paris, passing through Turin, Modane and Lyon. This means that Trenitalia also sells tickets for journeys between Paris and Lyon in the South-East corridor – the first time a foreign railway company has competed directly with SNCF in a high-speed domestic service. The Paris–Lyon connection is the jewel in SNCF's high-speed rail network and has always been the most attractive candidate for new competitors. Renfe also announced that it would start to run high-speed trains to France in 2023, starting with the Barcelona–Lyon route and followed by a service between Madrid and Marseille.

Trenitalia's average ticket price in 2022 was €37.40 compared to €54.20 for SNCF, which had large disparities: the TGV Ouigo was offering an average of €20.10 while the more expensive TGV Inoui was up to an average of €78.40, according to Rail Europe News. In December 2022, the millionth passenger was welcomed in one of the Frecciarossa – 'Red Arrow' – trains that Trenitalia operates in France. The competition has driven a 15 per cent increase in the number of trains on a line that is already considered saturated and whose market is relatively mature. Competition is stimulated in France by the French law which provides for a significant discount on tolls for any new entrant in the first year (−37 per cent), then decreasing thereafter to become zero in 2025.[56]

A success formula for rail?

Whereas airline privatization and liberalization are widely considered a success, competition in rail is only just ramping up and there does not appear to be a simple formula for success. A quarter of a century after the privatization of UK railways, Sir Malcom Rifkind, a member of the cabinets of both Thatcher and Major, tried to sum up the lessons. 'I had no problem with the principle of privatization,' he told the *Financial Times*. 'But the separation of responsibility for the railway track from the operating of the trains had been a mistake. To divorce from the person who's running the railway the ability to manage the track as well in the most economic and sensible way was irrational, bad economics, and bad business sense.'[57]

However, some form of private sector participation can have a positive impact on rail services, as the companies will find ways to optimize use of available tracks. (They will usually first aim for high-traffic routes with plenty of business travellers, such as Paris–Lyon and Madrid–Barcelona.) Privatization appears to have been an important ingredient in Japan's continued success with its shinkansen and other train services. But it has not been part of Switzerland's rail success. In most parts of the world, it is not realistic to keep government out of rail, as some of the lines required for a nationwide service will be unprofitable and will have to be run as a public good.

But competition in high-speed rail based on a separation of train and track is demonstrably improving services and reducing prices in parts of Europe and it is likely to grow as a trend. The liberalization of rail – whether or not accompanied by privatization – works best when done in a focused way, route by route or corridor by corridor. Competition in rail services also needs a single infrastructure manager to coordinate competing carriers within a larger system, as well as a convergence of the norms and standards applied in each rail network. Rail will then be safer and its capacity can be maximized. However, these measures won't keep it running in the event of a calamity.

KEY TAKEAWAYS

- In some industries, such as aviation, standardization is global. It does not, however, prevent innovation in business models, as demonstrated by the low-cost air carriers, which have achieved market growth through simplicity and cost efficiencies.

- Air liberalization was a revolution, which triggered huge changes in consumer expectations and challenged other competing modes of transport.

- In some areas of mobility, such as rail, standardization is just beginning – and so the resulting growth has just started.

- The standardization of mass markets has historically been a key driver of European integration. Mobility could learn from industries that have already been through this transformation, such as telecoms.

- Transport – both passenger and freight – is a network industry, which requires span and density. The standardization of mobile vehicles and operations control systems is crucial in order to extend networks and achieve financial viability.

- There is no clear, simple governance formula for success in rail: there are examples of success and failure of both privately owned and publicly owned railways. However, if track and train operations are separated, they need to be tightly coordinated among multiple players.

Notes

1 Levinson, M. (2006) *The Box: How the shipping container made the world smaller and the world economy bigger*. Princeton University Press

2 *The Economist* (2006) The world in a box, 16 March. Available at: www.economist.com/books-and-arts/2006/03/16/the-world-in-a-box (archived at https://perma.cc/9JMD-CG66)

3 *The Economist* (2013) The humble hero, 18 May. Available at: www.economist.com/finance-and-economics/2013/05/18/the-humble-hero (archived at https://perma.cc/737K-822B)

4 United Nations Conference on Trade and Development (2022) Review of Maritime Transport 2022. UNCTAD. Available at: https://unctad.org/rmt2022 (archived at https://perma.cc/3H7K-47TW)

5 Parkinson, J. (2015) The world's biggest ship – for 53 days, *BBC News Magazine*, 8 January. Available at: www.bbc.co.uk/news/magazine-30696685 (archived at https://perma.cc/ZMF4-NTGU)

6 *The Economist* (2013) The humble hero, 18 May. Available at: www.economist.com/finance-and-economics/2013/05/18/the-humble-hero (archived at https://perma.cc/737K-822B)

7 Wenzlhuemer, R. (2010) The history of standardisation in Europe, Institute of European History. Available at: https://d-nb.info/1020545348/34 (archived at https://perma.cc/XG6R-CHLB)

8 Russel, A. (2005) Standardization in history: A review essay with an eye to the future, *The Standards Edge: Future Generations*, Vol. 247. Available at: www.arussell.org/papers/futuregeneration-russell.pdf (archived at https://perma.cc/2SXW-2KXX)

9   Imperial War Museums (n.d.) Transport and supply during the First World War. Available at: www.iwm.org.uk/history/transport-and-supply-during-the-first-world-war (archived at https://perma.cc/26Q2-R9GX)

10   The Great War (2017) The backbone of total war – Trains in WWI I The Great War Special. YouTube. Available at: www.youtube.com/watch?v=LUhDuZAKmzY (archived at https://perma.cc/2726-7ZJR)

11   Müller, U. (2020) Railways in northern East Central Europe before, during and after the First World War, Encyclopédie d'histoire numérique de l'Europe, 26 June. Available at: https://ehne.fr/en/node/21310 (archived at https://perma.cc/QL9Y-XEC2)

12   European Court of Auditors (2018) A European high-speed rail network: Not a reality but an ineffective patchwork. Available at: https://op.europa.eu/webpub/eca/special-reports/high-speed-rail-19-2018/en/#chapter0 (archived at https://perma.cc/2SNW-QD9K)

13   ERTMS (n.d.) ERTMS in brief. Available at: www.ertms.net/about-ertms/ertms-in-brief/ (archived at https://perma.cc/JXW8-KJVL)

14   European Commission (2013) Trans-European Transport Network (TEN-T). Available at: https://transport.ec.europa.eu/transport-themes/infrastructure-and-investment/trans-european-transport-network-ten-t_en (archived at https://perma.cc/G48E-UHTV)

15   www.era.europaeu (2018) European Rail Traffic Management System (ERTMS) | European Union Agency for Railways. Available at: www.era.europa.eu/domains/infrastructure/european-rail-traffic-management-system-ertms_en (archived at https://perma.cc/2P9R-7RST)

16   Peterson, R. (2018) Impacts of airline deregulation, TR News, 315, 10–17. Available at: https://onlinepubs.trb.org/onlinepubs/trnews/trnews315airlinedereg.pdf (archived at https://perma.cc/S2GC-H4GS)

17   Airlines for America (2023) Air travelers in America: Annual survey. Available at: www.airlines.org/dataset/air-travelers-in-america-annual-survey/ (archived at https://perma.cc/4FYJ-6CWP)

18   Cooper, M (2018). Michael O'Leary: Turbulent times for the man who made Ryanair. Penguin Business

19   Milmo, D. (2012) Ryanair plan for standing-only plane tickets foiled by regulator, The Guardian, 28 February 2012. Available at: www.theguardian.com/business/2012/feb/28/ryanair-standing-only-plane-tickets-regulator

20   Ait Ali, A. and Eliasson, J. (2021) European railway deregulation: An overview of market organization and capacity allocation. Transportmetrica A: Transport Science, pp. 1–25

21   Council of the European Communities (1991) Council Directive 91/440/EEC of 29 July 1991 on the development of the Community's railways, *Official Journal of the European Union*. Available at: https://eur-lex.europa.eu/legal-content/EN/TXT/HTML/?uri=CELEX:31991L0440&from=IT (archived at https://perma.cc/JW9P-QDHY)

22 www.youtube.com (n.d.) The UK's failed experiment in rail privatization. Available at: www.youtube.com/watch?v=DlTq8DbRs4k (archived at https://perma.cc/A6F4-7SZD)

23 www.youtube.com (n.d.) The UK's failed experiment in rail privatization. Available at: www.youtube.com/watch?v=DlTq8DbRs4k (archived at https://perma.cc/A6F4-7SZD)

24 Steer Davies Gleave (2011) Unbundling and regulatory bodies in the context of the recast of the 1st railway package. Available at: www.europarl.europa.eu/cmsdata/182910/20110418ATT18161EN.pdf (archived at https://perma.cc/UXG7-LLVZ)

25 www.ft.com (n.d.) Why did the UK sell off the railways? Available at: www.ft.com/video/f473c61c-5167-40f0-8d1c-db556d74d668 (archived at https://perma.cc/Q5RP-5HTS)

26 UK Secretary of State for Transport & Inter City Railways Limited & East Coast Main Line Company Limited (2014) Franchise Agreement – Intercity East Coast. Available at: https://assets.publishing.service.gov.uk/government/uploads/system/uploads/attachment_data/file/488196/intercity-east-coast-franchise.pdf (archived at https://perma.cc/L2A7-6WVC)

27 BBC News (2006) GNER to surrender top train route, 16 December. Available at: http://news.bbc.co.uk/1/hi/business/6182027.stm (archived at https://perma.cc/VNA4-LG7Y)

28 Topham, G. (2017) East Coast rail 'bailout' could cost taxpayers hundreds of millions, *The Guardian*, 29 November. Available at: www.theguardian.com/uk-news/2017/nov/29/east-coast-rail-franchise-terminated-three-years-early-virgin-trains (archived at https://perma.cc/K88N-H59Q)

29 Elder, B. (2017) Stagecoach soars after government intervenes on contract, *Financial Times*, 29 November. Available at: www.ft.com/content/cd4bf9c2-d51b-11e7-a303-9060cb1e5f44 (archived at https://perma.cc/BPQ7-3782)

30 BBC News (2018) Stagecoach East Coast rail franchise to end early, 6 February. Available at: www.bbc.com/news/business-42945709 (archived at https://perma.cc/844R-L9SE)

31 Davies, R. (2020) Covid-19: Government suspends rail franchise agreements', *The Guardian*, 23 March. Available at: www.theguardian.com/world/2020/mar/23/covid-19-government-suspends-rail-franchise-agreements (archived at https://perma.cc/J8UN-S3FS)

32 Kollewe, J. and Topham, G. (2020) UK ends rail franchising as Covid measures extended, *The Guardian*, 21 September. Available at: www.theguardian.com/business/2020/sep/21/uk-covid-19-rail-rescue-measures-dft-franchising (archived at https://perma.cc/T64B-PFYE)

33 Trainline plc (2023) Annual Report and Accounts 2023. Available at: https://trn-13455-s3.s3.eu-west-2.amazonaws.com/media/7316/8546/4076/Trainline_plc_-_FY2023_Annual_Report.pdf (archived at https://perma.cc/D2JN-GW4P)

34   Godsmark, C. and Rodgers, P. (1997) Exposed: Who gets what from Eversholt's great gravy train, *Independent*, 20 February. Available at: www.independent.co.uk/news/business/exposed-who-gets-what-from-eversholt-s-great-gravy-train-1279632.html (archived at https://perma.cc/ENG6-JN5F)

35   UK Department of Transport (2021) Great British Railways – The Williams-Shapps plan for rail. Available at: https://assets.publishing.service.gov.uk/government/uploads/system/uploads/attachment_data/file/994603/gbr-williams-shapps-plan-for-rail.pdf (archived at https://perma.cc/748M-4CP2)

36   Duncan, P. and Swann, G. (2017) Tracking the cost: UK and European rail commuter fares compared – in data, *The Guardian*, 6 January. Available at: www.theguardian.com/money/datablog/2017/jan/06/tracking-the-cost-uk-and-european-commuter-rail-fares-compared-in-data (archived at https://perma.cc/24PG-V4YG)

37   Eurostat (2023) Modal split of inland freight transport. Available at: https://ec.europa.eu/eurostat/databrowser/view/TRAN_HV_FRMOD__custom_975268/default/table?lang=en (archived at https://perma.cc/ZN2H-69WX)

38   www.ft.com (n.d.) Why did the UK sell off the railways? Available at: www.ft.com/video/f473c61c-5167-40f0-8d1c-db556d74d668 (archived at https://perma.cc/Q5RP-5HTS)

39   UK Department of Transport (2021) Great British Railways – The Williams-Shapps plan for rail. Available at: https://assets.publishing.service.gov.uk/government/uploads/system/uploads/attachment_data/file/994603/gbr-williams-shapps-plan-for-rail.pdf (archived at https://perma.cc/748M-4CP2)

40   Wolmar, C. (2022) *British Rail*. Penguin UK.

41   Full Fact (2018) Do the public want the railways renationalised? Available at: https://fullfact.org/economy/do-public-want-railways-renationalised/ (archived at https://perma.cc/M9FY-457H)

42   Smith, S. (2011) Why Tokyo's privately owned rail systems work so well, Bloomberg, 31 October. Available at: www.bloomberg.com/news/articles/2011-10-31/why-tokyo-s-privately-owned-rail-systems-work-so-well (archived at https://perma.cc/355T-CBQK)

43   The Japan News (2022) 3 JR group companies post 1st April-June net profits in 3 years. Available at: https://japannews.yomiuri.co.jp/business/companies/20220803-49215/ (archived at https://perma.cc/SX5Z-VLYZ)

44   Central Japan Railway Company (n.d.) About the Shinkansen. Available at: https://global.jr-central.co.jp/en/company/about_shinkansen/ (archived at https://perma.cc/XM67-QK7Z)

45   www.jreast.co.jp (n.d.) Suica | Fares & Passes | JR-EAST. Available at: www.jreast.co.jp/e/pass/suica.html#suicaMap (archived at https://perma.cc/KU76-B4BW)

46   ADB Institute (2019) The privatization of Japan railways and Japan post: Why, how, and now. Available at: www.adb.org/sites/default/files/publication/539746/adbi-wp1039.pdf (archived at https://perma.cc/J8HD-854B)

47 Shoji, K. (2001) Lessons from Japanese experiences of roles of public and private sectors in urban transport, *Japan Railway & Transport Review*, 29 (December), 12–18. Available at: www.ejrcf.or.jp/jrtr/jrtr29/pdf/f12_sho.pdf (archived at https://perma.cc/AKQ8-MLCN)

48 Bruce, H. (1997) *The Pig That Flew: The battle to privatize Canadian National, Douglas & McIntyre*

49 www.youtube.com (n.d.) Austrian railways: Where train ride is pure satisfaction. Available at: www.youtube.com/watch?v=JCaf3k70uJU (archived at https://perma.cc/S7K8-284U)

50 Eurostat (2020) Average passenger kilometers traveled per capita in European countries in 2020. Available at: www.statista.com/statistics/1257407/average-passenger-kilometers-traveled-per-capita-europe/ (archived at https://perma.cc/H68H-UVUD)

51 www.g2rail.com (n.d.) Swiss Railway | G2Rail. Available at: www.g2rail.com/help/railways/swiss-sbb (archived at https://perma.cc/Z9H4-MFVB)

52 company.sbb.ch (n.d.) History | SBB. Available at: https://company.sbb.ch/en/the-company/profile/history.html (archived at https://perma.cc/TG46-JJ9H)

53 Desmaris, C. (2014) Une réforme du transport ferroviaire de voyageurs en Suisse: Davantage de performances sans concurrence?, *Les Cahiers Scientifiques du Transport*, 65, 67–96.

54 Desmaris, C. (2016) High speed rail competition in Italy, OECD. Available at: www.itf-oecd.org/sites/default/files/docs/high-speed-rail-competition-italy.pdf (archived at https://perma.cc/FG7K-LXMQ)

55 Piquier, I. (2023) In Spain, the successful liberalization of high-speed rail traffic, *Le Monde*. Available at: www.lemonde.fr/en/international/article/2023/01/03/in-spain-the-successful-liberalization-of-high-speed-rail-traffic_6010102_4.html (archived at https://perma.cc/M7TB-NYUH)

56 De Kemmeter, F. (2023) Success for Trenitalia France, Mediarail.be. Available at: https://mediarail.wordpress.com/success-for-trenitalia-france/ (archived at https://perma.cc/UJ62-7CA7)

57 www.ft.com (n.d.) Why did the UK sell off the railways? Available at: www.ft.com/video/f473c61c-5167-40f0-8d1c-db556d74d668 (archived at https://perma.cc/Q5RP-5HTS)

The global illness

5

How Covid changed
the mobility industry

- How Covid was similar to – and how it was different from – other major disruptions.
- How long it takes to recover from disruptions such as Covid.
- What Covid's lasting impacts were on mobility.

Officials at the International Air Transport Association (IATA) quickly became concerned when they heard news of a disease outbreak in China. The first cases had been reported in December 2019 in and around the city of Wuhan. The following month, the virus claimed its first victim, and on 23 January 2020, China's central government imposed a lockdown in Wuhan, suspending flights and public transport.

To stay aware of the virus's spread, IATA initiated contacts with the World Health Organization (WHO) in Geneva and began to cross-reference data on the spread of the virus. By the end of January, the disease had reached Europe, notably with two tourists returning to Italy from China. In early February 2020, the outbreak had begun to look very similar to a deadly pandemic nearly 20 years earlier.

The first case of SARS (severe acute respiratory syndrome) was reported in southern China in 2002. It then spread in early 2003 to nearby countries and had also reached Canada and Europe. Those affected in the early stages were primarily travellers, showing the close links between SARS and travel. In March 2003 the World Health Organization began to issue an unprecedented series of travel advisories: to limit the spread of infection by international travel, people should postpone non-essential trips to SARS-affected areas. The travel and tourism industries suffered and the SARS outbreak created international anxiety because of its novelty, ease of transmission in certain settings – and its rapid spread through air travel.

I remember this period, as an airline consultant living in Canada at the time. In May 2003, Air Canada grounded 40 aircraft as passenger numbers slumped due to fears of SARS at its busiest hub in Toronto. Business travel had all but dried up due to fear of the virus and the airline's losses had widened from C$2 million to C$5 million a day. A month earlier, Air Canada already had filed for bankruptcy protection due to the fallout from the war in Iraq, the September 11 terrorist attacks and the global economic downturn. 'I do not expect international travel demand to Canada to recover in the near term,' the airline's Chief Executive Robert Milton declared at the time. 'The terrible revenue environment we are now facing with SARS immediately after the war with Iraq necessitates drastic action to survive what is expected to be one of our weakest second and third quarters in history.'[1,2]

But by July 2003, the WHO declared SARS contained. Of the more than 8,000 people who caught the disease, of whom around 800 died, of course a terrible number, only a few of these were outside Asia (see Figure 5.1).[3]

Based on the experience of SARS, IATA officials in 2020 at first thought the new outbreak – which had been named Coronavirus disease 2019, or Covid-19 – would likely remain limited in time and geographic scope. South-East Asia has a variety of close links with China to the north, with frequent flights for business travel and tourism, and supply links for the region's booming manufacturing industries. As a consequence, South-East Asian countries were some of the first to declare infections. In Europe, there was relatively little worry at first. The World Economic Forum was gathering in January 2020 in Davos and though participants had heard the news from China, I remember little concern about a possible outbreak in the Swiss village.

However, by the end of February, with cases reported in many European countries, IATA started to see that the crisis might be bigger. From the beginning of March, travel restrictions were being imposed in a wider range of countries and in mid-March Europe had emerged as the new pandemic epicentre. IATA launched a crisis management procedure. It organized more frequent meetings of worldwide airline CEOs, and its Executive Committee began an intense communications and decision-making process, meeting every day at noon via video conference.

At an IATA board meeting on 15–16 March, members were glued to their incoming emails, which were announcing commercial air service closures in an ever-growing range of countries. Sentiment in the room quickly swayed from incredulity to concerns around the scope and duration of the shutdown. 'Is this a nightmare we're experiencing?' one executive committee leader said, remembers Alexandre de Juniac, then Director General of IATA.

Figure 5.1   Correlation of Covid cases and world's airline capacity, 2019–2023 (cumulative Covid cases in millions, available seat miles in billions)

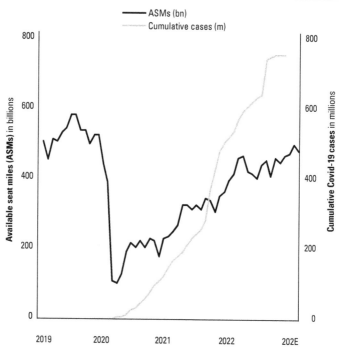

SOURCE World Health Organization, OAG schedule capacity via PlaneStats.com
NOTE 2023 ASMs based on forward-looking schedules. Covid case data NOT estimated for 2023.

After just a few weeks, IATA executives realized that the pandemic had become global and could be long lasting (see Figure 5.1). De Juniac described this as one of the most dramatic periods in his career. He was an important player amid a deadly global event that threatened countless lives. He and his IATA colleagues – those in the association's executive committee, plus airline CEOs – were in the control tower and making hourly decisions on how to limit impact and protect populations from the deadly virus. But they had little control over the disease itself. All they could do was take measures to limit its spread. So IATA leadership facilitated the set-up of travel restrictions around the entire world.

Mobility has long been linked to the spread of disease. In the fourteenth century, the bubonic plague spread most rapidly along the trade routes that crossed the Mediterranean Sea as infected rats and fleas made their way onto ships in contaminated food and supplies. It took much longer to move overland, where travel was then slower.

Thus, improvements in human mobility also represent opportunities for diseases. Of three nineteenth-century cholera epidemics in the United States (in 1832, 1844 and 1866), the third was the most rapid: the disease spread along the transport routes of the time and by 1866 the country's railroad network had expanded. Faster trips make it more likely that a person infected at the start of a journey will still be infectious at the end of that journey, meaning that infectious diseases spread far more easily in an age of high-speed travel. Now that millions of people make international air trips every week, diseases that might once have remained limited to specific regions can spread globally.[4]

Travel restrictions introduced worldwide

The Covid pandemic led to drastic travel restrictions almost everywhere in the world. In the vicinity of mainland China, Singapore, Taiwan and Hong Kong imposed restrictions on flights departing from China between 22 and 26 days after the outbreak in Wuhan in December 2019. South Korea waited until 34 days after the outbreak. Singapore, Taiwan and Hong Kong imposed travel restrictions on all countries 78–80 days after the outbreak and South Korea 91 days.[5]

Public transport operators, aware of the possibility of virus transmission in trains, buses and trams, established new vehicle and aircraft cleaning procedures. Once face masks became widely available, they were made compulsory in most jurisdictions. In Singapore, the Land Transport Authority (LTA) trained transport ambassadors to remind commuters to keep a safe distance from one another. Everywhere in stations (and at other public sites such as bank agencies or retail shops) one could see signs on the ground indicating safe distance between travellers. By early April 2020, public transport ridership had halved since the first cases there in January. 'We accept the fall in demand for buses and trains,' said then Transport Minister Khaw Boon Wan. 'It means that Singaporeans are staying at home more and doing what they need to do around their immediate neighbourhood. This is not the time to use our public transport to get to the other side of Singapore for your favourite hawker dish.'[6]

In many cities, the pandemic triggered unprecedented financial crises for the local transport authorities. Subway and bus ridership in New York City was down 90 per cent from pre-pandemic levels by April 2020. Commuter rail passengers had fallen 95 per cent, and bridge and tunnel traffic had declined 65 per cent. Even after a partial recovery, subway ridership was down 70 per cent in the summer of 2020 and commuter rail passenger down 80 per cent. Toll traffic was more resilient and was down only 15 per cent. Fares and tolls represented nearly 40 per cent of the operating revenue of the Metropolitan Transportation Authority (MTA) and the declines resulted in a cumulative budget gap of $16.2 billion from 2020 to 2024.

Air passenger transport was hit harder than any other sector besides hotels (and other lodging) and restaurants (and other forms of out-of-home catering). Air travel began to decline with the first Covid cases in January 2020, though the impact was at first limited to few countries. But, as the virus spread globally, passenger air transport activities fell rapidly (see Figures 5.1 and 5.2). Lockdowns, border closures and travel restrictions around the world led overall passenger numbers to decline 92 per cent from 2019 levels by April, with international air traffic down 98 per cent and domestic down 87 per cent. For the whole year of 2020, international passenger traffic suffered a dramatic 60 per cent drop over 2019, bringing air travel totals back to 2003 levels, according to a report by the International Civil Aviation Organization (ICAO), a United Nations agency. Seat capacity dropped by a half and the number of passengers fell to 1.8 billion, compared with 4.5 billion in 2019.

The aviation industry suffered huge financial losses: $370 billion by airlines, $115 billion by airports and $13 billion by air navigation services providers (ANSPs). IATA, concerned about the financial sustainability of its members, started to lobby governments and international bodies actively as early as March 2020. Over 18 months, governments injected $200 billion into the sector in forms such as subsidies, guaranteed loans and the underwriting of salaries. About $50 billion of this amount was in the United States. Airlines furloughed a majority of their staff to contain costs but maintained employees in critical operations – such as systems operations controllers, pilots and flight attendants – in order to be ready for the recovery, whenever it might come.

Figure 5.2 Scheduled available seat miles worldwide, 2019–2023
(billions available seat miles)

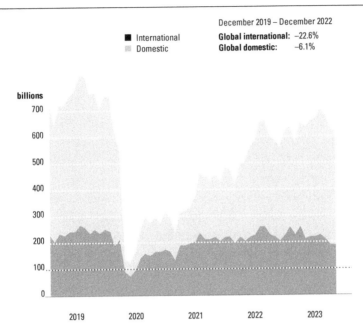

December 2019 – December 2022

■ International   **Global international:** −22.6%
▦ Domestic   **Global domestic:**   −6.1%

SOURCE OAG schedule capacity via PlaneStats.com
NOTE Domestic = capacity within individual countries.

Previous disasters and travel downturns

The travel industry had experienced major downturns before due to various shocks. After each crisis, traffic returned to the original underlying growth trend – but often with some structural changes.

The Persian Gulf War, from August 1990 to February 1991, led to oil supply disruptions, sending the price per barrel to a peak of $46 (about $94 in 2020 terms). The cost of air travel rose and many global companies imposed corporate travel bans, replacing face-to-face meetings with telephone-conferencing. Moreover, even people who could afford expensive transatlantic flights cancelled by the thousands due to the fear of terrorism. The downturn in travel came just as the early 1990s' recession hit and all major European airlines – including British Airways, Air France and SAS – suffered significant downturns in passenger numbers and revenue. Traffic at then the world's busiest airport, Heathrow, decreased by 21 per cent. Travel from North America to Jordan dropped by 48 per cent, to Egypt by 36 per cent and to Israel by 30 per cent, according to the World Tourism Organization (WTO). By the end of the war, about three million people engaged in tourism had lost their jobs.[7,8]

After the terrorist attacks on New York's World Trade Center on 11 September 2001, North American air space was closed for two days – the first time in history that US and Canadian airspace had been shut down. Flights then resumed, but the attack had a lasting impact on the industry. Before 9/11, aviation security experts had not envisioned the possibility of terrorists using commercial airplanes as weapons and being willing to sacrifice themselves in order to kill thousands of innocent people. Now, counter-terrorism and homeland security officials – in the US federal government and globally – work to imagine the unimaginable and enhance defences against ever-changing threats to aviation security.

Security measures at all steps in the travel chain significantly altered – and worsened – the traveller experience. Travellers now have to stand in long lines at security checkpoints, regularly waiting more than 30 minutes. They may have to take off their shoes, empty their pockets and remove laptops and other electronic devices from their carry-on bags. Then they step into high-resolution, full-body scanners, while their bags pass through 3D-imaging X-ray machines. And they mustn't forget to take liquids of more than 100 ml (3.4 ounces) out of their hand baggage.

Processing times, data requirements and controls are all a burden, and the extended time spent in airports has caused air travel to lose market share to road and rail for short and medium-distance trips. And, as security checks take longer, air passengers spend less time – and money – in airport lounges, restaurants and shops. 'September 11, 2001 had a massive, lasting impact on the aviation industry,' says James Cherry, then Chief Executive Officer of Montreal Airport. 'Nothing has been the same afterwards, from airport design and passenger flows to passenger experience and commercial services in airports.'

After SARS broke out in East Asia, advisories not to travel reduced air travel dramatically. Tourist arrivals to Singapore dropped by 41 per cent between 1 April and 21 April 2003 compared with the same period in 2002, according to the Department of Infectious Diseases. China, Hong Kong, Vietnam and Singapore suffered the most. Arrivals in the Asia and Pacific region as a whole fell 12 million during the epidemic, a 9 per cent drop compared with the previous year. International tourism arrivals fell 1.2 per cent to 694 million in 2003, according to WTO figures. The broader travel and tourism economy, which measures visitor spending around the world as well as capital investment, grew just 2.9 per cent – down from about 5 per cent in previous years.

The financial crisis in 2007 and 2008 wiped out more than $2 trillion in global GDP. In the immediate aftermath, consumers pulled back on discretionary spending, cancelling or downsizing planned vacations. Businesses tightened their belts and cut corporate travel expense accounts. Between January 2007 and March 2009, airline stock prices declined 68 per cent, while shares in hotel, resorts and cruise lines fell 74 per cent.

The recovery was slow and both business and leisure travel declined. But much changed in the travel industry in the years that followed. In the United States, some industries, such as hotels and airlines, have seen cyclical recoveries in line with the broader business cycle. Other travel areas, such as online bookings or emerging market outbound travel, experienced growth seemingly uninterrupted by the Great Recession. But some sectors, such as offline travel agents, sunk into a broader decline.

The long path back to normal

The recovery patterns from these past crises informed the aviation industry's plans for after the Covid pandemic. Immediately after total shutdown,

"9/11 had a massive, lasting impact on the aviation industry. Nothing has been the same afterwards"

James Cherry

IATA's board began to prepare for the future recovery phase. It worked with the International Civil Aviation Organization to define conditions and processes that would be needed to restart air traffic, such as mask requirements, health controls and testing procedures. In only around six weeks, airline executives from around the world got pretty much the entire industry aligned on these standards. Airlines started to operate again in June and July 2020.

'When the Covid crisis hit, we in the airline community did our job,' says then Director General Alexandre de Juniac. 'We aligned most carriers and closed down commercial airline operations in four days. After lockdown, it took us just six weeks to agree on how to restart operations. However, misalignment among nations over cross-border sanitary conditions meant it took longer before business actually recovered.'

Though IATA members agreed relatively easily on the recovery process, governments did not. The pandemic was evolving and spreading in each country at different rates and at different times. National health systems varied in their ability to cope with infected patients who needed treatment. For air travel, there were still no common procedures for screening passengers. Because the industry was so interdependent, international travel still struggled in spite of the resumption of flights. By April 2021, the industry was 12 months into the crisis and global flight volumes were still 43 per cent lower than two years previously. Some airlines had already gone bankrupt and the rest were losing tens of billions of dollars between them despite government support.

For IATA, the pandemic and its handling carried important lessons for the future. First, Deputy Director General Conrad Clifford noted that restrictions were applied more for political than scientific reasons. Another lesson was that it is difficult to remove restrictions once they have been

"When the Covid crisis hit, we in the airline community did our job. We aligned most carriers and closed down airline operations in four days"
Alexandre de Juniac

applied, particularly where the reason for a restriction was not clear in the first place.

In May 2023, Clifford outlined three recommendations for governments to ensure a better response to future global health crises. One was to recognize that border measures that restrict travel and trade come at a huge economic and social cost for, at best, a marginal and temporary benefit in population health. Another was to quickly implement a set of proportionate, risk-based, time-limited health measures. Third, IATA wanted to enable passengers to demonstrate their health status via a government portal.

Global recovery

By early autumn 2022, large majorities of the populations of most countries had Covid antibodies and the pandemic was seen as effectively over. Travel restrictions were lifted at the end of the year in the European Union and global air traffic mostly recovered. By the end of April 2023, planned global airline passenger seat capacity was just 3 per cent below its level in the same week of 2019, according to Katharina Buchholz of Statista.

Other factors led to large regional variations, however. In the United States, which accounts for almost 30 per cent of global seat capacity, the market bounced back in 2022–2023 and exceeded its 2019 level. The rest of the Americas grew even more strongly: planned passenger capacity in Central America was 16 per cent above its April 2019 level. But Russia's invasion of Ukraine in February 2022 reduced passenger numbers in Eastern Europe. At the end of April 2023, they were almost 25 per cent lower than four years previously, according to travel data service Official Airline Guide.[9]

However, some carriers never returned to operation. These included airlines that might not be familiar to the average traveller, such as Jet Time, NokScoot and Fly My Sky, as well as world-famous names such as Alitalia (although Italy now has a successor national airline in ITA Airways). Air Namibia, another national flag-carrier, also went under in 2021.

For some airlines, employee attrition made the return to operations challenging. Ground staff in airports were especially severely affected by this, according to de Juniac, who believes this is a sign that their jobs were undervalued, coming with lower wages despite their physical demands and importance. Airports also accelerated their introduction of digital technology for customer services – another previously existing trend boosted by the pandemic.

Other service industries thrived. Many people in much of the world learned to live and work with travel far more limited than in the past. However, that did not mean they wanted to stop travelling altogether. Rather, it encouraged them to avoid unnecessary trips and think more carefully about the purpose and benefits of the trips they did make. That meant commuting less frequently, new ideas for business and leisure travel, and the avoidance of dull shopping (for washing-up liquid and kitchen roll) – but not of shopping that is more fun (for shoes or fine food). In short, some of the pandemic's new living and working habits stuck, raising the prospect of lasting impacts on mobility and the transport sector.

Hybrid working

One quick impact of the pandemic was companies' decisions to let people work from home when possible. The success of this – helped by readily available video-conferencing technology and home broadband connections (although it took time for some companies to provide their non-travelling staff with mobile laptops and other equipment) – led to initial forecasts of a dramatic long-term shift to frequent (or full) remote working.[10]

In May 2021, Google, which has large headquarters buildings in Silicon Valley, expected 60 per cent of its employees to be on site for a few days a week, with 20 per cent working in new office locations and 20 per cent working from home. In October of the same year, PricewaterhouseCoopers, the accounting and consulting firm, announced it would allow all its 40,000 US-based client-service employees to work virtually from anywhere in the United States. The company said this was the first announcement of its kind from a professional services firm in the country, marking a shift away from the work culture prevalent before the pandemic. In Oliver Wyman's 2021 Travel Sentiment survey, 69 per cent of global respondents agreed that they could collaborate effectively with others via teleconferencing – a 10 percentage point rise in one year – and respondents were planning to spend on average 1.8 more days per week working from home, compared to before Covid.

However, this trend did not continue. Some US banks demanded a return to the office, with several major ones requiring employees to turn up five days a week. Europeans did not push so hard. One global Swiss bank estimated that around 75 per cent of its employees could work in either hybrid model or full-time remote work long term. In Canada, over 30 per cent of the workforce was estimated to be in jobs that could be performed remotely and a February 2021 Gartner survey showed that 82 per cent of Canadian company leaders were planning to allow some form of remote work after the pandemic.

The 2021 Traveler Sentiment Survey indicated that most age groups were ready to embrace a hybrid approach – a combination of working from home and in the office. In the United States, only 20 per cent of the respondents were able to work from home but didn't plan to, with those numbers concentrated among the over-55 age group. Gartner research in 2023 suggested that 48 per cent of employees would work remotely at least some of the time in the post-pandemic world, compared with 30 per cent before.

Remote – or at least flexible – working could ease some of the burden on rush-hour commuting capacity, both road and rail. Daily commuter numbers in large Western cities are expected to drop 15 per cent or 20 per cent on average, according to the experts we talked to. Beyond this reduction, being able to work partly from home helps commuters avoid peak hours: they can start work at home early in the morning, for instance, and then travel to a city centre outside the rush hour, easing the pressure on road and rail services while reducing their transit times and increasing productivity. This trend is also facilitated by differential pricing (that is, prices that vary according to the time of travel), which a growing number of public transit authorities have introduced. Alex Bayen, Professor of Electrical Engineering and Computer Science at University of California, Berkeley, notes: 'In a post-Covid world, transit operations need to adapt to the new urban landscape, which has changed greatly with new trends, such as work-from-home patterns, declined ridership in some geographies, and in some cases free transit like in Luxembourg.'

....

"In a post-Covid world, transit operations need to adapt to the new urban landscape, such as work-from-home patterns, declined ridership and in some cases free transit"
Alex Bayen

....

This is another sense in which the pandemic accelerated a trend already under way. Even before Covid, many office workers were starting to work from home one or two days a week, as part of corporate efforts to improve employees' work-life balance. 'Covid has exacerbated an ongoing redefinition of working habits, as white-collar workers avoid city congestion through WFH,' says Olivier Brousse, President of Veolia Transportation North America from 2004 to 2008. 'This trend has actually been under way in the US since the mid-2000s.'

For rail operators facing capacity constraints in commuter traffic – such as SNCF in the Ile de France region – the falloff in passenger numbers provided some relief. The changes may also necessitate a reorganization of mass transit offerings and timetables, suggests Jean-Pierre Farandou, Chairman and CEO of SNCF Group. Some commuters have decided to leave the city and live in a remote suburb or the countryside. They are now travelling longer distances, less frequently, but they remain railway customers so train operators need to cater for evolving traveller patterns.

Purposeful business travel

The increasing popularity of remote working has the potential to challenge business travel over the long term. Most business travel had to be cancelled during the Covid pandemic and collaborative software such as Microsoft Teams and Zoom seemed ready to replace it. Microsoft founder Bill Gates predicted during the pandemic that more than half of business travel would disappear, and even some senior airline industry bosses thought a significant chunk was gone forever.

"Covid has exacerbated an ongoing redefinition of working habits"
Olivier Brousse

Despite the reduced need to travel for meetings, old habits steadily returned and business executives have been quick to get back on the road. Business trips of shorter duration – to see customers, for example – were first to return, followed by events and conferences, says Andrew Watterson, Chief Operating Officer at Southwest Airlines. While Teams and Zoom have reduced travel for internal meetings, business travel as a whole will still grow, he says – though perhaps at a slower rate than the overall economy. In 2022, global business travel was 25 per cent to 30 per cent below comparable levels in 2019, according to Airlines Reporting Corp (ARC), which processes tickets sold through travel agencies. That shortfall was an improvement on the 50 per cent decline that persisted until the end of 2021. But recovery in business travel had clearly stalled through the first half of 2022.

The trend towards fewer trips goes well with the greater corporate emphasis on environmental, social and governance (ESG) considerations. Companies were already searching for ways to have employees travel less to reduce emissions. Some 60 per cent of CEOs are actively engaging in their company's sustainability programmes, according to GreenBiz Group's 'WHG – State of the Profession' report, 2022.[11] That was 25 percentage points higher than in the 2020 report. Industry leaders are also pressuring their suppliers to become more sustainable.

Sustainability is likely to rise in importance, as more potential employees now try to investigate a recruiting firm's efforts to reduce its climate impact. This is an existential challenge for many airlines, as business travel generates a large proportion of their profits on international routes in particular. Even if the number of leisure flights increases, and even if there is a growing share of high-paying first- and business-class leisure travellers, a question remains over whether they can compensate for erosion in lucrative corporate travellers.

New opportunities for the travel industry could come from shifts in the way people structure their trips. For example, greater flexibility in work schedules and location has fuelled a 'bleisure' movement, where leisure is added to a business trip, according to Oliver Wyman's 2022–2023 Airline Economic Analysis Report: 41 per cent of corporate travel managers reported an increase in employees asking for such blended travel, a survey by the Global Business Travel Association (GBTA) found.

The same poll of corporate travel managers by GBTA from October 2022 supports the likelihood of prolonged displacement of trips. Asked how current bookings for domestic business travel compared with pre-pandemic bookings, the managers reported an average of 63 per cent of pre-pandemic bookings (see Figure 5.3).

Figure 5.3   GBTA travel survey – percentage of 2022 bookings vs 2019 levels
(% of respondents)

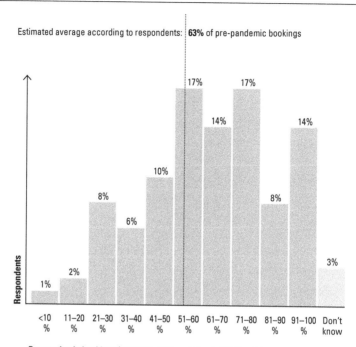

Estimated average according to respondents: **63%** of pre-pandemic bookings

Pre-pandemic bookings (current booking relative to 2019 levels)

SOURCE Global Business Travel Association (GBTA) October 2022 survey
NOTE Answers could be based on best estimate.

Combining work and vacation could reduce the total number of trips, which would erode airlines' revenues. But airline networks have evolved to serve more leisure destinations and leisure might open up new growth opportunities for airlines if family members are taken along on corporate-booked trips. One possibility could be to extend the discounts and corporate benefits in loyalty plans to family and friends who might fly in with a business traveller for a weekend.

New growth in leisure travel

Outside lockdowns, demand for leisure travel remained significant even during Covid, leading industry leaders in most regions to anticipate a surge as soon as restrictions were lifted. That was the case: people wanted to travel to new places, presenting new growth opportunities in leisure markets. Leisure travel rebounded faster than business trips and by May 2022 had recovered its 2019 level, according to data from Airlines Reporting Corp (ARC) based on a four-week moving average of tickets booked for domestic and international travel. Since then, leisure travel has remained above this level (see Figure 5.4).

When the pandemic hit, Southwest Airlines, like much of the aviation industry, went into crisis mode, cutting many of its routes and parking a chunk of its fleet. But Southwest, consistent with its employer brand, decided not to put employees on furlough or to carry out non-voluntary pay cuts. That meant it had excess capacity, which it used to study and test new markets. The high degree of uncertainty made it counter-productive to try to analyse what-if scenarios, so these tests were a way to manage forward, motivate teams and leverage one of the airline's core skills: airline planning and management.

Through an ad-hoc process, called internally 'Act and React', Southwest dynamically created 30-day, 60-day and 90-day plans with a focus on financial break-even to maintain airline operations and preserve employment. Within these planning horizons, the management team decided once a week the number of flights they would run to various destinations based on the latest assessment of demand, so as to stick as closely as possible to actual travel demand. By mid-2021, Southwest had added 18 new airports to its route map since the outbreak of Covid, more than any other US carrier.[12, 13, 14]

That meant the airline was able to maintain momentum in the leisure market and it also remained consistent with its brand employee proposition. Two years after the start of the pandemic, Southwest's operations had largely recovered to pre-pandemic levels, though some routes – primarily longer domestic ones – had still not yet returned to the schedule. However, this growth was largely opportunistic, said CEO Bob Jordan in an interview, and many of the new cities were already under consideration before the pandemic.

In 2023, rather than rolling out numerous new destinations, Southwest planned to first rebuild its network, with a goal of bringing most pre-pandemic routes back by the third quarter of the year. In August, the airline announced a range of new or revived routes to build on the growth in leisure

Figure 5.4 2020–2022 seat capacity in North American and European airports compared to 2019 (rolling 12-month seat totals, indexed to January 2019)

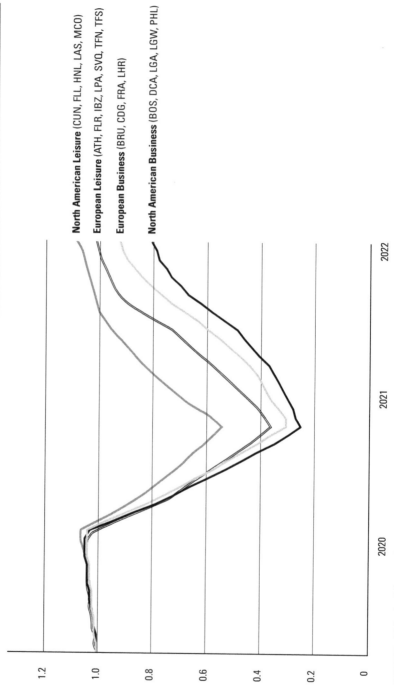

North American Leisure (CUN, FLL, HNL, LAS, MCO)

European Leisure (ATH, FLR, IBZ, LPA, SVQ, TFN, TFS)

European Business (BRU, CDG, FRA, LHR)

North American Business (BOS, DCA, LGA, LGW, PHL)

SOURCE OAG schedule capacity via PlaneStats.com

demand. New routes added for the 2024 spring break included Baltimore to Belize, Grand Cayman, Turks and Caicos, and Cabo San Lucas; St Louis to Los Cabos (Mexico); and Austin to San Juan (Puerto Rico). Other airlines, too, are now focusing more on premium leisure travellers who are willing to pay higher fares. All have learned the need to use a crisis period to prepare for post-crisis business by maintaining key operations teams and developing new services in segments with high growth potential.[15]

How shipping struggled and then recovered

About 80 per cent of goods around the globe are transported by sea, making maritime shipping the main pillar of international trade. The shocks unleashed by the pandemic caused havoc and sent freight costs fluctuating aggressively.

At first, the global economic crisis triggered a negative demand shock and there was less need to transport goods such as raw materials. Later, the pandemic triggered a surprise surge in demand for shipping services. Consumption and shopping patterns changed as people adopted or increased their use of electronic commerce. In richer countries, the appetite grew for manufactured consumer goods, a large share of which are moved in container ships. Economic stimulus packages boosted demand further.

While demand shot up, the global maritime shipping supply chain was slowed or even blocked as a result of restrictions to control the spread of the coronavirus. Some ports closed for periods. Those that still ran struggled with shortages of labour and necessary materials. Local sanitary regulations forced carriers to disrupt their regular rotations, so they skipped port calls, exacerbating the mismatch between supply and demand for containers.

Starting in late 2020, container ships began to anchor off the west coast of North America as they waited for berths to free up in ports. Containers got stuck on ships, intensifying the shortage in capacity, and empty containers became unavailable to move exports from China, an unprecedented phenomenon. Freight rates on the main East–West routes reached historic highs by late 2020, surging further in 2021 (see Figure 5.5). The rise in rates was even higher in some developing parts of Africa and Latin America. This global disruption was only absorbed over several months starting in 2022, after which the system resumed smoother operations.

Figure 5.5 2017–2023 40-foot container rates (USD)

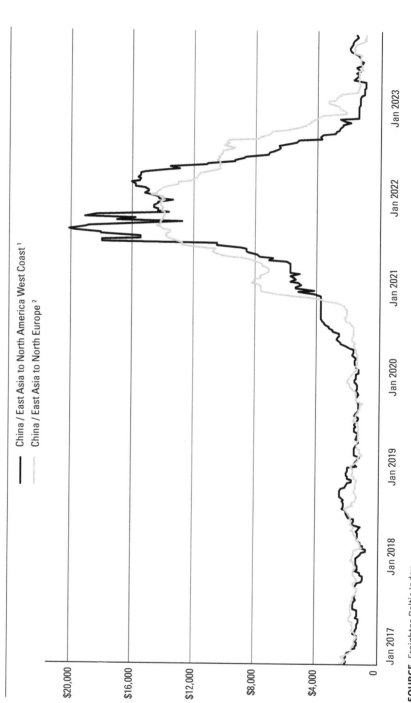

— China / East Asia to North America West Coast [1]
········ China / East Asia to North Europe [2]

SOURCE Freightos Baltic Index
NOTES 1. FBX China EA/WCNA Container Index; 2. FBX CHN EA to N EUR Container Index.

The pandemic took carriers, ports and shippers all by surprise and no contingency plans had been in place to mitigate the negative impacts of container shortages. In the midst of the crisis, the shipping industry suffered another shock, as the 224,000-ton container ship from Evergreen Marine ran aground in the Suez Canal in March 2021. Wedged across the canal, it blocked passage for six days and at one point at least 369 ships were queuing to pass through the canal, stranding an estimated $9.6 billion worth of trade.[16]

The pandemic disruption combined with the Evergreen ship incident were stark reminders of several challenges for shipping. Jan Hoffmann, Head of the Trade Logistics Branch, Division on Technology and Logistics at the United Nations Conference on Trade and Development, pointed to three in particular.

1 The importance of resilient supply chains: boosting these will require measures to digitize trade procedures, thereby making maritime transport more transparent and making close collaboration easier.

2 The potential imbalances between carriers and shippers: the surge in freight rates led to very strong earnings among carriers and caused difficulties for shippers. This contrast underlines the importance of ongoing regulatory oversight by competition authorities.

3 The energy transition for shipping: the maritime transport industry needs to assume responsibility and play its role in the fight to decarbonize the global industry as a whole. That implies developing some form of zero-carbon shipping – a change that will be as fundamental as the past switching of the primary fuel source from wind to coal and later from coal to oil.

The (even faster) rise of online commerce

Covid restrictions on both mobility and traditional shops drove a lot of consumers to shop more – or to start shopping – online. While shopping from home was already common in several Western economies, with the United States and the United Kingdom leading, it increased in all markets, especially in urban areas. To survive, businesses turned to pandemic-proof e-commerce sales.

In the United States, e-commerce sales increased from $571.2 billion in 2019 to $815.4 billion in 2020, a rise of 43 per cent, according to the US

Census Bureau Annual Retail Trade Survey. Globally, the e-commerce share of total retail sales jumped from 14.0 per cent in 2019 to 18.2 per cent in 2020, according to Insider Intelligence (see Figure 5.6). It had already been rising steadily, but the pandemic gave it a sharp boost and it has continued to rise since: the share for 2024 was forecast at 20.3 per cent. The crisis thus appears to have accelerated an ongoing shift towards the digital economy, which has had a negative impact on traditional physical retail business models. The biggest increases in businesses selling online were in Brazil, Spain and Japan.

Demand for e-commerce logistics exploded. To give one example, the UK Royal Mail reported a 39 per cent rise in parcel trade in the fiscal year ending in March 2021, as parcel revenues topped letters for the first time in its history. That drove revenues to £12.6 billion, an increase of 17 per cent over the previous year. The former state-owned company's pre-tax profits hit £726 million for the year, despite surging costs related to the pandemic – a fourfold rise from £180 million in the year to March 2020.

Figure 5.6   2015–2024 retail e-commerce sales worldwide (retail e-commerce sales as percentage of total retail sales)

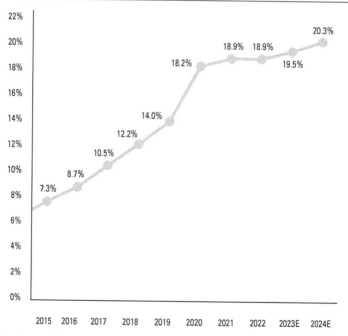

SOURCE Insider Intelligence

The unexpected disruptions caused big impacts on the courier industry. Many businesses transformed their mix of offerings between physical shops and online sales, expanding delivery options thanks to courier services. Some of these changes will last beyond the pandemic.

In the United Kingdom, demand for couriers surged nationwide, both same-day and overnight deliveries. The demand was mainly for food but also included medicine and clothing. In the food sector, much of the hospitality industry had to close during the pandemic. To continue operations, businesses turned to courier services and customers became used to the convenience of ordering food at the click of a button. Especially in London, this demand necessitated the development of specialist courier services, for example those offering temperature-controlled delivery.[17]

The pandemic both caused a surge in demand for medical and healthcare services and made it hard to fulfil this demand. To provide an alternative system, couriers designed services that handled, stored and delivered medical products in an appropriate way. Couriers also helped local businesses survive the pandemic without compromising on the health and safety of their colleagues, enabling customers to get hold of their products without physically having to step inside a store.[18]

Lessons from Covid

The Covid pandemic and the subsequent recovery showed, first, how resilient the demand is for mobility and transportation. Despite short-term downturns – in some cases severe – due to the restrictions put in place, all transport modes returned to a growth trajectory. That said, they underwent structural shifts. These were mostly the acceleration of underlying trends, such as remote working, purposeful business travel, online shopping and e-commerce logistics, and digitization and decarbonization. Just as before, transport and mobility continued to become more varied, complex and fragmented – only they have done this at a faster pace.

Covid, like previous shocks that disrupted transport and mobility, was temporary. The consequences were large, one-off impacts, followed by recovery, albeit with some important changes. But another global challenge linked to transportation has the potential to be long term and perhaps permanent: climate change.

> **KEY TAKEAWAYS**
>
> - Mobility services are vectors for diseases, which will travel as far and as fast as transport options allow.
> - Throughout history, epidemics and disasters have disrupted travel and stopped services regionally or globally for periods of varying length.
> - Mobility services tend to bounce back after disasters to their previous historical trends, though often with major differences. Covid did not trigger a lasting revolution in travel or transport of goods, but it did accelerate ongoing shifts – such as those towards hybrid work, online shopping and purposeful travel.
> - Even in the thick of a crisis, transport operators need to maintain some planning capacity and skills in order to strategically design their recovery and future growth.

Notes

1 Clark, A. (2003) Air Canada grounds planes as 'ruinous' Sars and war hit home, *The Guardian*, 15 May. Available at: www.theguardian.com/business/2003/may/15/theairlineindustry.travelnews (archived at https://perma.cc/XA2A-AADX)

2 Weber, T. (2003) Air Canada granted bankruptcy protection, *The Globe and Mail*, 1 April. Available at: www.theglobeandmail.com/report-on-business/air-canada-granted-bankruptcy-protection/article20448619/ (archived at https://perma.cc/QFR2-4GMR)

3 World Health Organization (2015) Summary of probable SARS cases with onset of illness from 1 November 2002 to 31 July 2003. Available at: www.who.int/publications/m/item/summary-of-probable-sars-cases-with-onset-of-illness-from-1-november-2002-to-31-july-2003 (archived at https://perma.cc/58UV-XM53)

4 Bowen, J.T. and Laroe, C. (2006) Airline networks and the international diffusion of severe acute respiratory syndrome (SARS). *The Geographical Journal*, 172(2), 130–144. doi: https://doi.org/10.1111/j.1475-4959.2006.00196.x (archived at https://perma.cc/3XB6-SFKV)

5 Gwee, S.X.W., Chua, P.E.Y., Wang, M.X. and Pang, J. (2021) Impact of travel ban implementation on COVID-19 spread in Singapore, Taiwan, Hong Kong and South Korea during the early phase of the pandemic: A comparative study. *BMC Infectious Diseases*, 21(1). doi: https://doi.org/10.1186/s12879-021-06449-1 (archived at https://perma.cc/VYG3-VURA)

6 The Straits Times (2020) Coronavirus 101: What do you want to know? Available at: www.straitstimes.com/multimedia/graphics/2020/02/virus101/index.html?shell (archived at https://perma.cc/83F3-Y5TX)

7 Special Report... World Tourism Organization Impact of the Gulf Crisis on International Tourism (1991) *Journal of Travel Research*, 30(2), 34–36. doi: https://doi.org/10.1177/004728759103000206 (archived at https://perma.cc/D3VJ-M865)

8 Golding, C. (2003) Iraq conflict 'will not have Gulf War impact', *The Caterer*, 19 March. Available at: www.thecaterer.com/archive/iraq-conflict-will-not-have-gulf-war-impact (archived at https://perma.cc/RGY6-P7AD)

9 www.oag.com. (n.d.) COVID-19 Airline Recovery | OAG. Available at: www.oag.com/en-gb/coronavirus-airline-schedules-data (archived at https://perma.cc/8CF9-F3KD)

10 Krugman, P. (2023) Working from home and realizing what matters, *The New York Times*, 22 May. Available at: www.nytimes.com/2023/05/22/opinion/work-from-home-commuting-gdp.html (archived at https://perma.cc/EJ7S-9C3T)

11 Davies, J. (2022) WHG – State of the Profession 2022, GreenBiz Group. Available at: www.greenbiz.com/report/state-profession-2022-report (archived at https://perma.cc/3FLE-CDNJ)

12 Russel, E. (2020) Southwest Airlines is cutting more than 100 routes from its 'full' schedule this winter, The Points Guy, 30 May. Available at: https://thepointsguy.com/news/southwest-airlines-cutting-routes-from-winter-schedule/ (archived at https://perma.cc/VT9U-B5VR)

13 Griff, Z. (2020) This is where U.S. airlines are parking their biggest planes during the coronavirus pandemic, The Points Guy, 7 April. Available at: https://thepointsguy.com/news/airlines-parking-planes-coronavirus/ (archived at https://perma.cc/8CUT-PY2U)

14 Griff, Z. (2021) Southwest unveils major expansion with 2 new cities, 78 new and returning routes, The Points Guy, 10 June. Available at: https://thepointsguy.com/news/southwest-major-expansion-syr-bli-fall-2021/ (archived at https://perma.cc/X2SF-AFS9)

15 Southwest Airlines (2023) Southwest Airlines extends flight schedule through April 8, 2020, Southwest Media, 3 August. Available at: https://swamedia.com/releases/release-7aaeaba8e0ec055676f9032728192df4-southwest-airlines-extends-flight-schedule-through-april-8-2024 (archived at https://perma.cc/V5MQ-UM3W)

16 BBC News (2021) Suez blockage is holding up $9.6bn of goods a day, 26 March. Available at: www.bbc.com/news/business-56533250 (archived at https://perma.cc/7GYR-JVAX)

17 Absolutely Courier (2023) Services. Available at: www.absolutelycourier.com/
our-services/ (archived at https://perma.cc/T6QG-HZTH)

18 Business Wire (2023) Courier Services Market Report 2022. Available at:
www.businesswire.com/news/home/20230125005453/en/Courier-Services-
Market-Report-2022-Rise-in-Use-for-Transportation-of-Official-Documents-
Boosts-Growth---ResearchAndMarkets.com (archived at https://perma.cc/
MX6B-2WCK)

New values for a new era

6

Gender inclusivity and decarbonization

- How the industry can accelerate gender diversity.
- What is being done to decarbonize the mobility value chain at pace.
- Why aviation faces the greatest challenges.
- How electrification gives China a new opportunity to lead.

Focusing relentlessly on the efficient movement of people and goods, the mobility and transport industries may have often considered some environmental and social considerations as more nice-to-haves – or they have simply neglected them. This may seem a paradox for an industry that aims to improve people's quality of life and develop the planet's economy.

Some of the challenges are intrinsic to what the industry does: moving people and goods requires energy. If this energy is generated from fossils – whether through engines that burn liquid fossil fuels or run on electricity generated from coal or natural gas – it will contribute to global warming. Huge efforts are already under way in this field and it's no stretch to say that these will dominate the industry for the coming decades.

But other considerations do not need technology solutions and the industry should simply do better. Women are underrepresented in most of the industry, but it is now widely recognized that all forms of underrepresentation of certain groups of people reduce the available pool of talent and will hinder performance. On some indicators, the record of transport companies has been worse than other industries: in the world's top 100 aviation organizations, for example, women currently hold only 14 per cent of C-suite roles and account for just 5 per cent of CEOs, recently increased from 3 per cent before 2022. That is still lower than the 6.4 per cent of women CEOs in the companies making up the S&P 500.[1]

These are more than simply values that it would be agreeable to uphold. They are crucial for survival. Environmental, social and governance (ESG) criteria are playing an increasingly important role in investment decisions and younger people are already taking environmental impact into account when deciding travel arrangements. Failure to develop a more inclusive workforce will eventually lead to a company's decline as rivals become more creative and attract the best talent.

Gender inclusivity

One surprise social media hit these past few years has been a truck driver based in North Carolina – not a 'typical' trucker, however, but one of the minority who are women. Clarissa Rankin has attracted 1.8 million online followers with clips of life on the road. She talks about rates for a job and the cost of a new truck. She points out parking areas. And she shows off her fingers after a visit to a nail bar. Most importantly, she tells other women about the satisfaction they can have from a trucking life. 'If you want to travel, if you want to make a great living, take that chance… because trucking is a different lifestyle,' she told followers. 'It's a whole different world, so if you always wanted to do it, just do it. Don't make up excuses.'[2,3,4]

Amid an ongoing shortage of truck drivers – exacerbated by supply chain disruptions during the Covid pandemic – women are helping to make up the numbers. In the United States, for example, they made up 8.1 per cent of all truck drivers in 2022, up from 5.4 per cent a decade previously. Women appear to be well suited to the job. They are less likely than men to take risks on the road, and male commercial drivers are 20 per cent more likely to be involved in a crash in areas such as traversing intersections, according to the American Transportation Research Institute. Other research indicates that female truckers are less likely than their male colleagues to feel lonely on the job and less likely to regret becoming a truck driver.[5]

In Europe, too, several TV channels have been running reality shows on women truckers, some of which have inspiring titles such as France's 'Les Reines de la Route' (Queens of the Road) – and Flemish TV's 'Lady Truckers'. These emphasize the job's challenges – getting stuck in the mud while picking up a load in a forest, for example, and unloading in a parking lot full of impatient, honking car drivers – and the protagonists' can-do spirit and freedom from the office grind. Brenda, from Flanders, decorated her truck with a picture of her heroine, the film and video-game action hero Lara

Croft. 'Lara solves every problem, does not shy away from a challenge and brings everything to a successful conclusion,' says Brenda. 'That's how I am.'[6,7]

Truck makers are trying various ways to attract more women drivers. Volvo Group sponsors Iron Women, a truck-driving programme for women that started in Peru and then expanded to southern Africa. It aims to help women to qualify as heavy-duty commercial truck drivers and so address driver shortages. But there are still plenty of barriers to overcome, starting with cabin design, which was done with male bodies in mind. Women seem to be at higher risk of injury than men driving the same vehicles with similar crash conditions, something that might be caused by the cabins designed for male bodies and the use of crash-test dummies based on the average man. Drivers' uniforms were traditionally made for men, and many truck stops do not have showers or other amenities for women.[8]

Safety concerns go beyond vulnerability in the case of a crash. In the United States, 68 per cent of women truckers reported feeling safe when working on the whole, compared with 78 per cent of male truckers, according to one survey from JW Surety Bonds. Some of the women surveyed reported carrying pepper spray and a knife to defend themselves in the event of harassment or assault.[9]

Only 25 per cent of women would consider offering driver services through a ride-hailing app such as Uber, according to research by that company. This is largely due to concerns around having strangers in their vehicle, driving at night, the efforts associated with the licensing process or not having a suitable vehicle. Uber has introduced more safety features, such as 'Follow my ride', an emergency assistance button in its app.[10,11]

It's not just trucking. Women are underrepresented in the transport and mobility industry as a whole, and businesses could gain a lot by employing more of them. All forms of underrepresentation of certain groups of people in the workforce reduce the available pool of talent and will hinder performance, in an industry where many segments suffer from talent shortages. If women earned the same as men, the World Bank found in 2020, global human capital wealth could increase by about one-fifth. For the aviation industry, the International Air Transport Association considers that the loss is of leadership talent that could improve a variety of areas, including safety, sustainability, innovation and risk management.[12] A similar point applies to other forms of diversity, such as ethnic or socio-economic. In these areas, it is hard to find data being tracked and little may be available. However, in many countries, there is a long way to go to make senior representation in transport diverse, inclusive and accessible to all.

To analyse the impact of women in leadership roles, an Australian study looked at six years of Australian companies' gender reporting to the federal Workplace Gender Equality Agency. It concluded that firms that appointed a female CEO increased their market value by 5 per cent. A rise of 10 percentage points or more in the share of women in other key leadership positions boosted a company's market value by 6.6 per cent.[13]

Moreover, ESG-oriented investing is growing, so performance in diversity and environment increasingly affects companies' ability to raise financing. In the 2021 proxy season, three shareholder resolutions were filed at US companies requesting public disclosure of demographic workforce data, according to IATA. Of these, two received over 80 per cent support. Six proposals requested enhanced reporting with respect to equality of opportunity, promotion and retention. Of these, three received majority support. If aviation does not take action now, it will be disadvantaged in a highly competitive environment.[12–78 to 14–80]

To understand the challenge, Oliver Wyman and the International Aviation Women's Association (IAWA) in 2021 carried out a survey of 450 women and men in aviation leadership roles and interviewed successful female leaders. The study found that, relative to men in the industry, women report more negative experiences, slower career advancement and fewer opportunities to take on senior or challenging roles. As a result, women are more likely to be pushed out of the industry because of adverse experiences, while men are more often pulled away by the lure of better opportunities: 59 per cent of women have considered leaving aviation, but just 45 per cent of men. And the top reason for women is implicit bias discrimination, while that for men is interest in another career or industry.[16]

While women are more likely than men to encounter a range of negative experiences throughout their careers, these become more pronounced at senior leadership levels: 71 per cent of women have felt overlooked for opportunities, compared with 54 per cent of men. Other experiences include being interrupted, having ideas dismissed or misattributed and being viewed as overly aggressive. These add up over the course of a career and women need additional energy to confront them. Consequently, mid-career women often consider opting out.

This phenomenon is not specific to aviation within mobility. One industry senior leader told me that when she was a junior manager in railway operations, her male supervisor told her bluntly that she had no chance of a successful career in the organization – or the industry – because she was a woman. She would not be able to withstand the operational challenges of railways, or manage male colleagues, he added. But she was tenacious.

She told me she decided to ignore these warnings and keep trying. She has had a 25-year career in a European railway organization, rising to the C-suite of the company.

Sumati Sharma, a partner in Oliver Wyman's global Aviation practice based in London, but formerly an airline senior executive, remembers that progression was relatively easy in the earlier part of her career in an airline, when capabilities and hard work were sufficient. Higher up, however, these are simply minimum requirements. 'When you get more senior, you start to think, 'Have the rules changed, or do I just not know what they are?' she says. 'To make sure you're not left on the sidelines, number one is confidence.'

However, there is a vast confidence gap between genders: compared with men, women generally don't consider themselves as ready for promotion, they predict they'll do worse in tests, and they generally underestimate their abilities. 'A growing body of evidence shows that that can be devastating, that lack of confidence,' she says. 'Success correlates just as closely with confidence as it does with competence.'

Confidence can be threatened by feeling out of place. When Sharma worked in a senior role at an airline, she found herself in a meeting to discuss the commercial and financial terms of a joint venture and it was remarked that she was the only woman in the room. Still, she says, 'The good news is that you can work on your confidence. It can be acquired.'[17,18]

Over the past decade, aviation has put significant energy and investment into inclusion and diversity programming. Men in the industry broadly believe their companies are doing a good job of offering effective and accessible programmes to help develop and promote gender equity, according to the Oliver Wyman study.

···

"When you get more senior, you start to think, **Have the rules changed, or do I just not know what they are?"**
Sumati Sharma

···

But existing inclusion and diversity programming is still somewhat ineffective. A major factor is that aviation leadership is predominantly male, so it is mostly men who decide what initiatives will enhance gender balance. However, it can be hard to know what to change if the people in charge cannot see what's wrong, because it's not wrong for them. While senior executive compensation typically is tied to metrics related to goals for growth in company value, 93 per cent of survey respondents did not know if there was a link between compensation and inclusion and diversity goals.

There are significant gaps between women's and men's perceptions of a company's priorities. Women are more likely to prioritize female representation in leadership but are less likely to have a role in improving representation. Men, however, are more likely to believe that the representation of women in leadership roles is already well supported.

The most prevalent initiatives in women's leadership programming are those that men believe will solve the problem – or that they believe have already solved the problem – such as paid family leave and clear processes to report harassment. But women view these as minimum requirements, not as true enablers of success. Instead, women want a systemic focus on growth that takes into account the barriers they face. Without women at the table, obstacles to their success will be difficult to understand and the best solutions will remain out of reach.

To go further, three changes can be particularly meaningful and lasting. One is to redesign systems for balance by including women in the development of solutions to achieve gender balance in leadership. It is important that women's voices and lived experiences inform the development of targeted initiatives that specifically address women's career development needs. Another is culture change – that is, making inclusive leadership a requirement and prioritizing gender balance as a strategic imperative. To accelerate culture change, women should be made visible so that their voices are regularly heard in leadership discussions and public presentations. They should feature on interview panels, deliver keynote presentations, be profiled in company communications and present to the board and senior executives.

Perhaps the biggest contribution could come from making sure women have sponsors who speak out on their behalf. Sponsorship is widely considered essential for achieving a senior leadership position: only sponsors can advocate with key influencers and act as a guide to challenging roles or projects. But sponsorship often arises from informal networks. Such groupings are dominated by men and women have greater difficulty in developing the trust and relationships that come naturally from these networks. Of the women surveyed, 65 per cent had never had a sponsor and respondents of both genders cited a lack of sponsorship as a top-three career challenge for women in aviation.

The role of sponsors is often poorly defined or confused with coaching and mentorship. But coaching generally focuses on developing certain competencies, and mentoring serves as a sounding board for ideas and long-term knowledge transfer and the skills development. Sponsorship involves in-depth, proactive support and advocacy, and only sponsors can help women identify career-enhancing opportunities and advocate on their behalf. Women can end-up 'over-mentored and under-sponsored' – receiving lots of advice, without direct, vocal support. Both women and men responding to the survey also agreed that investment in sponsorship programmes should be the top industry initiative to improve the retention and advancement of women. This should consist of formal sponsorship programmes that explicitly serve women and encouraging leaders to diversify their advocacy.[19]

In general, leaders must take responsibility for implementing, tracking and championing new programming and be ready to quickly change tactics if initiatives are not delivering results. At the moment, there might be a disconnect between the intent and the impact of efforts designed to encourage and elevate women. When this is the case, leaders must acknowledge and understand it, so that they can better address systemic issues and develop more effective career programmes for women. Ultimately, real change needs top leadership to treat inclusion and diversity as a business imperative and create accountability for real results.

Government can also make a difference. In the UK, gender pay gap reporting was mandated in 2018 and it quickly highlighted how far behind the airline industry was. The data was the trigger for Sumati Sharma to found the Women in Aviation and Aerospace Charter, which was supported by the British government. So far, Scandinavian companies are the leading representation of women at senior levels thanks to government rules in those countries.

One area in which companies could benefit from having more women in leadership positions is sustainability. However, for women to have an impact, they need to be in key decision-making roles that have substantial influence on the board and on a company's strategic direction, such as C-suite positions and heads of major business units. A study of Chinese companies showed that having a female CEO or chair and increased representation of female directors both significantly increase environmental investment – in non-polluting as well as polluting enterprises. Another study, of US data, showed that firms with female CEOs produce less air and water pollution, generate lower greenhouse gas emissions and receive fewer environmental penalties, compared with firms with male CEOs. After a transition from a male to a female CEO, firms might reduce greenhouse gas emissions and toxic discharges into water and the air, and they receive, according to the study, fewer environmental penalties.[20,21]

The same principle applies to environmental policy as to diversity: it cannot be treated as an add-on – a project separate from a company's main business. It has to become part of the strategic core.

Decarbonization

Transportation is the second largest source of greenhouse gas emissions after the energy sector, representing around 23 per cent of the global total. That means that – as with other sectors – there is great pressure to decarbonize.

One way the environmental challenge is unlikely to be solved is by people travelling less, which would go against human nature. Instead, transport will have to become greener. But not all transport modes are environmentally equal, raising important questions: Will the energy transition simply mean a switch to new kinds of propulsion, with various transport modes operating much as they do today? Or will it significantly benefit those modes of transport that transform fastest? And could that lead to a shift in industrial power to the countries that are fastest to develop the tools of carbon-free travel? 'The idea that human beings will be less mobile and travel less is a non-starter,' says Rupert Duchesne, formerly Vice President of Marketing for Air Canada and President and CEO of loyalty management pioneer firm Aimia. 'They will just travel green, which means transport modes will and must decarbonize over time.'[22]

"The idea that human beings will be less mobile and travel less is a non-starter. They will just travel green"
Rupert Duchesne

A glance at various common forms of mobility shows that some need to change very little before becoming carbon neutral. Others need some effort, for example, to convert to electric propulsion. And some modes have serious challenges for which no clear and stable solutions currently exist.

Cycling results in effectively zero greenhouse gas emissions – just those from manufacturing a bicycle, which are far less than for a car, plus those from growing whatever food the rider burns while in the saddle – very little if they eat locally grown vegetables. Even an electric bicycle will generate emissions equivalent to just 0.3 kg of CO_2 for a 30 km trip, with that amount coming mainly from the bike's manufacture. That's one-tenth of the emissions for an electric car – which, again, are mostly generated during the manufacturing process – and less than one-twentieth of the emissions for a car powered by an internal combustion engine.[23,24]

Rail travel has long been on a decarbonization path. More than half of Europe's train network is now electrified, so they don't cause direct emissions.

But their manufacture does, as does the construction of rail lines. And the generation of the electricity they use varies according to country. In France, much electricity comes from nuclear power stations and a 30 km journey for a single person generates 0.2 kg of CO_2-equivalent. But the figure would likely be higher for countries such as Germany and Italy, where much electric power is generated from either coal or natural gas.

At the other end of the spectrum, sea and air travel face high hurdles. Maritime transport emits 1 billion tons of carbon dioxide per year, or 4 per cent of the global total, due to its major role in supporting international trade. At present, 98 per cent of vessels run on fossil fuels, though this does not emit greenhouse gases to the extent of road and air transport. Shipping produces 135 grammes of CO_2 per ton per kilometre, around the same as road transport. But emissions from rail freight are one-ninth of that level, while those from air freight are seven times as high as those from maritime transport, at around 1 kg per ton per kilometre.[25]

Imperatives for change

Consciousness of climate and sustainability has grown strongly over the past decade and is having an impact on the way different modes of transportation are perceived and regulated, at least in Europe. Because of rail's relatively low carbon footprint, the French government in 2023 prohibited passenger flights on routes with few long-haul connections and where the equivalent rail trip is under about 2.5 hours. That ended domestic point-to-point air traffic from Paris Orly Airport to Nantes and Bordeaux. Generation Z (born between 1997 and 2012) are highly sustainability conscious and recent Oliver Wyman Forum research suggests that many would swap air travel for a longer journey by electric train. Further impact could come if carbon regulations raise the cost of flying. 'We should not have to choose between transport and ecology,' says Guillaume Pepy, former Chairman and CEO of SNCF Group, the French national railway and mobility group. 'Sustainable mobility is the goal of having no more impact on the planet.'[26,27]

Pressure to reduce greenhouse gas emissions is coming from all sides. Governments increasingly embrace the climate change agenda: since 1995, the 'Conference of the Parties' (COP) summit brings together signatory states to the United Nations Framework Convention on Climate Change (UNFCCC).

Regulators are also pushing for a reduction in or elimination of the use of fossil fuels. The European Green Deal, presented in 2019, aims to transform the European Union into a modern, resource-efficient and competitive economy, with no net greenhouse gas emissions by 2050 and economic growth decoupled from resource use. The European Commission has adopted a midway target for 2030 of reducing emissions by at least 55 per cent from 1990 levels.[28,29]

Financial institutions have developed alliances such as the Glasgow Financial Alliance for Net Zero (GFANZ), which aims to accelerate decarbonization and limit global temperature rises to 1.5 C from pre-industrial levels. GFANZ works to develop the tools and methodologies needed to turn financial institutions' net-zero commitments into action.

The general public and consumers are increasingly conscious of climate challenges. Nearly one in four Americans was considering climate change to

"We should not have to choose between transport and ecology"
Guillaume Pepy

be the most important social challenge facing the country, according to a 2021 study from Cornerstone Advisors and Meniga.[30] Among consumers who didn't mention climate change as the most important challenge, 44 per cent still said they consider climate change to be a very important issue.

But the Cornerstone and Meniga survey showed that people do not yet collectively act strongly enough on it. Car journeys and flights have become part of the fabric of life in many countries, whether for daily commuting and weekly shopping trips or for annual holidays. Many people in developed countries now think of them as a basic right and it's hard to persuade them to do without them. A recent Cornerstone survey showed that even among consumers who consider climate change to be the most important social challenge, just 9 per cent were tracking their carbon footprint. Another survey, by the Oliver Wyman Forum in 2023, found that Generation Z understand the importance of protecting the environment: 93 per cent in the United States said addressing climate change is critical for the future of the planet. But only 20 per cent of US Gen Z members said they minimized their waste and only 37 per cent said they reduced their energy and utility usage. 'When developing new services,' says Adrian Slywotzky, former Boston-based senior Partner at Oliver Wyman and author of acclaimed business books such as *Profit Zone* and *Value Migration*, 'the most difficult factor to predict is NOT technology evolution and innovations, but rather future customer behaviour.'[31]

Overall, though, pressure on decarbonization is mounting. Whatever the short-term trends in politics and public opinion, transport (like all industry) will only prosper in the long term if it decarbonizes. If a transportation mode does not decarbonize, demand will shift over time to another mode. If an operator within a mode falls behind, customers will eventually turn to other, greener, operators. Leaders in the transport and mobility industries are taking action.

"The most difficult factor to predict is not technology evolution and innovations, but rather future customer behaviour"
Adrian Slywotzky

Maritime shipping

Today, the maritime sector relies almost entirely on fossil fuels and shipping emissions are growing rapidly. The International Maritime Organization (IMO), the United Nations agency responsible for regulating shipping, aims to achieve net-zero emissions from international shipping around 2050, first cutting emissions by between 20 per cent and 30 per cent by 2030.[32,33]

Numerous initiatives are under way to decarbonize the shipping industry in line with the goals of the European Green Deal. In December 2022, a provisional agreement was reached to include shipping emissions in the EU Emissions Trading System (EU ETS). That was followed in July 2023 by the 'FuelEU Maritime' initiative, a new regulation to ensure that the greenhouse gas intensity of fuels used by the shipping sector will be gradually lowered over time, starting with a reduction of 2 per cent in 2025 and achieving a decrease of 80 per cent by 2050.[34,35]

One approach is to swap diesel for liquified natural gas (LNG), which is natural gas (methane) cooled into liquid form, so its volume decreases to 600 times less than that of gas at standard atmospheric pressure, making it easier to transport and store. Although LNG is still a fossil fuel, it is included in the EU Taxonomy, which includes it as a transitional fuel for activities that cannot yet feasibly be replaced by low-carbon alternatives but do contribute to climate change mitigation and so will assist the switch to renewable energy in the future.[36]

Many more avenues are being explored. In September 2023, Maersk and CMA-CGM, respectively the world's second and third largest maritime shipping companies, announced a partnership aiming to pool investment and R&D efforts into sustainable alternative fuels to accelerate their journey towards net zero.[37]

Aviation: The biggest challenge?

However, the biggest barriers to sustainability in the mobility sector are in aviation, which accounted for roughly 2.4 per cent of global emissions before the Covid pandemic. Aviation has not been covered by the EU carbon pricing system, but the EU decided in 2022 to introduce carbon pricing on flights by the end of 2026. 'Business-model challenges for point-to-point low-cost air travel should increase, as taxes and a true carbon price transform its cost structure,' says Barbara Dalibard, President of the Board of Michelin and former CEO of Voyages SNCF, SNCF's long-distance business unit.[38]

"Business-model challenges for low-cost air travel should increase, as taxes and a true carbon price transform its cost structure"
Barbara Dalibard

Adrian Slywotzky adds: 'Depending on what region they are in, some airlines will struggle to comply with environmental requirements before sustainable energy becomes available. It is difficult to predict this.'

At the end of November 2022, Jean-Marc Jancovici, an engineer and president of the Shift Project think tank, declared on a radio programme, 'The plane was born with oil and will die with it,' arguing that since air transport took off in the 1970s, it benefits only a minority and 1 per cent of travellers emit 50 per cent of CO_2. He added that it wouldn't be outrageous to introduce 'a quota of four flights per person' during their lifetime. Leaving aside politics, this seems a rather radical and pessimistic view of the future of air transport. It will not surprise our readers that our expert panel is rather adopting a stance to encourage the development of solutions towards sustainable mobility, including the trickier topic of sustainable aviation, and will expect some modal share redistribution.

Aircraft manufacturers have a proud history of technology innovation and in recent decades they have made aircraft lighter and more aerodynamic via design changes and the use of light metals and composite materials. They have significantly cut energy consumption, enabling longer ranges at a lower cost.

"Some airlines will struggle to comply with environmental requirements"
Adrian Slywotzy

But those efficiency gains will not reduce the sector's total emissions nearly enough to reach their agreed target of net zero by 2050 via carbon regulation. Traffic has been doubling every 15 years, a trend that is expected to be maintained, so sustainability requires new technologies and alternative fuels that are not yet in commercial use. 'Technology improvements in aircraft have been impressive over the years,' says Fabrice Brégier, former Chief Executive Officer of Airbus Group, currently CEO of Palantir France and Chairman of the Board of reinsurance firm SCOR. 'Airplanes are much lighter, have longer ranges and a fuel consumption reduced by 80 per cent. Engines contribute a lot to it with a better performance, lower noise and emissions, a higher reliability and a compatibility with the SAF. However, this continuous improvement is not sufficient to compensate for the doubling of traffic we have observed over the past 15 years.'

One solution being worked on is aircraft powered by electric batteries. A number of start-ups are aiming to develop small electric aircraft that could make short trips before the end of the decade. Heart Aerospace in Sweden, for example, has been planning to start flight tests in 2024 of 19-seat planes, with the intention of following with commercial flights by 2026. The initial plan is to use the planes for purposes such as crossing fjords in Scandinavia or other routes that are difficult to replace with ground transport.[39]

However, battery-powered flight is challenging because of the weight. Batteries would need to double their energy density for the kind of range (about 400 km, or 250 miles) start-ups such as Heart are aiming for, according to an analysis by the International Council on Clean Transportation (ICCT). Such an improvement would likely approach the limit of lithium-ion batteries. And even this would enable battery-powered planes to replace only very few flights by conventional aircraft.[40]

Hydrogen fuel cells have a higher energy density, giving them potential to fuel longer flights. Anglo-US start-up ZeroAvia announced the successful

"Technology improvements in aircraft have been impressive over the years. However, this continuous improvement is not sufficient"

Fabrice Brégier

completion of a 10-minute test flight in January 2023 of a propeller aircraft partially powered by hydrogen fuel cells. The test plane was a Dornier 228, the largest aircraft to fly using a hydrogen-electric engine, according to the company. Seats were taken out to make room for hydrogen tanks and a fuel cell propulsion system. The plane's left-side engines derived about half their power from hydrogen fuel cells and half from batteries. The right side used traditional kerosene as fuel. To reduce the time to market, the firm plans to transform the old Dornier aircraft into a zero-emission airplane, which could carry 19 passengers for a 500 km range. ZeroAvia said the technology would also reduce operating and maintenance costs by 20 per cent compared to thermic engines.

As of January 2023, ZeroAvia had raised over $140 million in funding from investors, such as Jeff Bezos and Breakthrough Energy Ventures, Bill Gates's energy venture fund. They also included airlines – British Airways, United Airlines and American Airlines – and Shell, which is supplying it with the hydrogen. The company hopes to have a turboprop seating between 9 and 19 passengers ready for commercial flights by 2025 and a 40-to-80 seat aircraft to enter service by 2027. It had already received 1,500 pre-orders for its engines, including 600 or 700 for the size used during the test flight.[41]

However, hydrogen faces numerous hurdles. So far, 95 per cent of global hydrogen production is so-called grey hydrogen: it is produced from natural gas through steam reforming. But this does not lead to long-term sustainable fuel as the process emits carbon dioxide. An alternative, blue hydrogen, uses a similar process but captures most of the resulting carbon emissions. Some CO_2 capture technologies are commercially available now, while others are still in development.

Green hydrogen, in contrast, is sustainable. It uses electric power generated from renewable energy sources to split water into hydrogen and oxygen through electrolysis. Once stored in a fuel cell, hydrogen is very energy-intense, producing a lot of energy from relatively little weight. However, the process to date is inefficient and expensive, and green hydrogen makes up less than 2 per cent of global hydrogen production. Fuel cells also face questions over commercial viability. Hydrogen is expensive to produce, transport and store at the moment, and it is also highly inflammable and explosive, famously demonstrated when the Hindenburg zeppelin caught fire in 1937 during its attempt to dock with its mooring mast in New Jersey. It was destroyed and 36 people were killed.

The European Union Aviation Safety Agency (EASA) has already certified a small, battery-powered electric aircraft, the Velis Electro by Slovenia-based Pipistrel, a maker of gliders and light aircraft that is now owned by US conglomerate Textron. But EASA has not so far approved any hydrogen-powered aircraft for commercial flights.[42]

Certification, too, is no easy task. The final design by ZeroAvia was scheduled to be submitted to the UK Civil Aviation Authority by the end of 2023, after which new tests will be carried out with the aim of achieving final certification by the end of 2024. In order to get this green light, ZeroAvia will have to demonstrate that its technology is reliable and safe enough, compared with traditional thermic powered engines which the Agency is used to and which have been perfected over about a hundred years.

Though experts say small, short-range commercial aircraft could be powered by hydrogen fuel cells within the decade, that would represent only a small fraction of the emissions from flying. Technologies for larger aircraft over longer distances would have a greater impact, but this will be hard with fuel cells because they are far less energy-dense than kerosene. So more work is needed for larger commercial aircraft, and the topic is at the top of executive teams' agendas. As Andrew Watterson, Chief Operating Officer of Southwest Airlines, recognizes, 'The Southwest brand stands for trust and authenticity. Greenwashing would be against our brand culture.'[43]

While fuel cells and hybrid batteries still show cost and weight limitations for sizable commercial aircraft of the calibre of A320 or B737, let alone wide-body aircrafts for long-haul flying, alternative fuels still require substantial amounts of R&D funding. One way forward could be an expanded R&D plan for alternative fuels and aircraft design, which would likely need substantial government funding. The administration of US President Joe Biden in 2021 called for sustainable alternative fuel (SAF) production of 3 billion gallons a year by 2030, to reduce aviation emissions by 20 per cent. The EU wants 20 per cent of fuels used at its airports to be SAFs by 2035. In the meantime, some long-haul freight might shift to the sea, while

"Greenwashing would be against Southwest's brand culture"
Andrew Watterson

passengers increasingly take trains. Rupert Duchesne believes that 'reducing the total carbon load of travel is utterly fundamental and must be tackled in multiple ways that redistribute modal shares and minimize natural resource usage. Rail and electric transit should be used for short- and medium-haul journeys, and new jet fuel technology is needed for longer-range air travel'.

"Reducing the total carbon load of travel is utterly fundamental"
Rupert Duchesne

One should not ignore the mounting concerns about sustainable mobility and potential impact of modal share distribution. I was surprised recently when one of our Gen Z children took a strong stance against a direct, point-to-point 1 hour 15 minute flight to our vacation destination and instead selected a 6 hour 40 minute train ride to the South of France. While the 'flygskam' (shame of flying) phenomenon has not yet fully proliferated across Europe, there is growing evidence that new generations, and corporates alike, are increasingly carefully watching their usage of flying.

Timing of aviation's innovation may dictate the extent to which competitive modal mix will evolve as climate consciousness increases. 'We need government assistance for sustainable fuel development to achieve a cost-effective energy transition,' says Andrew Watterson.[44,45]

"We need government assistance for sustainable fuel development"
Andrew Watterson

Trucks, supertrucks and beyond

Trucks are an integral part of the global economy. They move over 70 per cent of all the freight in the United States and have grown ever larger and heavier. In Europe, heavy-duty road transport accounts for about 5 per cent of carbon dioxide emissions. But reducing the carbon footprint of trucking is difficult in similar ways to aviation and shipping – that is, it is difficult to carry a heavy battery or alternative fuel source over a long distance.

One partial solution is the improvement of existing technology. The US Department of Energy (DOE) launched its SuperTruck programme in 2009 with the aim of improving heavy-duty truck freight efficiency by 50 per cent. It directed hundreds of millions of dollars through a cost-shared, public-private partnership to finance R&D into aerodynamic equipment, lighter-weight tractors and trailers, and more efficient engines. Four teams participated in SuperTruck I, the first programme: Daimler Trucks, Volvo Trucks, Navistar, and a joint effort involving Cummins and Peterbilt. Each tractor team partnered with a trailer manufacturer to produce a trailer optimized for fuel efficiency.[46]

SuperTruck I technologies that have already been commercialized include improvements in aerodynamics, such as tighter close-outs around wheels, the replacement of mirrors with cameras, airflow modifiers at the rear and full-height, full-length side skirts. Combining these advances in aerodynamics with low-rolling-resistance tyres and other friction-reducing technologies, participants found they needed only 100 horsepower to maintain 100 kph (65 mph) on flat ground – about a third of the power for a traditional truck. The engines were significantly down speeded too. 'Back in 2009, the OEMs [original equipment manufacturers] thought the goal of increasing freight efficiency by 50 per cent would be a very challenging target,' said Rick Mihelic, the Director of Emerging Technologies Studies at the North American Council for Freight Efficiency (NACFE). 'In the end, everyone greatly exceeded that target.'

The SuperTruck II initiative that followed focused on aerodynamics, rolling resistance, powertrain efficiency and weight-reduction technology. In late June 2023, US Truck OEM Navistar revealed the latest fuel efficiency achievement of its international SuperTruck II. The experimental truck recorded a claimed 6.5 km per litre (16 miles per US gallon) at a maximum loaded weight of 36 tonnes. That compares with an average of less than seven miles per gallon in an experiment run in 2016 and 2017 for lighter (class 7 and 8) trucks.[47]

Further reductions in truck emissions will require new sources of power, but there are greater challenges for trucks than there are for cars. Trucks that make short trips into cities – daily runs of 100 km to 200 km – will, like cars and vans, be able to use battery electric vehicle (BEV) solutions, some of which are already on the market. 'In Europe, where the economy is much more concentrated and distances are shorter than in the US, the advent of electric trucks will have a greater negative impact on freight rail, given the challenging economics of short-haul rail,' says Hugh Randall, retired Senior Partner at Oliver Wyman and former head of the firm's global Transportation practice.[48,49]

Beyond that distance, batteries become unfeasible – especially with five-axle, 44-ton trucks that have to cover distances over 300 km. A long-distance truck typically has to carry all the energy it needs to complete a mission. Diesel, which these trucks use at present, is dense in energy and a truck can cover over 3,000 km on a single tank of fuel. But a battery is heavier and extending the range soon leads to a point at which the battery takes up all the weight the truck can carry – leaving no capacity for the actual load.

So far, there are two alternative, credible technologies for green trucking. One is electric road systems, which are based essentially on the technology used for electric railways: an overhead power line from which a train receives power via a pantograph. A similar infrastructure could be built on highways, so a truck would not have to carry all the power it needs. It would have a small auxiliary battery for short distances travelled off major highways. Another concept – based on the same idea and currently under development – is electric road surfaces, where trucks would acquire energy from the ground.

However, that would require the electrification of thousands of kilometres of highways and it would work only if the whole highway network was

"In Europe, the advent of electric trucks will have a greater negative impact on freight rail"

Hugh Randall

electrified, a huge investment. In addition, Europe would face a compatibility challenge. A journey from, say, Palermo to Rotterdam crosses several borders and the system would need the same electricity standard in each country. But aligning European countries on single standards has traditionally been a struggle. Railway systems in different countries typically have different electrical standards, and to cross borders, locomotives need to be designed to run on various voltages.

A harmonized start-up phase across Europe might be feasible, but such a system would also lead to sharp peaks in demand when traffic is busy, requiring extra power plants available just for these times. And if these plants used renewable sources (as the aim is to reduce carbon emissions), they would generate power only intermittently – when the sun shone on solar panels or the wind blew on wind turbines.

Hydrogen fuel cells are another potential solution. But apart from the expense of producing green hydrogen, truckers would need a new refuelling infrastructure – a bit like the current system of fuel stations. However, hydrogen transport would require fewer of these than there are petrol stations at present: they would be needed just along the main corridors used by heavy-duty trucks. Hydrogen is also difficult to store. One way is at a very high level of compression – up to 700 bars – which implies containers that are thick and expensive. Another is to convert it to liquid form, but this implies temperatures below minus 250°C, which also leads to great expense. Complicating the challenge, H_2 molecules are very small and tend to escape easily. All these challenges would have to be met throughout a wide network of refuelling stations.

Several factors would, over time, reduce the cost of hydrogen relative to its alternatives. One is the continuing fall in the cost of renewables, while another is carbon pricing, which will make hydrogen more competitive against less-green forms of energy. As a result, the cost of green hydrogen has the potential to be at parity with grey hydrogen by 2030. Another advantage is that hydrogen-powered vehicles consist essentially of electric vehicles powered by fuel cells (rather than batteries). They thus benefit from some of the technology that already works for electric vehicles (EVs).

The eventual market has the potential to be worth tens of billions of euros, and the complexity of the endeavour means that a range of actors is required for success. Collaboration is needed between a number of technology companies, including some outside the current automotive industry, such as energy companies. Governments will also be involved and hydrogen will have to be standardized by a regulator to serve multiple vehicle types and benefit from scale.

Some partnerships already exist. The Port of Rotterdam is working with Shell and Iveco, which bases its fuel cell technology on the technology developed by US-based alternative energy truck producer Nikola. The EU Green Deal includes numerous hydrogen initiatives, such as the European Clean Hydrogen Alliance. This has a pipeline of more than 750 projects extending along the full hydrogen value chain, from production, transmission and distribution to consumption in the industrial and transport sectors, energy systems and buildings. The projects are based throughout Europe and many of them aim to become operational by the end of 2025.[50,51]

One way to compare the strengths of electric road systems and hydrogen fuel cells is through the lens of usage versus investment costs. Hydrogen requires less upfront investment because it needs just a number of stations in strategic locations. But its unit costs would be much higher as making hydrogen requires more transformations of the energy used. Electric road systems, in contrast, would need a vast new power-carrying infrastructure, an investment five times higher than that needed to set up a hydrogen network, according to Oliver Wyman estimates. But once this was set up, the unit costs of the electricity would be relatively low.

With no clear winner yet, truck manufacturers have to work on both solutions while still not being sure which will prevail. Most are forming alliances to limit their investment risks. The H2Accelerate collaboration, for example, secured funding in early 2023 for two primary initiatives: the deployment of eight heavy-duty hydrogen refuelling stations under the Connecting Europe Facility and a project for 150 fuel-cell trucks funded by the Clean Hydrogen Partnership. These projects will enable trucks and refuelling equipment to be tested under real-world conditions and are expected to be a crucial step towards mass commercialization.[52]

Developers of these systems could take a lesson from the electric vehicle industry. There, the successful companies did not only offer new technology but also new models and approaches. Tesla, in particular, thought in ways that traditional car manufacturers did not, forging up- and down-stream alliances. With these partners, it set up an end-to-end vertically integrated system for customers, for example offering them a digital interface from its inception, as well as superchargers. For the past few years, there has been a clear division between the plug type for Teslas and for other EVs: Teslas have a custom plug, the NACS, and non-Teslas have the CCS port, similar to the difference between ports for iPhones and for other smartphones. However, Tesla has since opened up some of its superchargers to other cars and several automakers have said they will make their cars with the Tesla charging port. Tesla's high market share in EVs and the speed of its infrastructure deployment have enabled it to position itself as a key standard-setter in the North American automotive industry. Tesla is thus solidifying its position in the EV market and also creating demand for its lucrative supercharger business.

Developers of hydrogen electric vehicles should take the same approach. As well as selling trucks, they should consider the ancillary services and the infrastructure these will need. And they should talk to end-customers, many of whom are under pressure to achieve net zero throughout their operations and are therefore willing to pay a little more for sustainable transport.

For freight providers, the decarbonization of the supply chain will have to be demonstrated both at customer and supplier levels. But even those countries with high carbon dioxide emissions in their energy mix have planned pathways to reach net zero in coming decades. An Oliver Wyman report dated May 2023 reviewed the largest European member states decarbonization roadmap for parcel delivery and found that roadmaps exist across the EU to reduce emissions by 30 per cent by 2030 and 50 per cent beyond 2040.

A new era for trains?

Train operators and services recognize their lead in decarbonization and are advertising it. Reservations service Trainline partnered with singer-songwriter Craig David in 2022 on an original song for a campaign to boost awareness of rail's environmental advantages. In the song, called 'Better Days', David sings, 'It's just the little things we know can make a beautiful change – that's why I'm happy that I came by train.' He said, 'I wrote this as a reminder that by making one small change, we can have such a big impact on all our relationships and our beautiful planet.' A video made for the song states, 'Trains create 70 per cent less CO_2 than cars.'

Eurostar's website trumpets its train services' relatively low environmental impact, displaying a comparison table of carbon emissions per passenger: one flight between London and Paris is equivalent to 14 Eurostar trips, while a flight between London and Amsterdam is equivalent to seven. 'Here at Eurostar, we try our very best to leave the lightest carbon footprint we can as we travel between London, Paris, Lille, Brussels and Amsterdam,' the company says. 'And compared to air travel, we think we're already pretty green.'[53,54]

These moves to publicize trains as a green mode of transport come after years of preference for road investment over rail. Between 1995 and 2020, the length of motorways in Europe grew 60 per cent, while that of railways shrank 6.5 per cent, the German thinktanks Wuppertal Institute and T3 Transportation said in 2023. For every €1 governments spent building railways, they spent €1.6 building roads. The EU, Norway, Switzerland and the UK spent €1.5 trillion between 1995 and 2018 to extend their roads but just €930 billion to extend their rail networks, according to the report. The UK had a plan for a new high-speed network from London to the north of England, but in 2023 decided to reduce its scope amid pressure on the national budget.[55,56]

In several countries, however, massive investments are being committed to building, maintaining and expanding rail networks, at least partly in the name of environmental action. A 2022 TV advertisement for SNCF featured a 10-year-old rapper, Rayad, asking people what they are doing for the environment: Driving more slowly? Separating rubbish? Eating home-grown organic vegetables? 'What kind of environmentalist are you?' he asks. 'Well, anyway, always going by train.'[57]

France announced in February 2023 an investment of €100 billion up to 2040 to expand and upgrade the country's rail network to reduce carbon emissions. The plan includes launching express commuter trains similar to the Paris RER (Réseau Express Régional – the suburban rail system in the Paris region) system in other cities, to reduce the gap between public transport in the capital and in French provinces. 'Our strategy must benefit all French people, wherever they live,' said Prime Minister Élisabeth Borne, 'from small communes to the big cities.'[58,59]

The funds for rail came under the broad plan 'France nation verte – Green nation France' to achieve the goals of the Paris COP 21 Agreement and meet the European Green Deal target of a 55 per cent reduction in emissions by 2030. It includes 22 areas of investment, including mobility, housing and the way goods are produced and consumed. 'From a 10 per cent modal share today, I believe rail in France can reach 10 per cent to 20 per cent over time thanks to its climate friendliness,' says Jean-Pierre Farandou, Chairman and Chief Executive Officer of SNCF Group. 'It is also a question of quality of service and price.'

But not all rail is electrified – just 40 per cent of the European rail network, according to the European Commission, though 80 per cent of rail traffic runs on electrified lines. Most of the non-electric trains run on diesel – that is, a fossil fuel. While there are no technical obstacles to further electrification, it is very expensive to upgrade and electrify existing rail infrastructure. That means the cost and the expected carbon reduction need to be considered case by case. On busy lines electrification makes sense, but the goal for low-density lines is to develop cost-efficient replacements for diesel trains.[60]

Over history, energy innovation has been closely linked with transport technology. Some trains in France's Transport express regional (TER) already run on a biofuel based on rapeseed oil. Others will run either on onboard electrical sources such as batteries or hydrogen cells: battery-powered trains can now travel about 100 km on a single charge and hydrogen-based fuel cell locomotives up to 1,000 km. Alstom said its Coradia iLint regional train is the world's first passenger train powered by a hydrogen fuel cell. However, hydrogen trains will only reach scale and fully replace diesel when the production and distribution of hydrogen is secured, a significant industrial and logistics challenge.[61]

And trains are being developed that need less power, such as a light train being developed by SNCF and industry partners under the EU Tech4Rail programme. The light train would reduce track wear, use digital technology to ease traffic management and shrink the costs of operation and maintenance. The first tests were scheduled for 2024.[62]

Another route is to produce energy locally, as is being done in Australia. Queensland has a goal of supplying 50 per cent of the state's energy needs through renewables by 2030, up from 20 per cent in 2022. Its Zero Emission Vehicle Strategy 2022–2032 aims to reduce the emissions generated by a range of transport modes and includes increasing local manufacturing, recycling batteries and building local hydrogen production facilities. Queensland-based Aurizon, Australia's largest freight railway, is exploring the application

"From a 10% modal share today, I believe rail in France can reach 10% to 20% over time thanks to its climate friendliness"
Jean-Pierre Farandou

of mining company Anglo American's proprietary hydrogen fuel cell and battery hybrid power units for its heavy-haul freight rail operations in two corridors serving Anglo American's local operations.

Germany has fallen behind in rail investment in recent decades, according to its Federal Ministry for Digital Affairs and Transport (BMDV), which says rail will require additional funding of up to €45 billion by 2027. Some of that amount was allocated in August from the country's Klima- und Transformationsfonds (KTF, or Climate and Transformation Fund), which will provide €212 billion in green transition funding between 2024 and 2027. One German plan for green electricity already up and running is a 40-hectare photovoltaic system in Schleswig-Holstein at the end of April 2023, which feeds up to 42 MW of electricity directly into the railway grid.[63,64]

A Swiss company, Sun-Ways, has developed a pilot project to place solar modules in between rails. Standard-size photovoltaic panels will be joined in a chain and the train will unroll them between the rails, as if they formed a carpet. The design allows factory pre-assembly of the string of photovoltaic panels. The system is also reversible and the panels can be removed for maintenance as easily as they were laid.[65]

Electric cars and a geopolitical shift

Cars, because of their sheer number, are one of the greatest challenges in the decarbonization of transport: car travel is responsible for 61 per cent of the EU's carbon dioxide emissions by the transportation sector, according to the European Parliament's fact base. The industry's solution is electric vehicles and EV sales exceeded 10 million in 2022: the share of electric cars in total sales more than tripled from around 4 per cent in 2020 to 14 per cent in 2022, according to the International Energy Agency (IEA).

But the EV era could bring about more than just a shift in propulsion. It could also lead to a shift in industrial power, away from the West. China is using the shift to battery electric vehicles as a way to challenge the dominance of incumbent car players from countries known globally for their automotive industries – that is, the US, Japan, Korea, Germany and France. Chinese automakers have already significantly upgraded their capabilities in areas ranging from software and infotainment to interior and exterior styling.[66]

In the early 2000s, China had no domestic brands that were capable of rivalling the US, German and Japanese automakers, which dominated world export markets. Though China was able to manufacture traditional cars, it appeared unlikely to be able to overtake the global incumbents in thermic (internal-combustion engine) cars. Battery electric vehicles were a chance for China to become a global automotive power. They were also an opportunity to help curb China's severe air pollution and reduce its reliance on imported oil.

The country's Tenth Five-Year Plan, from 2001 to 2005, made EV technology a priority research project. In 2007, Wan Gang, an auto engineer who had worked for Audi in Germany for a decade, became China's minister of science and technology. He was an EV enthusiast and tested Tesla's first model, the Roadster, when it was released in 2008. Wan has been credited with the decision to make EV development a priority for China's national economic planning.

Starting in 2009, China began providing financial subsidies to EV companies to make buses, taxis and cars. From 2009 to 2022, the government put over 200 billion RMB ($29 billion) into relevant subsidies and tax breaks. The government also helped domestic EV companies through procurement contracts for public transport systems. From 2010, well before the consumer market for EVs took off, China began to have BEV buses and taxis, providing reliable streams of revenue for EV manufacturers, which, in addition, gained valuable road-test data.

Another push for EVs came through policies on car licence plates, which were rationed in big cities such as Beijing. While it might take years and thousands of dollars to get one for an internal-combustion car, it became very easy to get one to buy an EV. Some local governments developed relationships with EV companies. BYD, for example, worked closely with the southern city of Shenzhen, which became the world's first to completely electrify its public bus fleet.

China did not limit subsidies to domestic companies but included foreign firms such as Tesla, which local governments courted to set up production facilities. The company built a Gigafactory in Shanghai in 2019 thanks to favourable policies there and this was Tesla's most productive manufacturing hub in 2022, accounting for over half its cars delivered. The facility has made China an important part of Tesla's supply chain, while Tesla's presence in China has pushed Chinese brands to innovate to catch up in aspects of EV production, from technology to pricing.

Chinese companies are also leading in batteries, which can make up about 40 per cent of the cost of a vehicle. Western manufacturers pursued a type based on lithium nickel manganese cobalt (NMC), which have a relatively high energy density – so a longer range – but are expensive. An alternative type, lithium iron phosphate (LFP) batteries, have lower energy density and perform relatively poorly in low temperatures, but they cost less and could be appropriate for smaller and entry-level EVs.[67]

But a few Chinese battery companies, such as Contemporary Amperex Technology Co. Limited (CATL), worked on LFP technology and narrowed the gap in energy density. CATL was reported to have developed a battery system, called Qilin, that will power a Zeekr car and give it a range of 1,000 km, albeit under optimistic test conditions. CATL also announced a confidential partnership to further develop its products in civil aviation (see Figure 6.1).[68,69]

In addition, China controls a lot of the ingredients needed to make batteries – such as cobalt, nickel, lithium, and graphite – because either it has mines for the raw materials or it dominates their refining. Chinese manufacturers (notably, CATL, BYD, LGES and CALB) have a share of more than 60 per cent of the overall (that is, not just for cars) global battery market, with the rest of the production mainly Korean (see Figure 6.1).

In Europe, EV technology was developed relatively quickly, but adoption has been slower than initially hoped due to price and a lack of charging infrastructure. Recently, however, the EU has made climate and sustainability considerations a major priority for its regulation. This is one of the biggest evolutions in mobility regulation in the last decade and EVs are now expected to help replace fossil-fuel vehicles in the coming decade or two.

However, the EU is a union of sovereign member states and answers, ultimately, to their governments. Sometimes, these oppose the majority view. That tension flared up in 2023 over plans to ban the sale in the EU of new vehicles powered by thermic engines by 2035, as part of the campaign to achieve carbon neutrality by 2050.

Such a drastic change in technology will have a huge impact on workforces. Electric motors have fewer parts than thermic engines, so they need fewer people to make them. The engineers the industry does need will have to retrain. Scrapping internal combustion engines could mean the motor industry needs 40 per cent fewer workers, according to the chief executive of Ford, which in 2023 announced it would cut 3,800 jobs in Europe. Automotive supplier association CLEPA has said the switch to electric cars could cost hundreds of thousands of jobs over the coming decades.[70] These changes would hit Germany particularly hard. The EU's largest economy relies heavily on the global success of its traditional car industry, which accounts for a fifth of the country's industrial revenues. In 2022, the EU's three institutions – the European Commission, the European Parliament and the

Figure 6.1 2022–2030 market shares of global battery market

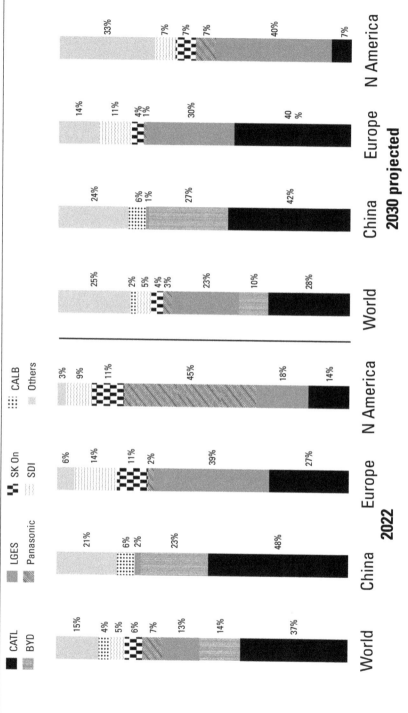

SOURCE Bernstein Research

Council of member states – agreed a directive to ban the sale of combustion engines from 2035. Normally, such an agreement marks the end of the EU law-making process and it is rare for such deals to be reopened.

But in March 2023, German Transport Minister Volker Wissing said that Berlin would block the directive days before it was due to be finally approved, unless an exception was granted for cars that run on CO_2-neutral fuels. A deal was made to create a new category of 'e-fuel' cars, which would need vehicles with engines adapted to run only on these e-fuels and not on traditional fossil fuels. Green groups and other EU member states, including France, were critical. Even rival, non-German car manufacturers such as Volvo and Ford attacked the idea, saying that the industry had already invested heavily in electric vehicles. (Such cars may have limited value in the future, however, as numerous large cities announce that they will ban thermic cars from around 2030 or in the following decade.)[71]

China can often regulate faster than the EU – for a market 1.8 times the size: 26 million vehicles sold in 2021 versus 14.3 million in the EU. China has a top-down system of government without the need to balance competing interests, such as those of EU member states. Moreover, it does not face public resistance to fast-paced, large-scale change, as when Europeans use courts to fight new infrastructure projects. For example, some Chinese cities have simply banned the use of motorcycles from many of their roads: they were involved in high numbers of traffic accidents and motorcycle robbers were snatching belongings from pedestrians. Shenzhen, for instance, banned motorcycles from most roads in 2003.

More importantly, the Chinese government's powers go beyond regulation. While China does not have a regulatory framework like that in the EU, it has been effectively coordinating the electrification of the car fleet across multiple sectors and players: automakers, digital technology developers, telecom operators and developers of charging infrastructure. China's government and business structures enable both fast technological progress and the creation of an ecosystem to rapidly introduce electric – and, later, autonomous – cars.

China's close coordination of the EV ecosystem can be seen in its roll-out of charging stations to encourage EV sales. According to one report, China operated an EV infrastructure network of more than 1.9 million public chargers as of March 2023. Another report put the figure at just 1.15 million, but this still would have accounted for 65 per cent of global public EV charging stations. The government is said to be aiming for 20 million by 2025.[72,73]

In the West, however, there is currently more limited coordination between car manufacturers, battery producers, charging infrastructure developers, state aid and regulations. Battery EVs have jumped from 20 per cent of new cars to 80 per cent in less than five years in Norway thanks to tax breaks, but the charging infrastructure has struggled to keep pace and there are often long lines at highway charging stations on holiday weekends.[74]

The United States has the world's second highest number of public charging stations in 2023, at some 114,000, and the Biden administration has announced plans for 500,000 by 2030. But concerns over charging have been a factor in a return to the internal combustion engine by a quarter of early US electric car buyers, according to a US government study. California, for example, had about 1.1 million electric cars and plug-in hybrids as of September 2023, but only just over 90,000 chargers, according to state data. By 2030, about 1.2 million chargers will be needed for 8 million vehicles, according to a state report, with an interim goal of 250,000 by 2025. Mostly, private companies are responsible for installing them, although state grants help.[75,76,77]

China's lead in the various parts of the EV ecosystem has made it by far the biggest market for EVs. The number of EVs sold there grew in just two years from 1.3 million to a whopping 6.8 million in 2022, more than half of global EV registrations. That made 2022 the eighth consecutive year in which China was the world's largest EV market. Growth in 2023 was expected to slow, due to the removal of state subsidies, a turbulent business environment and a gloomy outlook for the world economy. But by 2025, EVs (including plug-in hybrids) vehicles were expected to be 40 per cent out of the total passenger vehicle sales of 27 million. For comparison, only about 800,000 EVs were sold in the United States in 2022.

This lead has had a big impact on Chinese consumers' awareness of EVs. In 2021, more than half of Chinese respondents to a survey were considering an EV as their next car, the highest proportion in the world and twice the global average. These prospective customers now have plenty of options. Thanks to generous government subsidies, tax breaks, procurement contracts and other policy incentives, a slew of homegrown EV brands has emerged, including BYD, SAIC-GM-Wuling and Geely, which started out as producers of traditional cars, and Nio, Xpeng and LiAuto, which only make EVs.

They have optimized new technologies to meet the real-life needs of Chinese consumers, thus cultivating young car buyers. Unlike their parents, who prefer German or Japanese brands, the new generation of Chinese car buyers do not see domestic brands as less prestigious than foreign brands. In 2022, 11 out of the top 15 best-selling EV brands in China were domestic and 7 of those players achieved annual growth of over 100 per cent (see Figure 6.2).[78]

Figure 6.2 Top 15 new energy vehicles (NEV) passenger vehicle companies by retail sales in 2022 (thousand units)

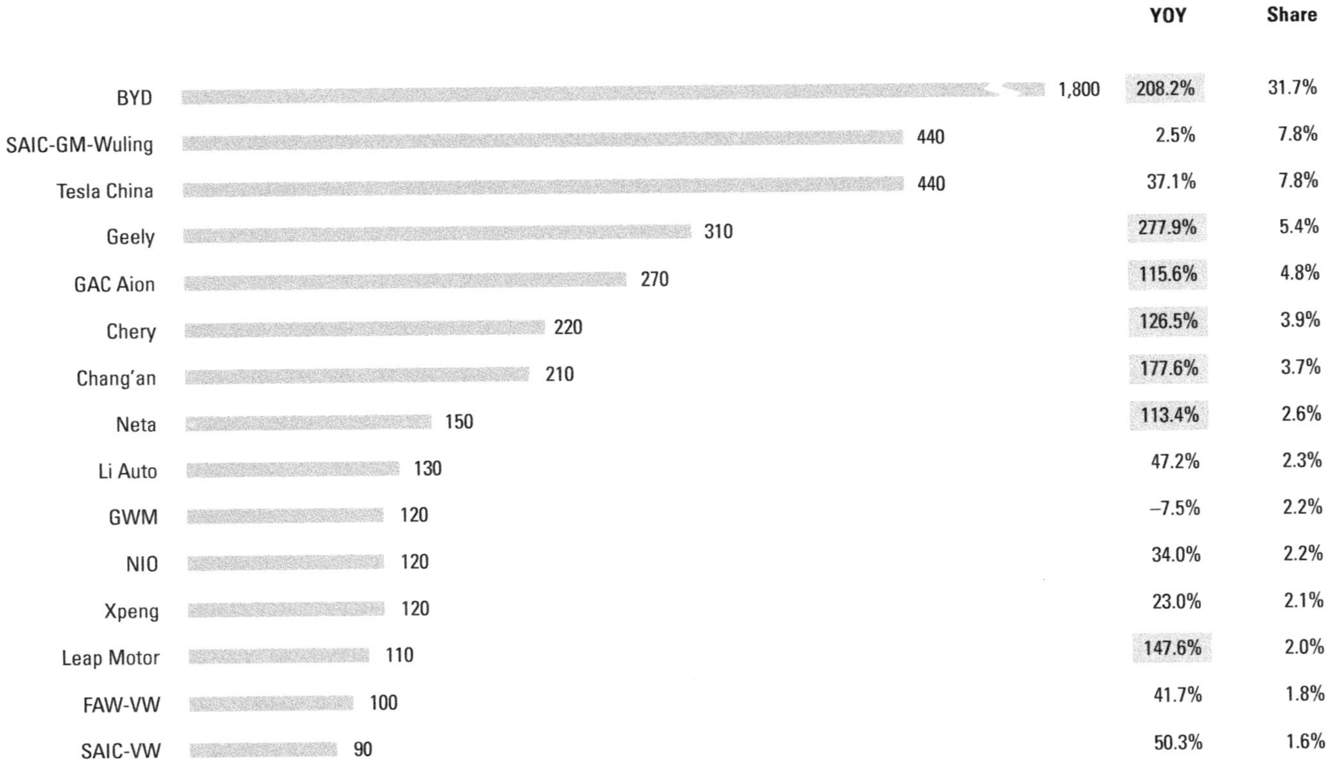

	Sales	YOY	Share
BYD	1,800	208.2%	31.7%
SAIC-GM-Wuling	440	2.5%	7.8%
Tesla China	440	37.1%	7.8%
Geely	310	277.9%	5.4%
GAC Aion	270	115.6%	4.8%
Chery	220	126.5%	3.9%
Chang'an	210	177.6%	3.7%
Neta	150	113.4%	2.6%
Li Auto	130	47.2%	2.3%
GWM	120	−7.5%	2.2%
NIO	120	34.0%	2.2%
Xpeng	120	23.0%	2.1%
Leap Motor	110	147.6%	2.0%
FAW-VW	100	41.7%	1.8%
SAIC-VW	90	50.3%	1.6%

SOURCE China Association of Automobile Manufacturers, Oliver Wyman

China's international expansion

Chinese automakers' dominance of their domestic EV market is helping them take market share from overseas manufacturers, which are present in China mainly through joint ventures with Chinese partners. These have been the world leaders in traditional cars and they had less incentive to pursue EVs, especially battery-only cars. Some Japanese automakers, for example, had become leaders in hybrid vehicles, which are some 40 per cent more energy-efficient than cars powered purely by thermic engines. The growth of China's domestic EV manufacturers raises the prospect that some of the overseas companies might withdraw from the Chinese market.

The strength of Chinese EV manufacturers also presents the first opportunity for Chinese automakers to expand overseas and become global brands. It will not be easy. Japanese and Korean car brands became successful in Europe and the United States only after decades of effort, shifting gradually from an export-based model to local production so as to avoid trade disputes. Current geopolitical tensions with the West may mean that the greatest potential growth will come from emerging markets and many EVs made in China have gone to Africa, South America, India and South-East Asia. So far, Chinese EV companies are also building manufacturing bases in South-east Asia to expand and diversify their footprint, and countries such as Indonesia are already courting Chinese investment in the EV industry (see Figure 6.3).

In 2022, China exported 679,000 EVs, a 120 per cent increase from the year before. In 2023, EV exports were expected to reach 1 million, or 29 per cent of China's total exports (see Figure 6.4) and China was expected to overtake Japan as the world's biggest car exporter.[79,80]

By 2023, China's share of EVs sold in Europe had risen to 8 per cent, according to the European Commission, which added it could reach 15 per cent in 2025. In September of that year, the Commission launched an investigation into whether to impose punitive tariffs on Chinese imports, noting prices were typically 20 per cent below EU-made models. The standard EU tariff on car imports is currently 10 per cent.

The EU investigation will look at a broad range of possible unfair subsidies, from prices for raw materials and batteries to preferential lending or cheap provision of land. Chinese state subsidies for electric and hybrid vehicles were $57 billion from 2016 to 2022, according to consulting firm AlixPartners. 'Global markets are now flooded with cheaper electric cars. And their price is kept artificially low by huge state subsidies,' European Commission President Ursula von der Leyen told the European Parliament.[81]

Figure 6.3 China NEV expansion in South-East Asia

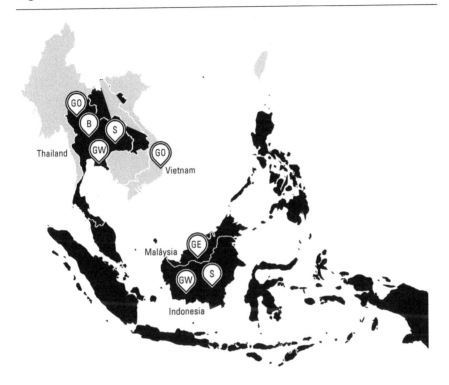

NEV Original Equipment Manufacturers

(S) SAIC **Thailand (since 2014):** Joint Venture with Charoen Pokphand Group

(GE) GEELY **Malaysia (2017):** Strategic partnered with Malaysia Proton

(GW) GWM **Thailand (2021):** Built production base in Rayong, the second largest manufacturing facilities outside China

(B) BYD **Thailand (2024):** Signed with Thai industrial developer WHA Group to build BYD first Electric Vehicles plant in South-East Asia

Electric Vehicles Battery

(GO) GOTION **Vietnam (2023):** Co-invest with Vingroup to construct battery plant with planned annual capacity of 5 GWh

(C) CATL **Thailand (2024):** Licensed CTP technology to Arun Plus (PTT subsidiary), gained deals to supply Foxconn in Thailand by 2024.

SOURCE Official websites, Oliver Wyman

Figure 6.4   China automotive exports 2019–2023E (thousand units)

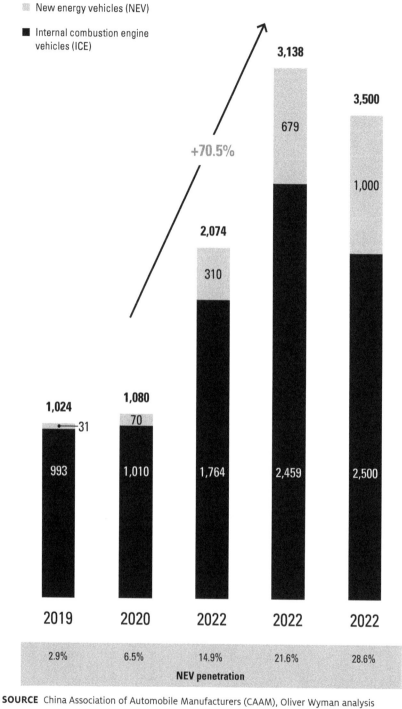

SOURCE China Association of Automobile Manufacturers (CAAM), Oliver Wyman analysis

Other emerging economies might see China's EV experience as a model. But it may not be that easy to achieve the same success. Other countries don't have China's strong traditional auto industry to build on, nor do they have the Chinese government's background in handling massive industrial policies through diverse policy tools.

The shift to electric vehicles is an opportunity for China to position itself as a leader – perhaps *the* leader – in future mobility, a shift that could have enormous geopolitical ramifications.

As China expands its EV production overseas, the country could increase its zone of economic influence and position itself as a contributor to global sustainability – a sharp contrast to its past reputation as a major polluter and source of greenhouse gas emissions.

While EVs are a welcome contribution to sustainability in the mobility industry, they also represent yet another moving part for players and nations to consider in an increasingly complicated mobility industry.

KEY TAKEAWAYS

- The mobility industry is under pressure to keep up with the times. That implies improving its gender inclusivity and reducing its environmental footprint. The industry can – and should – work faster on much of this. But some of these tasks are challenging.

- Diversity is still a work in progress in the transport industry. In much of it, advances for women are only nascent, in particular in leadership roles.

- Transport's use of fossil fuels makes it a major contributor to CO_2 emissions and all subsectors have set reduction goals. Most modes have developed technology that could enable them to achieve net zero emissions by 2050.

- The key to much decarbonization is electrification. This has been implemented in much of rail and is under way in cars and trucks. However, it is not seen as a viable option for aviation for larger aviation.

- That leaves the air industry with a significant challenge, which may curtail its growth potential in some market segments. Government support is needed to help develop adequate pathways towards green aviation.

- China appears to be taking the lead in the electrification of the global automotive industry.

Notes

1 IATA (2022) IATA Economics' Chart of the Week. Available at: www.iata.org/en/iata-repository/publications/economic-reports/women-are-still-under-represented-in-leading-positions-at-airlines/ (archived at https://perma.cc/7K5T-HLQF)

2 www.youtube.com. (n.d.) TikTok superstar Clarissa Rankin. Available at: www.youtube.com/watch?v=j4tM9Pi4RR4 (archived at https://perma.cc/D7RT-J4JT)

3 TikTok. (n.d.) ClarissaRankin (@clarissarankin) Official. Available at: www.tiktok.com/@clarissarankin (archived at https://perma.cc/6Z8R-7C8U)

4 www.youtube.com. (n.d.) Lady Trucker Clarissa Rankin wants more women behind big rigs. Available at: www.youtube.com/watch?v=ADFzV8PywyY (archived at https://perma.cc/6AV9-VP7H)

5 Sheidlower, N. (2023) More women become truckers as the industry tries to overcome a shortage of drivers, CNBC, 25 March. Available at: www.cnbc.com/2023/03/25/women-truck-driving-shortage.html (archived at https://perma.cc/P9JL-4QRB)

6 6play (n.d.) Les reines de la route. Available at: www.6play.fr/les-reines-de-la-route-p_18855 (archived at https://perma.cc/5UZN-24WS)

7 VTM.be (n.d.) Lady truckers. Available at: https://vtm.be/lady-truckers (archived at https://perma.cc/GB38-8LTQ)

8 Volvo (2023) Volvo Trucks is accelerating women in transport. Available at: www.volvotrucks.com/en-en/news-stories/press-releases/2021/jun/volvo-trucks-is-accelerating-women-in-transport.html (archived at https://perma.cc/GS93-NVLK)

9 JW Surety Bonds (2023). Women Making a Living Behind the Wheel. Available at: www.jwsuretybonds.com/blog/women-in-trucking

10 Uber.BE (2022) Making Uber the most accessible platform for women in Europe. Available at: www.uber.com/en-BE/newsroom/uber-for-women-in-europe/ (archived at https://perma.cc/J7KA-K6K9)

11 Uber (n.d.) Safety with the Uber app. Available at: www.uber.com/be/en/drive/basics/staying-safe-with-the-uber-app/ (archived at https://perma.cc/F2L8-QMB2)

12 IATA (2022) IATA Economics' Chart of the Week. Available at: www.iata.org/en/iata-repository/publications/economic-reports/women-are-still-under-represented-in-leading-positions-at-airlines/ (archived at https://perma.cc/7K5T-HLQF)

13 Workplace Gender Equality Agency (2020). More women at the top proves better for business. Available at: www.wgea.gov.au/newsroom/more-women-at-the-top-proves-better-for-business

14 IATA (2022) IATA Economics' Chart of the Week. Available at: www.iata.org/
    en/iata-repository/publications/economic-reports/women-are-still-under-
    represented-in-leading-positions-at-airlines/ (archived at https://perma.cc/7K5T-
    HLQF)

15 Oliver Wyman – International Aviation Women's Association (2021) Lift off to
    leadership: Advancing women in aviation. Available at: www.oliverwyman.
    com/content/dam/oliver-wyman/v2/publications/2021/IAWA_OW_Women%20
    in%20Aviation_FINAL_Copy.pdf (archived at https://perma.cc/6DH4-XUEK)

16 Oliver Wyman – International Aviation Women's Association (2021) Lift off to
    leadership: Advancing women in aviation. Available at: www.oliverwyman.
    com/content/dam/oliver-wyman/v2/publications/2021/IAWA_OW_Women%20
    in%20Aviation_FINAL_Copy.pdf (archived at https://perma.cc/6DH4-XUEK)

17 Jonga, M. (2021) Inclusion should be a business strategy: Sumati Sharma on
    building diversity, Aerotime Hub, 9 September. Available at: www.aerotime.
    aero/articles/28819-sumati-sharma-on-building-diversity-in-aviation (archived
    at https://perma.cc/L4BA-Z3R6)

18 Sharma, S. (2021) Podcast: Tackling gender imbalance in aviation, Oliver
    Wyman. Available at: www.oliverwyman.com/our-expertise/insights/2021/mar/
    international-womens-day-2021-sumati-sharma-gender-podcast.html (archived
    at https://perma.cc/W9X5-DGV2)

19 Oliver Wyman – International Aviation Women's Association (2021) Lift off to
    leadership: Advancing women in aviation. Available at: www.oliverwyman.
    com/content/dam/oliver-wyman/v2/publications/2021/IAWA_OW_Women%20
    in%20Aviation_FINAL_Copy.pdf (archived at https://perma.cc/6DH4-XUEK)

20 Jiang, X. and Akbar, A. (2018) Does increased representation of female
    executives improve corporate environmental investment? Evidence from China,
    Sustainability, 10(12), 4750. doi: https://doi.org/10.3390/su10124750
    (archived at https://perma.cc/JBY6-PRKU)

21 Wang, Z. and Yu, L. (n.d.) Are firms with female CEOs more environmentally
    friendly?, The University of Hong-Kong.

22 IEA (2020) Global energy-related CO2 emissions by sector. Available at: www.
    iea.org/data-and-statistics/charts/global-energy-related-co2-emissions-by-sector
    (archived at https://perma.cc/C282-QWC9)

23 Isopp, B. (2021) Why aren't more big bike firms tracking their environmental
    impact?, *The Guardian*, 23 September. Available at: www.theguardian.com/
    environment/bike-blog/2021/sep/23/why-arent-more-big-bike-firms-tracking-
    their-environmental-impact (archived at https://perma.cc/5MFS-TMW2)

24 ADEME (2020) Calculer les émmissions de carbone de vos trajets. Available
    at: https://agirpourlatransition.ademe.fr/particuliers/bureau/deplacements/
    calculer-emissions-carbone-trajets (archived at https://perma.cc/5QPX-3NZY)

25 European Environment Agency (2017) Specific CO_2 emissions per tonne-km
    and per mode of transport in Europe. Available at: www.eea.europa.eu/
    data-and-maps/daviz/specific-co2-emissions-per-tonne-2#tab-chart_1 (archived
    at https://perma.cc/8QLB-NU5D)

26 European Environment Agency (2023) Rail and waterborne – best for low-carbon motorised transport. Available at: www.eea.europa.eu/publications/rail-and-waterborne-transport (archived at https://perma.cc/Q97Z-Y4Q2)

27 Parsons, M. (2023) Trains, not planes, are increasingly business travelers' preferred choice in Europe, Skift, 17 April. Available at: https://skift.com/2023/04/17/trains-not-planes-are-increasingly-business-travelers-preferred-choice-in-europe/ (archived at https://perma.cc/UQL8-6EY5)

28 European Commission (n.d.) The European Green Deal. Available at: https://commission.europa.eu/strategy-and-policy/priorities-2019-2024/european-green-deal_en (archived at https://perma.cc/6UGM-JDJD)

29 European Commission (2022) Questions and answers on the EU Taxonomy Complementary Climate Delegated Act covering certain nuclear and gas activities, 2 February. Available at: https://ec.europa.eu/commission/presscorner/detail/en/QANDA_22_712 (archived at https://perma.cc/9HMY-VAL4)

30 Meniga (2021). Going Green – The climate change opportunity in banking. Available at:www.meniga.com/download/going-green-the-climate-change-opportunity-in-banking/

31 Kreacic, A. and Cooper, S. (2022) How to help Gen Z turn climate anxiety into action, Oliver Wyman Forum, 10 November. Available at: www.oliverwymanforum.com/global-consumer-sentiment/2022/nov/how-to-help-gen-z-turn-climate-anxiety-into-action.html (archived at https://perma.cc/K362-H5YY)

32 International Maritime Organization (n.d.) IMO's work to cut GHG emissions from ships. Available at: www.imo.org/en/MediaCentre/HotTopics/Pages/Cutting-GHG-emissions.aspx (archived at https://perma.cc/8X8W-U6RW)

33 Transport & Environment (2021) FuelEU Maritime. Available at: www.transportenvironment.org/wp-content/uploads/2021/08/FuelEU-Maritime.pdf (archived at https://perma.cc/P9ZU-2QES)

34 European Council (2023) FuelEU Maritime initiative: Council adopts new law to decarbonise the maritime sector, 25 July. Available at: www.consilium.europa.eu/en/press/press-releases/2023/07/25/fueleu-maritime-initiative-council-adopts-new-law-to-decarbonise-the-maritime-sector/ (archived at https://perma.cc/3CYQ-4D2N)

35 European Council (2023) Fit for 55: Increasing the uptake of greener fuels in the aviation and maritime sectors. Available at: www.consilium.europa.eu/en/infographics/fit-for-55-refueleu-and-fueleu/ (archived at https://perma.cc/9WYC-WKW7)

36 European Commission (n.d.) Liquefied natural gas. Available at: https://energy.ec.europa.eu/topics/oil-gas-and-coal/liquefied-natural-gas_en (archived at https://perma.cc/WPX8-QH5R)

37 Maersk (2023) CMA CGM and Maersk join forces to accelerate the decarbonization of the shipping industry, 10 September. Available at: www. maersk.com/news/articles/2023/09/19/cma-cgm-and-maersk-join-forces-to-accelerate-the-decarbonization-of-the-shipping-industry (archived at https:// perma.cc/EA5F-8K44)

38 European Commission (2022) European Green Deal: New rules agreed on applying the EU emissions trading system in the aviation sector, 9 December. Available at: https://ec.europa.eu/commission/presscorner/detail/en/ip_22_7609 (archived at https://perma.cc/ZDP2-MT2E)

39 Heart Aerospace (n.d.) Electrifying regional air travel. Available at: https:// heartaerospace.com/ (archived at https://perma.cc/BUF4-NP7M)

40 Crownhart, C. (2022) This is what's keeping electric planes from taking off, *MIT Technology Review*, 17 August. Available at: www.technologyreview. com/2022/08/17/1058013/electric-planes-taking-off-challenges/ (archived at https://perma.cc/Z45G-EE59)

41 Crownhart, C. (2023) Hydrogen-powered planes take off with startup's test flight, *MIT Technology Review*, 19 January. Available at: www. technologyreview.com/2023/01/19/1067113/hydrogen-planes-test-flight/ (archived at https://perma.cc/7YKL-CFQE)

42 Bauer, A. (2020) L'Europe certifie son premier avion 100 per cent électrique, *Les Echos*, 11 June. Available at: www.lesechos.fr/industrie-services/air-defense/ leurope-certifie-son-premier-avion-100-electrique-1210353 (archived at https:// perma.cc/Q4JL-HKM8)

43 Crownhart, C. (2023) Hydrogen-powered planes take off with startup's test flight, *MIT Technology Review*, 19 January. Available at: www. technologyreview.com/2023/01/19/1067113/hydrogen-planes-test-flight/ (archived at https://perma.cc/7YKL-CFQE)

44 De Bellaigue, C. (2023) Will flying ever be green, *The Guardian*, 6 April. Available at: www.theguardian.com/world/2023/apr/06/will-flying-ever-be-green-aviation-electric-planes-evtol (archived at https://perma.cc/5RV5-27B6)

45 US White House (2021) Biden administration advances the future of sustainable fuels in American aviation, 9 September. Available at: www. whitehouse.gov/briefing-room/statements-releases/2021/09/09/fact-sheet-biden-administration-advances-the-future-of-sustainable-fuels-in-american-aviation/ (archived at https://perma.cc/G8WM-PQK2)

46 Ucci, F. and Schnurrer, S. (2021) Hydrogen for the long haul, Oliver Wyman. Available at: www.oliverwyman.com/our-expertise/insights/2021/jan/hydrogen-for-the-long-haul.html (archived at https://perma.cc/VT3V-DGBS)

47 Geotab (n.d.) The state of fuel economy in trucking. Available at: www.geotab. com/truck-mpg-benchmark/ (archived at https://perma.cc/79S5-LR9C)

48 Ucci, F. and Schnurrer, S. (2021) Hydrogen for the long haul, Oliver Wyman. Available at: www.oliverwyman.com/our-expertise/insights/2021/jan/hydrogen-for-the-long-haul.html (archived at https://perma.cc/VT3V-DGBS)

49 Marchant, N. (2021) Grey, blue, green – why are there so many colours of hydrogen?, World Economic Forum. Available at: www.weforum.org/agenda/2021/07/clean-energy-green-hydrogen (archived at https://perma.cc/VHG5-R874)

50 European Commission (n.d.) European Clean Hydrogen Alliance. Available at: https://single-market-economy.ec.europa.eu/industry/strategy/industrial-alliances/european-clean-hydrogen-alliance_en (archived at https://perma.cc/ZN62-EA9S)

51 Hydrogen Europe (2021) Project pipeline of the European Clean Hydrogen Alliance. Available at: https://hydrogeneurope.eu/project-pipeline-of-the-european-clean-hydrogen-alliance/ (archived at https://perma.cc/J242-BA4G)

52 H2Accelerate (2023) The H2Accelerate collaboration announces acquisition of funding to enable deployment of 150 hydrogen trucks and 8 heavy-duty hydrogen refuelling stations, 14 March. Available at: https://h2accelerate.eu/the-h2accelerate-collaboration-announces-acquisition-of-funding-to-enable-deployment-of-150-hydrogen-trucks-and-8-heavy-duty-hydrogen-refuelling-stations/ (archived at https://perma.cc/G5WJ-TTEB)

53 Branding in Asia (2022) Craig David promotes eco-friendly train travel with 'Better Days (I Came by Train)', 31 October. Available at: www.brandinginasia.com/craig-david-promotes-eco-friendly-train-travel-with-better-days-i-came-by-train/ (archived at https://perma.cc/6E4R-DNAP)

54 Mendenhall, J. (2022) Behind the scenes with Craig David and Francis Bourgeois, Trainline. Available at: www.thetrainline.com/via/sustainable-travel-news/behind-the-scenes-with-craig-david-and-francis-bourgeois (archived at https://perma.cc/AP47-6DE2)

55 Niranjan, A. (2023) European governments shrinking railways in favour of road-building, report finds, *The Guardian*, 19 September. Available at: www.theguardian.com/world/2023/sep/19/european-governments-railways-road-building-report-motorways-funding-rail (archived at https://perma.cc/78F7-KY88)

56 Swinford, S., Wright, O. and Clatworthy, B. (2023) Rishi Sunak set to scrap second leg of HS2 to Manchester, *The Times*, 23 September. Available at: www.thetimes.co.uk/article/rishi-sunak-set-to-scrap-second-leg-of-hs2-to-manchester-qlgkxmntr (archived at https://perma.cc/6GF6-V7F6)

57 www.youtube.com. (n.d.) RAYAD & @sncf Quel écolo tu es? (Pub). Available at: www.youtube.com/watch?v=xNMBhxHx6Dk (archived at https://perma.cc/MZ7T-K5GY)

58 Borne, E. (2023) Twitter post, 24 February. Available at: https://twitter.com/Elisabeth_Borne/status/1629182979112161280 (archived at https://perma.cc/64ZD-3K5W)

59 Borne, E. (2023) Déclaration de Mme Élisabeth Borne, Première ministre, sur la remise du rapport du Conseil d'orientation des infrastructures et le plan d'avenir pour les transports […], 24 February. Available at: www.vie-publique.fr/discours/288342-elisabeth-borne-24022023plan-d-avenir-pour-les-transports-2040 (archived at https://perma.cc/W2BT-TJN7)

60 European Commission (2017) Electrification of the Transport System. Available at: https://ec.europa.eu/newsroom/horizon2020/document.cfm? doc_id=46372 (archived at https://perma.cc/L9EH-JL9Q)

61 Alstom. (n.d.) Alstom Coradia iLint – the world's 1st hydrogen powered passenger train. Available at: www.alstom.com/solutions/rolling-stock/ alstom-coradia-ilint-worlds-1st-hydrogen-powered-passenger-train (archived at https://perma.cc/8M7Z-DJEY)

62 SNCF.com (2023) Local Mobility for all. Available at: www.sncf.com/en/ innovation-development/innovation-research/local-mobility-for-all (archived at https://perma.cc/J997-SGSL)

63 Preston, R. (2023) German government provides €12.5bn more for rail investment, International Rail Journal, 15 August. Available at: www. railjournal.com/financial/german-government-provides-e12-5bn-more-for-rail-investment/ (archived at https://perma.cc/N5LA-P52P)

64 Hansen, H. and Alkousaa, R. (2023) German cabinet approves 58 bln euro green investment plan for 2024, Reuters, 9 August. Available at: www.reuters. com/world/europe/german-cabinet-approves-58-bln-eur-green-investments-plan-2024-2023-08-09/ (archived at https://perma.cc/LX6E-RCWS)

65 Ruiz, M. (2023) Power could soon be generated from solar panels placed between railway tracks, *Travel Tomorrow*, 22 March. Available at: https:// traveltomorrow.com/power-could-soon-be-generated-from-solar-panels-placed-between-railway-tracks/ (archived at https://perma.cc/D955-2DQY)

66 Yang, Z. (2023) How did China come to dominate the world of electric cars?, *MIT Technology Review*, 21 February. Available at: www.technologyreview. com/2023/02/21/1068880/how-did-china-dominate-electric-cars-policy/ (archived at https://perma.cc/5FHR-QXV4)

67 Man, H. (2023) What are LFP, NMC, NCA batteries in electric cars?, ZeCar, 19 February. Available at: https://zecar.com/resources/what-are-lfp-nmc-nca-batteries-in-electric-cars (archived at https://perma.cc/M6WH-M88A)

68 Kane, M (2023) Report: CATL's new Qilin Battery Enters Series Production, InsideEVs, 22 March. Available at: https://insideevs.com/news/658474/ report-catl-qilin-battery-series-production/ (archived at https://perma.cc/ V49V-RH6Q)

69 CATL.com (2023) Together for better: CATL shines at Auto Shanghai with carbon neutral ambition and advanced technologies. Available at: www.catl. com/en/news/6017.html (archived at https://perma.cc/3HGY-N2L8)

70 Iordache, R. (2023) Ford to cut 3,800 jobs in Europe in shift to electric vehicle production, CNBC, 14 February. Available at: www.cnbc.com/2023/02/14/ ford-to-eliminate-3800-engineering-administration-jobs-in-europe.html (archived at https://perma.cc/HQ67-QSWE)

71 Kottasova, I. (2023) EU was set to ban internal combustion engine cars. Then Germany suddenly changed its mind, CNN Business, 27 March. Available at: https://edition.cnn.com/2023/03/24/cars/eu-combustion-engine-debate-climate-intl/ (archived at https://perma.cc/6B8E-AWKD)

72 Sickels, D. (2022) China has 65 per cent of public EV charging stations worldwide, The Buzz EV News, 17 August. Available at: www.thebuzzevnews. com/china-public-ev-charging-stations/ (archived at https://perma.cc/8TRZ-3TCH)

73 Shen, J. (2023) Chinese government makes big push for EV adoption in rural areas, lower-tier cities, Technode, 8 May. Available at: https://technode.com/2023/05/08/Chinese-government-makes-big-push-for-ev-adoption-in-rural-areas-lower-tier-cities/ (archived at https://perma.cc/W4V9-ATMM)

74 Masters, B (2023) Taking an electric car on the road is still a gamble in America, *Financial Times*, 28 May. Available at: www.ft.com/content/e85297a6-6f95-4f77-891b-0afe9e0c66b2 (archived at https://perma.cc/G3WN-BDQC)

75 California Energy Commission (n.d.) Light-duty vehicle population in California. Available at: www.energy.ca.gov/data-reports/energy-almanac/zero-emission-vehicle-and-infrastructure-statistics/light-duty-vehicle (archived at https://perma.cc/ZT4H-EAJG)

76 California Energy Commission (n.d.) Assembly Bill 2127 electric vehicle charging infrastructure assessment: Analyzing charging needs to support zero-emission vehicles in 2030. Available at: www.energy.ca.gov/publications/2020/assembly-bill-2127-electric-vehicle-charging-infrastructure-assessment-analyzing (archived at https://perma.cc/57F8-VL3P)

77 California Energy Commission (n.d.) Electric vehicle chargers in California. Available at: www.energy.ca.gov/data-reports/energy-almanac/zero-emission-vehicle-and-infrastructure-statistics/electric-vehicle (archived at https://perma.cc/LG6Y-HXZ5)

78 China Association of Automobile Manufacturers (n.d.) Sales of automobiles in December 2023. Available at: http://en.caam.org.cn/Index/lists/catid/64.html (archived at https://perma.cc/BH4A-MQ8J)

79 Fusheng, L. (2023) Big overseas potential for China's EV makers, ChinaDaily, 3 July. Available at: www.chinadaily.com.cn/a/202307/03/WS64a1f823a310bf8a75d6cc81.html (archived at https://perma.cc/G4ZZ-CZ3S)

80 Ying Shan, L. (2023) China is on course to overtake Japan and become the world's No. 1 car exporter, CNBC, 15 August. Available at: www.cnbc.com/2023/08/15/china-can-become-worlds-number-1-car-exporter-by-2023-moodys.html (archived at https://perma.cc/M38D-RXNY)

81 Blenkinsop, P. (2023) EU to investigate 'flood' of Chinese electric cars, weigh tariffs, Reuters, 13 September. Available at: www.reuters.com/world/europe/eu-launches-anti-subsidy-investigation-into-chinese-electric-vehicles-2023-09-13/ (archived at https://perma.cc/S5ZA-WSBT)

Fragmentation and digital connections

7

- How digital search and social media give power to consumers.
- How digital innovation unlocks growth in intermodal connectivity.
- Why shared vehicle services are taking off.
- How operators are seeking new, digital relationships with consumers.

In the 2000s, SNCF's long-distance high-speed business (in the form of TGV) was growing well, but it was under pressure from new competitors. After the liberalization of the European air travel market, low-cost airlines such as Ryanair and easyJet had expanded to a variety of European destinations and they were now capturing much of the high-growth, price-sensitive leisure market. These airlines had schedules that were much more flexible than those of rail operators and they altered them to meet seasonal demand – flights to ski areas in winter and beach resorts in summer. Unlike the TGV, which was augmenting its network in France with a range of secondary stops, the low-cost carriers focused their operating models tightly on efficient point-to-point operations to achieve the highest possible productivity for their assets.

Rail operators would have to reduce their fares to compete, but they were still obliged to invest in and maintain vast fixed infrastructure, the cost of which can reach up to 30 per cent of an operator's revenues for high-speed rail. Competitors – that is, airlines and later in 2015 the newly liberalized long-distance bus services – did not have to bear such a burden of fixed infrastructure. In addition, the European market for international rail passenger services was liberalized in 2010, further increasing competitive pressures.

Guillaume Pepy, then Chairman and CEO of SNCF, felt he needed to mobilize his giant organization around the low-cost threat and competition from other rail services. The company had already developed a website, voyagesSNCF.com, to digitize ticket distribution and respond to the growing threat from the big tech companies (sometimes referred to as GAFAM for Google, Amazon, Facebook, Apple and Microsoft), which had begun to target the travel industry. But Pepy now needed a fresh set of eyes to develop products for the future – products that would be low-cost, digital and accessible.

His solution in 2010: appoint a telecom executive as chief executive officer of Voyages SNCF, the railways' long distance business unit. Barbara Dalibard had worked for nearly 30 years in telecoms and had always been focused on capturing early warning indicators of changes in business sectors. In particular, she had experience of sectoral disruption and how to react to it. She had been an executive at France Telecom, the French telecom monopoly, when Europe liberalized the telecommunications sector, and she had been part of the team leading it through its emergence under a new brand, Orange, where she also worked for a decade.

One effect of these new digital services from big tech and other companies was that they would lead consumers to do their own research into journeys, which would often lead them to choose convenient, flexible, low-cost alternatives to incumbent national air carriers and rail services. This was Barbara Dalibard's challenge at SNCF.

Not the usual kind of change

The greatest change in mobility today is not the result of a new type of engine (though many are being developed and commercialized especially in the wake of mobility de-carbonization), a new mode of transport (despite the promising ideas in the pipeline) or an interesting new vehicle concept (of which there are plenty). It is the way consumers – that is, travellers – access mobility. And that is increasingly via an app on a smartphone or some equivalent digital means.

In each of the interviews I carried out for this book with senior mobility leaders and experts, I asked them for a vision of the future of mobility in the next decade. By far the most common reply was that, instead of providers pushing services, customers would 'pull' them: mobility would be on demand in a fragmented, multi-modal and data-rich environment. 'I go where I want and how I want, thanks to my digital assistant, which helps me plan and execute a trip on my own,' was one typical summary. 'Digitalization has changed customers from captive modal users into clients that are empowered by an application that creates and manages a multi-modal journey,' says Patrick Jeantet, former Chief Executive Officer of the French rail infrastructure manager, SNCF Réseau.

Digital search and payment, developed since the early 2000s, has transformed the way in which people seek out travel opportunities. Digital innovators have reversed the value chain: instead of being limited to one or two reasonable options for how to complete a journey, the customer is now in charge. Digital services offer customers an array of choices and parts of a journey can be carried out by a variety of modes and service operators, at different speeds and via a choice of routes. Customers find it relatively easy to navigate an array of trip scenarios via apps and internet searches, which lay out journey times and prices in an instant.

Market power will be with cross-sector platforms that can help travellers plan their trips, pay for them and adapt their itineraries to new circumstances in real time. Data will become a critical asset as it will help to predict the options a traveller might choose and the price they might be willing to pay for them. Platforms will therefore capture customer data to increase their range of services and value will migrate along the mobility value chain towards data holders and managers. Aggregators will buy content that builds up their offerings.

Moreover, digital technology has made shared mobility practical and a growing number of younger people seem happy to forgo car ownership in favour of various kinds of renting and sharing. Shared micro-mobility – notably e-scooters and bicycles – is also taking off, as flexible, easy-to-use apps make mobility-on-demand possible in cities. As travellers gain control over their trips and itineraries, city mobility may cease to be a chore and instead become a pleasure. 'The most formidable disruption in mobility has been the advent of data and GAFAMs,' says Marc Ivaldi, Professor of Economics at the Toulouse School of Economics. 'They have dramatically improved people's quality of life when travelling and commuting, by providing enhanced, accelerated access to information.'

"Digitalization has changed customers from captive modal users into clients that are empowered"
Patrick Jeantet

Digital disruption has hit mobility relatively late. The digitization of media and certain types of retail offered instant rewards in speed and convenience when selling or delivering their products. The first wave of internet disruption hit consumer-facing industries from the late 1990s, as the dot-com boom empowered consumers to make purchases in new ways, starting with books and spreading to household items and banking.

But mobility needs high levels of capital expenditure, as well as long-term network design to serve a multitude of itineraries. It must have vehicles, which are usually expensive, and ground transport needs roads or rail tracks. Many modes require some kind of port or station for departure and arrival. Moreover, many mobility services are local, so they don't benefit from digital technology's power to eliminate distance. And transport systems are often well developed and run by solid incumbent operators.

In the past – which in digital terms means the 1990s and earlier – a traveller from the outskirts of Paris who wanted to go to the island of Sylt in northern Germany would have needed a travel agent to book a taxi, flight, train and boat. To do this, they would need to rely heavily on a well-trained travel agent to learn about service options and fares. The travel agent's computer terminal would have been connected to its global distribution system – the airline reservation systems that were later branded as Amadeus, Galileo, Sabre or Worldspan at that time. The travel agent would have had to navigate a primitive graphical user interface full of complex technical terms and lacking images because of the limitations to bandwidth and computer memory. However, for a cross-border trip, the agent in France may or may not have been able to access domestic German services such as trains and ferries, or with only basic messaging and product features. They would therefore have had to call a dedicated customer-care centre. The process was cumbersome and labour-intensive, therefore costly, and it limited the options that could be made available to the traveller.

"The most formidable disruption in mobility has been the advent of data and GAFAMs"
Marc Ivaldi

Eventually, the traveller would receive a paper ticket or voucher as a proof of booking and payment. The travel agent would receive a percentage of the price as revenue, often between 10 per cent and 25 per cent. Any change of plans would mean the traveller going back to the agent to ask them to reschedule the various legs of the journey, which would often incur a penalty charge. In 1993 and 1994, I was involved in a project that aimed to modernize such a travel distribution network. At its inception, Eurostar was a joint venture between the UK government, the French national railway SNCF and the Belgian national railway SNCB. All market studies identified the UK market as the largest future originating market for the product, with around a 60 per cent share.

However, selling Eurostar in the UK would not be easy. Eurostar inventory was hosted in SNCF's reservation system (called Resarail), physically located in Lille in northern France, and Eurostar did not yet have a web-based distribution channel. The only way to sell SNCF products in the UK was via an SNCF affiliate, French Railway Ltd (FRL). So FRL brought dozens of desktop terminals over from France that were directly connected to SNCF's system. These were installed in FRL offices, which were hosting a UK-based call centre, and also at a few contracted local UK travel agents. Overseas, for example in the United States and Asia, Eurostar products initially could only be bought via SNCF affiliates and their agents, as these were the only distribution companies connected to SNCF inventory.

It was expected that the rail service would grow quickly, seizing market share from airlines and ferries for travel between London and Paris, especially after a high-speed line would be built in the UK in 2003 to complement that between Paris and Calais in the north of France. That meant SNCF's direct-access solution would not be robust and scalable enough for the long term, so a different approach was taken. SNCF decided to connect Eurostar inventory to all airline reservation systems, ultimately placing Eurostar product competitively on the same screen as other London–Paris travel services. I was among the lucky consultants tasked with the end-to-end management of this project and I came away with a souvenir. A project steering committee meeting was scheduled in London on the day of the first commercial Eurostar service between Paris and London and they asked me to act as a testing agent. I took a ticket and ran it through the machine at the boarding gates – and I can proudly claim to possess the very first ticket in Eurostar history stamped for boarding! Eurostar was a resounding success despite a fire incident in the tunnel which slowed down the phase of traffic ramp-up. By the year 2000, more than 7 million passengers a year were travelling on the cross-Channel service, a figure that rose to 11.1 million in 2019.[1]

Power to the consumers

Today, consumer-travellers can do pretty much all their booking online by themselves in just a few clicks. They have access to multiple options and plenty of information on each one, and embedded comparators make the choices easier. New booking and price-comparison sites mushroomed and the effect was amplified and spread in the 2000s with the rise of social networking. This phenomenon has been called disintermediation. It is one of the major disruptions in travel over the past three decades. Specifically, it has completely disrupted the business model of travel agencies.

Where travel agents used to be an essential component of the mass travel market, they now serve more select customer segments – the case with corporate travel services – or they specialize in certain types of products, such as exotic tours or cultural trips. Otherwise, it is difficult for them to survive financially if they do not gain significant scale or do not attract a highly focused and service-orientated client base prepared to pay high commissions for complex service.

For consumer-facing businesses, the birth of web-based search led to a vast expansion of customer choice. In travel, e-commerce sites allowed customers to purchase travel products such as hotels, flights and rental cars. Travel companies, such as airlines, set up their own websites so that a consumer could have a direct dialogue with the carrier. In addition to the direct booking of flights, airlines could then offer – or point the way to – other travel services such as car hire and hotels.

But consumers needed their task simplified and a wave of online travel agencies emerged to help. Online travel intermediaries make booking easier, they enlarge the scope of accessible service offerings and often provide discounts by buying up travel services – package tours or flights – in bulk. Online travel agencies (OTAs) often worked like travel agencies, but online. They forged agreements with hotels, car rentals and other suppliers of travel services, which they then sold on to end-customers. Some worked with an agency model: customers booked a hotel via the website and paid the hotel directly. That way, the agency would not need a payment infrastructure. It could just collect the commission fees later from the service providers. Others used a merchant model: they bought blocks of rooms from hotels and seats from air carriers and they collected payments from the end-customers. The traditional role of travel agencies had gone beyond that of booking, they also served as curators and advisors to help consumers navigate the expanded array of choices. How could a consumer be sure that what they were booking was going to be good value and of high quality?

In 1998, Stephen Kaufer, a software entrepreneur, was trying to find a hotel for a trip to Mexico but decided that the only information available was from tourism providers – and, therefore, biased. He founded a website that would collect consumer opinions and help travellers plan their trips in advance. He called it Tripadvisor and users could rate hotels from one to five. Tripadvisor would go on to set the industry standards for consumer interaction in digital services. In particular, other travel and mobility sites began to offer users the chance to comment on services and assign scores.

It began to take off from around 2000 with the advent of what later became known as Web 2.0 – the internet's evolution beyond search to greater interactivity in the form of blogs and social networks. This enabled internet users to participate more in the content found online – and was the cue for the founding of Wikipedia, Myspace and Facebook. Crowdsourcing, as such user-generated content became known, is supposed to mean that the reviews are genuine: they should have been written by other customers who have visited a destination and who also use the same website and are therefore members of the same community.

In 2010, Tripadvisor added a feature that allows users to connect to their Facebook account, so they can find friends' profiles and follow their reviews. The site also went beyond flights and accommodation to include the experience at a destination – that is, restaurants and other tourist attractions. Tripadvisor later bought up review services – such as French site TheFork, for which it paid $150 million in 2014 – and provided links to these.[2,3]

Since around 2010, smartphones have become ubiquitous in much of the world, making the reviewers' advice available to all. The increased portability of a smartphone makes it even easier to consult advice and then provide it. Online mapping meant that a traveller could receive walking instructions to a destination and wander round with knowledge approaching that of a local resident. By 2023, Tripadvisor had 469 million unique visitors per month and 859 million reviews of 8.3 million establishments. Annual turnover was $2.52 billion in 2022.[4]

The travel agencies, especially brick and mortar models, lacked a high level of intimacy with customers and so had to figure out what consumers wanted. One of the most successful did this by nurturing a culture of experimentation. Bookings.nl was founded in Amsterdam in 1996 by Geert-Jan Bruinsma, who had become fascinated with the nascent internet. Later known as Booking.com, the company's slogan was 'to make it easier for everyone to experience the world'. It did this by endless experimentation,

CEO Gillian Tans told a Harvard Business School Case Study in 2018. Many companies develop a product that they can then market all over the world, Tans said. 'Booking did the opposite. We had a basic product and then worked hard to get it right for customers. But figuring out what they like is hard. We got it wrong so many times.'[5,6]

Starting in 2004, it ran simple tests to learn which product features customers preferred. It then adjusted the product based on these preferences. Typically, customers were randomly assigned to two different versions of the product experience and the resulting key metrics – mainly user conversion, measured as bookings per day – were computed and compared. The premise was that the company's predictions of what customers would like were typically wrong. 'We mistakenly believed that customers would like hotel offers packaged with other products since travel brochures are full of them. Or we thought that customers would want a chat line helping them through the booking process. Neither idea worked during our tests. It's how you learn,' Tans explained.

One example cited in the Harvard Business School study was a test to decide whether to add a walkability assessment to a hotel's user reviews. This was found not to have a significant impact, so it was rejected. Another was the addition of the actual checkout date to the statement of children's ages on checkout date (rather than just 'ages of children at check-out') in order to add clarity. This did have a significant positive impact and so was launched as a new feature. Other examples include experiments to find the right colour for the 'Book' button. On any day, the company ran more than 1,000 tests via its website, servers and apps.

The system was a kind of rapid prototyping and generated the cumulative effect of many small changes, according to Chief Product Officer David Vismans. He described it as a version of Amazon's flywheel concept. 'It's a virtuous cycle with network effects, where each component is an accelerator... It's very effective in building something that customers find most valuable or easy to use.'

The resulting online travel agent was a machine version of what people found in their high street, but one that offered vastly greater choice, as well as features such as real-time reviews. It was scalable, so cheaper and available to all, and based on real data. It was also connected with multitudes of providers and their online information was updated frequently. Hence, customers were much more up to date on the latest products and offers and providers were able to dynamically manage their supply and pricing to maximize choice.

In 2023, Booking.com launched an artificial intelligence-based trip planner in the United States. Built on the foundation of the company's existing machine learning models, the planner is also partially powered bya large-language model. This aims to create a conversational experience as travellers scope out potential destinations and accommodation in order to create an itinerary. In 2022, the global online travel market was $475 billion (up 20 per cent from 2020) and was expected to reach $521 billion in 2023. In 2021, the largest travel agencies worldwide in terms of revenues were Booking ($11.0 billion), Expedia ($8.6 billion) and Airbnb ($6.0 billion).[7]

Online travel agencies and digital search are becoming ever more important. In 2010, Google announced it would acquire flight data company ITA for $700 million. ITA organized data such as flight times, seat availability and prices, and its powerful engine was used by Hotwire, Orbitz and other online companies to search for flight options and quickly show fares and schedules. Google used ITA to launch Google Flights, which was later integrated into Google Travel. It said the acquisition would make it easier for customers to comparison shop for flights and airfares and boost the online travel market.[8]

This acquisition was an example of the GAFAM strategy to expand their global platforms into large, diverse markets such as travel, one of the largest consumer marketplaces. It has much in common with Facebook's acquisition of messaging service WhatsApp and Amazon's of grocery chain Whole Foods. 'It's such a gradual process,' wrote Pete Meyers, an expert on Google search algorithms who works as a marketing scientist at search engine optimization company Moz, – in a *Washington Post* article in 2020. 'It's often subtle in the moment. Six months later, when all of these small changes accumulate, Search can look very different.' Needless to say, back in 2010 Google's announcement met huge opposition from online travel players, which were concerned about unfair competition. The case has been subject to regulatory review since 2020.[9]

Shared mobility

The internet also helped launch another service that exploded in popularity and further fragmented travel demand: new ways to share cars.

One Christmas, Stanford University student Frédéric Mazzella wanted to get home to his family in the French countryside. He had no car and the trains were full. The roads, too, were full – of people driving home alone in their cars. An old-fashioned solution would have been to hitchhike – find a car to take you some of the way to your destination for free or for a small contribution to road tolls and petrol. It was the years after the dotcom boom and Mazzella started thinking. Surely hitchhiking could be organized more efficiently online – that is, to put lone drivers in touch with people needing a ride rather than the hitchhiker waiting on the side of the road. However, no such site existed at the time.

In 2006, Mazzella put a first site online and a small community began to develop. He then worked with Francis Nappez, an engineer, and Nicolas Brusson, another student, to build out the service so it could reach its potential. One of its features was to allow members to indicate on their profiles how much they like to chat in the car: 'Bla' indicated they like to watch the scenery go by, 'BlaBla' says they can be chatty and 'BlaBlaBla' means they won't keep quiet. They called the service BlaBlaCar and it grew into a pan-European community marketplace that connects drivers and passengers. In 2022, BlaBlaCar enabled 90 million shared rides, saving carpool drivers as much as €450 million.[10]

At the root of the idea was the observation that road mobility resources were not being used efficiently. A car that could carry several people was often only carrying one and it was taking up just as much road space as a vehicle with several passengers. 'Carpooling stems from the mere observation that the total capacity of cars in terms of seat-kilometres is hugely underutilized. Carpooling is gradually rising, as the desire to own a car fades, and the sharing community expands,' says Mazzella, Chief Executive Officer and Founder of BlaBlaCar. 'Carpooling is the natural response to the desire to save energy and money in transport and to the necessity to reduce our CO_2 emissions per passenger transported. Carpool lanes and incentive programmes also largely contribute to changing drivers' habits, who quickly become natural carpoolers.'

"The total capacity of cars' seats in terms of seat-kilometres is hugely underutilized"
Frédéric Mazzella

From car ownership to car sharing

For more than 100 years, the individual car was a symbol of individualism and freedom. At first they were a sign of prosperity, as cars were expensive compared to average incomes. Later, as incomes rose and cars became mass produced, they became a must-have product in richer countries. While cars have helped billions of people get to where they want to go, they have also become an environmental problem, a cause of global warming due to their use of fossil fuels, and of traffic jams and pollution in many cities. This environmental damage and pollution will rapidly diminish with the expansion of electric vehicles (see Chapter 6), and some more mature drivers maintain a strong emotional link with their cars. But a growing number of people – especially the youngest – are now uninterested in car ownership.

However, not everyone has easy access to public transport or safe cycling infrastructure, either because they live outside major cities or because the cities do not have adequate mass transit or dedicated cycling lanes. Some would still use a car from time to time – for heavy shopping, an out-of-the-way work trip, or a weekend in the countryside. For them, shared mobility is a solution. This includes micro-mobility, such as e-scooters, but by far the biggest markets so far are car rental and new ways to use cars, including ride-hailing and carsharing.

Carsharing comes in a variety of forms, which are effectively digital versions of previously existing services. BlaBlaCar is a digital form of hitchhiking, but much more efficient at matching supply and demand; other forms of carsharing are essentially digitally enabled car hire. In peer-to-peer carsharing, existing car owners make their vehicles available for others to rent for short periods of time. Other systems use cars owned and maintained by an operating company, which lets users – who have typically been pre-approved to drive – rent for short periods of time, from less than an hour to several weeks. In some systems, members pick up a car in a fixed location and return it there afterwards: this is often close to public transport for easy access. In others, known as free-floating, a user finds a car via an app, takes it for a ride and then leaves it somewhere else within a designated free-floating zone.

Carsharing is conceivable in a world without apps or internet. Car rental existed for decades before carsharing took off, just as hitchhiking was common before BlaBlaCar. But digital technology makes it far easier to dynamically manage offerings, inventory and bookings. Shared cars typically make use of onboard computers to record distance and time travelled and thus

calculate the price of a trip. Reservation, pickup and return are all self-ser-
vice, so, unlike traditional rental, carsharing is not limited by office hours.
Various carsharing schemes were tried from the 1970s but they mostly did
not survive. Carsharing only really took off in the internet era.

People could hail a ride, too, before widespread digital technology – think
of waving down a taxi in the street or phoning a mini-cab service. But ride-
hailing really took off because of the smartphone. In 2008, Garret Camp, a
Canadian tech entrepreneur, was annoyed because even in tech-savvy San
Francisco he couldn't get a taxi in under half an hour. The city's taxi system
was old and base station dispatchers took calls from customers and radioed
them to the taxi drivers. But it was unreliable and a requested taxi might not
arrive. Camp figured that one way to improve his chances was to call all the
major taxi services in the city to ask for a ride. When one arrived, he would
take that. Eventually, the cab companies refused to serve him.[11,12]

One New Year's Eve, Camp and some friends spent $800 hiring a private
driver for an evening and he thought that was too expensive. However, he
realized that sharing the costs of a private driver with other users could
make it affordable. But how to coordinate the right driver and the various
clients?

Reportedly, inspiration came from *Casino Royale*, the James Bond film,
and the latest piece of gadgetry it showed off. In one scene, the spy was driving through Nassau in the Bahamas and looking at a cell phone. This showed
a GPS-based map on its screen and Bond could see his progress through the
city, indicated by an arrow on the screen. While Bond films have long shown
off exotic, often futuristic devices, this one had something in common with
some new tech that had just been released. The iPhone came with Wi-Fi connectivity and future versions would feature GPS. These were the essential
technologies for calculating a user's location – and, therefore, working out
who were the best available drivers to serve a potential client.

UberCab, the first service that Camp set up with Uber cofounder Travis
Kalanick, allowed a user to summon a car by pressing a button on a smartphone or sending a text. The price was around 1.5 times that of a typical San
Francisco cab. The app automatically charges the passenger's credit card
once the transaction is complete. Then, both the customer and driver rate
each other on Uber's application. In 2023, Uber Technologies had over 130
million monthly active users and 6 million active drivers in the over 70
countries in which it is active. Since 2010, it has helped to arrange 42 billion
trips. Uber also branched out into services such as food delivery, which
made up nearly half of its 2022 gross bookings of $31 billion.

The rise of such car-hailing services, in the meantime, had a dramatic impact on incumbent public transport and taxi operators. As Mark Joseph, former CEO of Transdev North-America, a leading mass-transit operator, points out, the company's on-demand car service business, which was once a major source of profits, was not able to cope with such disruption and it proved extremely difficult to disrupt and transform the company's own business. 'Our on-demand car service was once a major source of profits,' he explains. 'But it was not able to cope with the new-economy disruptors such as Uber and Lyft. We, as a company, could not stop milking the cow, while we should have disrupted our own business. But that is very difficult to do!'

The world's leading mobile transportation platform is now Beijing-based DiDi Global, which operates in countries in Asia, Africa, Latin America, Eastern Europe and Oceania. DiDi was founded in 2012 by former Alibaba Group executive Will Wei Cheng and over the years it has acquired several Chinese rivals, including Kuaidi Dache and Uber China. It has over 90 per cent of China's ride-hailing market, according to Investopedia, and more than 550 million users worldwide. It offers them a full range of algorithm-optimized app-based services, which include ride-hailing, taxi-hailing and other forms of shared mobility, as well as food delivery, intra-city freight and financial services.[13]

Overall, the global ride-hailing market is expected to almost double from its 2020 level to $347 billion in 2030, according to Oliver Wyman Forum research. Car sharing is forecast to more than treble, to $24 billion.

Why shared mobility is growing

The rise of digital car sharing, along with other mobility services (see Figure 7.1), is one of the most remarkable phenomena in mobility of the past three

"Our on-demand car service was not able to cope with the new-economy disruptors"
Mark Joseph

Figure 7.1   Global value pool sizes by mobility services (US$ bn)

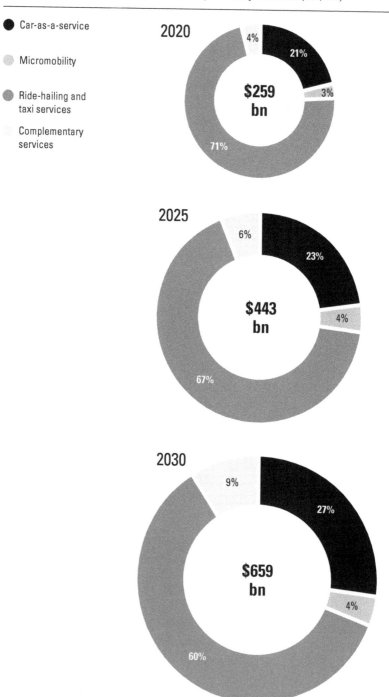

- Car-as-a-service
- Micromobility
- Ride-hailing and taxi services
- Complementary services

2020
$259 bn
4%
21%
3%
71%

2025
$443 bn
6%
23%
4%
67%

2030
$659 bn
9%
27%
4%
60%

SOURCE Oliver Wyman Forum Mobility Value Pool analysis

decades. While ride-hailing is available worldwide, carsharing has also spread to other global markets with dense urban populations. A look at its main drivers shows why it is likely to continue to expand.

First comes technology, such as large database management systems, web-based connectivity, GPS technology and search engines. Another – perhaps the most important – push will come when self-driving cars become common. These will convert many carsharing services into digital chauffeur-driven taxi services and they will slash the price of ride-hailing because they will not need a driver.

A second growth factor for shared mobility is the efficiency gains it enables. In cities, there is huge underutilization of individual car seat-km capacity, due to cars moving around with a driver but no passengers. They also spend 90 per cent or more of their time parked – often at the sides of crowded roads, when the space could be repurposed for pedestrians, cyclists or public transport.

A third factor is sharing services' organic, community-based growth. This often starts slowly, due to the need for sufficient scale to attract a large number of users. When there are relatively few available cars to share or hail in a city, the service is less practical. But as a service grows, it becomes easier to use: the probability falls that, at any given time, all ride-hailing drivers or cars for sharing are unavailable or too distant. And a service's advantages spread by word of mouth (the BlaBlaCar chattiness test is a sign that it is a friendly way to travel).

Shared mobility offers several kinds of contributions to society, the economy and the environment. It provides jobs for drivers, at least before the era of mass self-driving cars. These jobs are flexible, so drivers can work part-time while carrying out other forms of work. It also enables people without their own cars to travel to workplaces or shopping destinations that might not otherwise have been within reach as they do not have to commit to the upfront costs of car ownership. They might also use ride-hailing or some form of micro-mobility – an electric bike or an e-scooter – to get to a mass-transit station that would normally be too far from their home or a workplace.

Shared mobility services can also have a positive impact on commuting, leisure and tourism. One study of ridesharing in New York City showed the positive impact that ridesharing had on the restaurant business in the outer boroughs, which are not as well served as Manhattan by the subway system. Moreover, while yellow cabs have become well-known symbols of the city, they are concentrated in Manhattan and people in less affluent areas in the outer boroughs have long had trouble hailing them. Overall, these areas of New York City are harder to access and leave.

The launch of ridesharing services changed the way many New Yorkers got around, but this was especially the case in the previously under-served outer boroughs. While the total number of trips beginning in Manhattan remained around 15 million over a sample period in which new ridesharing services were launched, the number of trips originating in outer boroughs increased by 50 per cent.

This appears to have made some areas more accessible, making it possible to open businesses in them. In particular, outer boroughs' share of New York City's net creation of restaurants went from under 40 per cent to nearly 80 per cent, showing a huge boom in restaurant net creation in the outer boroughs. 'In short,' concluded Caitlin Gorback, the economist who carried out the research, 'ridesharing opens a new set of destinations for residents to travel for pleasure, rather than for business.'[14]

Shared mobility also has the potential to reduce urban problems such as air pollution and traffic congestion, but the overall impact is mixed so far. It is very hard to divert car users towards other forms of transport, whether mass transit or forms of micro-mobility. This means that new modes, such as bikes and e-scooters, often generate new trips rather than reducing car journeys. And if the various forms of car sharing encourage greater amounts of driving, then the effect on the environment would be negative as long as vehicles are still powered by fossil fuels.

However, the benefits of a service such as BlaBlaCar are clear: two or more people complete a journey that generates the same emissions as one transporting just a single driver. In 2022, BlaBlaCar's mobility services contributed to avoiding 1.5 million tons of CO_2 emissions, the company says. And shared mobility might persuade drivers to abandon car ownership, if not car use in itself. 'In a future of low-priced ride-hailing services, private car ownership will continue to decline, while fleet ownership and management will thrive,' predicts Mark Joseph.

"Private car ownership will continue to decline, while fleet ownership and management will thrive"

Mark Joseph

Such a shift could reduce the amount people use cars because of the way sharing services are charged. Much of the expense of an owned car is sunk costs – such as the price of the vehicle and insurance – and so independent of how much the car is driven. In contrast, sharing services are usually charged by distance and time used, providing an incentive to travel by car less.

Guillaume Thibault, partner and leader of Oliver Wyman's Global Mobility Forum, believes that the trend of eroding car ownership will continue as mobility digitalizes and consumers take over the process of mobility management. That's good news for the environment and the use of land in cities. But it's a challenge for mobility operators. 'As the mobility value chain is digitalized,' he says, 'the end-consumer is gaining power and will microsegment to use the right tool for each purpose.'

The challenge for traditional mobility companies

For incumbent mobility operators, shared mobility is both an opportunity and a challenge. If shared mobility discourages car ownership, it could encourage the use of public transport when the consumer doesn't feel the need to borrow a car, and it can also serve as a means to reach a transit station for people who live too far away to walk. But shared mobility adds yet more complication to an increasingly choice-filled digital landscape. 'Mobility players always need to catch up with ever-changing demand,' says André Navarri, former President and Chief Operating Officer of global rail integrator Bombardier Transportation.

"As the mobility value chain is digitalized, the end-consumer is gaining power"
Guillaume Thibault

"Mobility players always need to catch up with ever-changing demand"
André Navarri

Progress in mobility has long been based on technology innovation. In rail, this started with the industrial revolution of the nineteenth century, with steam engines. These were then followed by diesel, before a shift from mechanical to electro-mechanical propulsion. The most recent shift has been to digital technology and it is different from the changes in the past. The industry used to be a collection of single, vertically integrated organizations that arranged transport for a particular type of customer. It has changed to a horizontal, open and connected environment. 'A key disruption is that we have moved from a closed-loop mobility environment, where each operator managed its own infrastructure and movements, to an open and inter-connected ecosystem, where multiple operators' offerings are intertwined,' says Laurent Troger, former President and Chief Operating Officer at Bombardier Transportation.

Digital capabilities have triggered a transformation in the way people think about travel. In the past, technology pushed new services by creating ways to transport people and goods faster, more safely and in greater numbers or volumes. It was mostly a supply-driven market environment. For example, travelling from Paris to the Riviera in the south of France before high-speed

"We have moved from a closed-loop mobility environment to an open and interconnected ecosystem"
Laurent Troger

rail had not been possible for many people: it was too far to drive and too expensive to fly (including low available capacity). Then, the TGV created a new possibility – that normal people could travel previously unthinkable distances for purposes such as tourism or even visiting friends and relatives or commuting.

Today, however, there is a fundamental shift from the captive user of regional mobility services to active, digitally enabled customers. Instead of being the go-to service for a certain kind of journey, a rail operator or airline is merely one of a number of options that appear when a traveller plans a trip. That means they have to compete on price, speed and convenience in order to be chosen for a single leg of this customer's journey. And at the same time, they may not have any direct contact with the customer – so they risk becoming transport subcontractors with less prospect of developing their businesses through direct customer relationships.

This shift in demand is changing the value in the mobility ecosystem and also challenging a style of governance that still largely functions in silos. At a private leadership conference in 2019, I witnessed the president of a global manufacturer of equipment for metro and tramway networks alerting his top 300 managers about the risk of marginalization of mass transit systems by new virtual entrants such as DiDi. There was no threat to the existence of mass transit systems because of their superior ability to carry high numbers of passengers in dense urban areas. But he was concerned that value was migrating towards innovative, digital and asset-light business models. Meanwhile, incumbent mass transit and rail operators – and the manufacturers of their trains and other systems and components – continue with the challenge of keeping billions of dollars of fixed assets productive. 'The legacy operators are overwhelmed by the consumer's desire to choose increasingly late in the booking process, to change itinerary easily and to have fewer pain points,' says Troger.

"The legacy operators are overwhelmed by the consumer's desire to choose increasingly late in the booking process"
Laurent Troger

But the senior leaders and experts I talked to for this book believe there is a silver lining in the potential to digitize operations along the mobility value chain, helped (instead of being challenged) by new tech companies that are entering the sector.

Mobility operators take up tech

Ryanair appointed John Hurley as chief technical officer in 2013 and he observed that the company's tech policy had been to avoid spending money on IT. 'We didn't just miss the first wave [of digital],' he told an interviewer, 'we missed the second wave.' His way to persuade his CEO O'Leary of the benefits of IT was to show that it could save money for the company. A series of 'small data' projects saved around €20 million over the course of two years.

More creatively, Ryanair developed a mobile app that gathered information on customers. The company's website then stored customer payment, identity and passport details, as well as preferences such as seats. This meant the airline could target customers with offers and options and further boost Ryanair's ancillary revenues. The data would also streamline passenger processing before a flight.

A new service, 'My Ryanair Club', offered discounts and free flights. The app provided customers with information about destinations – warning families that a destination might be more suitable for stag and hen parties, giving them information about the arrival airport and how to travel on from it, and pointing them towards child-friendly hotels. Cabin crew were equipped with Android devices as point-of-sale devices, so that they had data for proper stock control for each flight – which were based on what passengers were likely to buy, including food and drink. A passenger who had shown consistent preferences in the past could be presented with tailor-made onboard offers. 'It's all about the data, sharing the right information, mining it, protecting it,' Hurley said. 'We're trying to get the line between knowing enough to not annoy you and use it in a smart way to almost read your mind.'

When SNCF's management recognized the threat of disintermediation in their distribution channels, they saw the trend in the airline industry, where global distribution systems – that is, Amadeus, Galileo and Sabre – were thriving. They partnered with online travel distributor Expedia to develop the web site voyagesSNCF.com, which was later renamed SNCF Connect. It has become one of Europe's top online commercial sites with €4.5 billion of sales in 2021, accounting for more than 60 per cent of TGV sales and targeting as much as €6.5 billion by 2025.[15]

As digitalization accelerated, SNCF Chief Executive Officer Guillaume Pepy decided the company needed to go further. 'The GAFAM entry into mobility was a shock that made us disrupt our own business faster,' says Pepy.

In a first of its kind for the railway organization, he developed a training programme for his executive team with Stanford University, aimed at changing the mindset at the top of the organization. This aimed at digital reinvention of the company – but with a healthy understanding of the limitations. SNCF did not have the financial resources or in-house skills and capabilities to be able to invest massively in new mobility services in the way that the big tech companies could. But it would strike out a new strategic direction as an 'industrial and platform enterprise'. One in aspect of this was a round of hires from outside the railway industry to inject fresh skills at senior-management level. The newcomers came from fields such as software integration, digital distribution and telecommunications, which had been through its own upheaval two decades earlier.

Yes, go

One of these was Barbara Dalibard, the France Telecom and Orange executive, who became CEO of SNCF's long-distance business. She instantly recognized the rise of low-cost models. Airlines had been using these to expand throughout Europe for two decades, and further competition was arriving in the form of long-distance bus services. Previously, long-distance coach ser-

"The GAFAM entry into mobility was a shock that made us disrupt our own business faster"
Guillaume Pepy

vices had been subject to various restrictions, the aim of which was to promote rail for long-distance travel. As a result, the market for long-distance coaches was a fraction of that in the United Kingdom, where long-distance rail was not so well developed. The 2015 'Loi Macron' (see Chapter 4) aimed to give coaches a boost and further liberalize the domestic mobility market.

To compete, SNCF launched a low-cost high-speed rail brand that it called Ouigo ('Yes, go'). This leaned heavily on digital capabilities. Booking and ticketing were online-only, removing the costs of station sales desks, call centres and travel agents. I estimate that the cost of selling a ticket fell from more than €10 to less than €4. Digital monitoring of train components enabled predictive maintenance, reduced maintenance costs and sharply increased the utilization of rolling stock. SNCF is a highly unionized organization, but the new operating model was acceptable to its staff because of its narratives of innovation and a service accessible to all – something that sat well with railway workers' public service DNA. With high-speed rail becoming price-competitive with low-cost airlines and providing digital enablement on board, the value of time is also shifting and longer transit times become more acceptable than before, as Jean-Marie Metzler, former Chief Executive of SNCF's long-distance business, points out.

Ouigo quickly became competitive in the price-sensitive market segment for leisure travel and visiting friend and relatives. In 2018, a Spanish version was launched, Ouigo España, which now operates in Spain's liberalized long-distance rail market. In 2023, SNCF claimed that Ouigo would soon represent up to 25 per cent of the company's high-speed rail domestic offering.[16] 'Competition has been a real trigger for incumbents to modernize,' says Dalibard, 'with car sharing services like BlaBlaCar leading to the launch of low-cost rail and GAFAM stimulating the expansion of digital rail distribution platforms.'

"The value of time has changed for the new generations"
Jean-Marie Metzler

"Competition has been a real trigger for incumbents to modernize"
Barbara Dalibard

Unifying the physical and the digital

Despite their digital products, traditional transport companies still have a weakness. 'Unlike GAFAM models,' says Jean-Marie Metzler, also the leader of the launch of the first TGV service in France, 'typical legacy carrier applications are focused on single-carrier offers. This limits their reach and hinders their focus on customer needs.'

Some are now changing that. One principle is that, as with Amazon in logistics, the future belongs to those players who combine software with hardware. Amazon isn't just successful because of its top-class search and payment facilities, it also depends on its own warehouses and last-mile delivery capabilities, which it continues to develop. From a retailer standpoint, coordinated combination of online and physical shopping is paramount, to provide consumers with a seamless experience and ability to navigate autonomously through hybrid shopping mode. As Deepak Chopra, former

"Typical legacy carrier applications are focused on single-carrier offers. This limits their reach"
Jean-Marie Metzler

President and Chief Executive Officer of Canada Post, puts it: 'I believe in a new balance of online and offline retailing driven by economic reality, societal needs, sustainability and other regulatory requirements. All activities must be based on trust, which is a growing currency in the digital world.'

Another principle is that most people do not want to have two or three mobility apps on their smartphones. Instead, they want a single app that provides access to all the mobility services they need under a variety of circumstances and needs. If they cannot develop a platform themselves, or are too late in the game, mobility incumbents can always seek strategic partnerships with platform-based enterprises.

That's what Arriva, the multinational bus and train operator, is trying to achieve in the Netherlands. In 2021, it teamed up with Moovit, creator of a successful mobility app, to develop 'glimble'. The app searches for mobility choices among all public transport options in the relevant market and regions (bus, trains, tram, metro, ferries), shared modes (such as bikes, cars, e-scooters and mopeds) and ride-hailing services. Users can find out which combination will get them from points A to B with the lowest CO_2 emissions, lowest cost, fastest journey time or fewest transfers. Or they ask for step-free journeys. Mike Cooper, President and Chief Executive Officer of Arriva, described the level of change this required for his organization: 'To build a digital platform such as glimble within Arriva, it takes a different set of capabilities and a fundamentally new culture. Hence the glimble team was established on the opposite side of the Netherlands from Arriva NL headquarters, to maintain its start-up mindset.'

The app goes beyond big tech-style search, however. Previously in the Netherlands, public transport riders had to pay with a dedicated contactless card, which they would have charged every so often. Drivers were not allowed to accept cash payments on buses, so some people would find they

"A new balance of online and offline retailing is being driven by economic reality"
Deepak Chopra

did not have enough credits left on their cards and would have to leave the bus, top up their card at a machine and wait for the next bus. Users of glimble can now pay via the app, which also provides real-time arrival information, alerts to remind passengers to disembark and service alerts that issue warnings over disruptions. Arriva says that 'being able to seamlessly connect across more than one mode of transport… is essential to make public transport the easy choice. This, in turn, will encourage people to get out of their cars more often and turn to public transport'. Arriva says it wants to roll out the app in other countries in Europe where data-sharing policies can support it (see Figure 7.2). Berlin has an app with similar capabilities, Jelbi, and the Brussels public transport company MIVB/STIB launched one in 2023 called Floya.

The European Union has identified data access as a key success factor for future mobility and has been drawing up a strategy to encourage glimble-type projects. The European Commission launched an initiative in 2022 called EMDS, the Common European Mobility Data Space, which lays out a strategic framework to tackle the problem of fragmented data sources and to facilitate the exchange of data. The EMDS aims to facilitate the access, sharing and pooling of data to make transport safer, more efficient, more sustainable and more resilient. The first steps are to identify data sources and facilitate access to them. Later, the strategy aims to optimize data collection and make it easily interoperable with other European data spaces. A publication on EMDS by the European Commission was planned for the end of 2023 and will describe the main features, support measures, objectives and milestones, as well as the related governance system. The

"To build a digital platform such as glimble within Arriva, it takes a different set of capabilities"

Mike Cooper

Figure 7.2   glimble app screenshots

Commission's approach to technology evolution seems to be a realistic one, which will eventually result in improved choice and service level for consumers.

The future is (even more) digital

As Patrick Jeantet adds, 'Tomorrow's travellers will use all modes of transport, they will be active "zappers" – switching from one to the other seamlessly. An efficient, smooth, anxiety-free intermodality at optimum cost is the future for the mobility sector. Working on a better complementarity of all modes of transport and their transition towards energies with low greenhouse or toxic gas emissions is the major challenge of the next decades.'

By integrating various components in mobility chains, which had been disjointed in the past, digital technology can coordinate among travel modes and improve the customer experience of a door-to-door journey. That marks a change from the past when different modes operated in their own worlds for particular types of populations: rail transit to take large populations over a fixed urban network, contrasted with the individual car as a symbol of freedom and prosperity. (Driving is still a symbol of emancipation for women in many countries where they are not yet allowed to drive.) 'While the twentieth century tended to set alternative transport modes against each other,' says Jean-Pierre Loubinoux, former CEO of the International Union of Railways (UIC), 'the competition today is within modes as well. Integration and cooperation are carried out between different modes and they are enabled by digital technology.'

"Tomorrow's travellers will use all modes of transport – they will be active 'zappers'"
Patrick Jeantet

The mobility sector is still just scratching the surface of digital technology's potential. The number of mobility start-ups increased by 15 per cent a year between 2007 and 2017, and in 2020 they attracted investment of $40 billion. The future will bring greater integration of various modes and services, better response to customer demands and increased automation.

KEY TAKEAWAYS

- Digital technology has profoundly disrupted the value chain of the mobility industry, complicating the businesses of large incumbent mobility operators. But it has also provided them with solutions by enabling them to connect with customers and provide new, value-added services.

- Digital connectivity also breaks down siloes, giving traditional mobility providers the opportunity to adapt through partnerships.

- Power has shifted to consumers. In particular, the growing market power of Generation Z means that digital services will continue to expand rapidly. Legacy providers have little time to adapt.

- Legacy players have an opportunity to fully leverage the coordinated physical and digital experience.

- Digital versions of traditional car use have transformed into new shared services that could one day fully replace car ownership.

- Even asset-heavy rail operators are developing low-cost services based on new, digital capabilities. These are helping them to compete with low-cost air carriers.

"The 20th century tended to set alternative transport modes against each other; the competition today is within modes as well"

Jean-Pierre Loubinoux

Notes

1 Eurostar (2020) Eurostar reports on 2019 performance. Available at: https://mediacentre.eurostar.com/mc_view?language=&article_Id=ka43z000000 kM6xAAE (archived at https://perma.cc/FYE8-AJ6N)

2 latribune.fr (2014) Le spécialiste de la reservation La Fourchette racheté par le géant américain Trip Advisor, La Tribune, 7 May. Available at: www.latribune.fr/technos-medias/internet/20140507trib000828833/le-specialiste-de-la-reservation-la-fourchette-rachete-par-le-geant-americain-trip-advisor.html (archived at https://perma.cc/3YZW-MAJ9)

3 Neveux, C. (2014) Un coup de Fourchette à 150 millions de dollars, Le JDD, 25 May. Available at: www.lejdd.fr/Economie/Le-site-La-Fourchette-rachete-a-150-millions-de-dollars-668151-3185408 (archived at https://perma.cc/GJL4-3N58)

4 TripAdvisor (n.d.) About TripAdvisor. Available at: https://tripadvisor.mediaroom.com/fr-about-us (archived at https://perma.cc/TZS4-YU6R)

5 Booking.com (2023) Booking.com launches new AI trip planner to enhance travel planning experience, 27 June. Available at: https://globalnews.booking.com/bookingcom-launches-new-ai-trip-planner-to-enhance-travel-planning-experience/ (archived at https://perma.cc/5BK6-PPS8)

6 Thomke, S. (2018) Case: Booking.com, Harvard Business School. Available at: www.hbs.edu/faculty/Pages/item.aspx?num=55158 (archived at https://perma.cc/2FP6-WALC)

7 Statista (2023) Online travel market size worldwide from 2020 to 2022, with a forecast for 2023 and 2030. Statista. Available at: www.statista.com/statistics/1179020/online-travel-agent-market-size-worldwide/ (archived at https://perma.cc/F78S-F2E4)

8 Carlson, N. (2010) Google buys huge flight search engine ITA for $700 million, Business Insider, 1 July. Available at: www.businessinsider.com/google-will-buy-ita-software-for-700-million-2010-7?r=US&IR=T (archived at https://perma.cc/2TGM-NB4N)

9 Lerman, R. (2020) Government kept to the sidelines as Google got big. Now regulators have the chance to rein the company back in, *The Washington Post*, 12 October. Available at: www.washingtonpost.com/technology/2020/10/12/google-antitrust-ita-merger/ (archived at https://perma.cc/P84E-83VD)

10 BlaBlaCar.com (n.d.) About us. Available at: https://blog.blablacar.com/about-us (archived at https://perma.cc/82XK-BPKJ)

11 Isaac, M. (2020) *Super Pumped: The battle for Uber*. W W Norton.

12 Shontell, A. (2014) All hail the Uber man! How sharp-elbowed salesman Travis Kalanick became Silicon Valley's newest star, Business Insider, 11 January.

Available at: www.businessinsider.com/uber-travis-kalanick-bio-2014-1?r=US&IR=T (archived at https://perma.cc/BFF4-B6TR)

13 Ciaccia, C. (2022) DiDi Chuxing: The Chinese ride-sharing giant, Investopedia, 15 February. Available at: www.investopedia.com/articles/small-business/012517/didi-chuxing.asp (archived at https://perma.cc/EV75-HHWJ)

14 Gorback, C. (2019) Your Uber has arrived – how ridesharing expands access, increases emissions and changes cities, Kleinman Center for Energy Policy. Available at: https://kleinmanenergy.upenn.edu/wp-content/uploads/2020/08/Your-Uber-Has-Arrived-1.pdf (archived at https://perma.cc/D4F5-RG4R)

15 SNCF (2022) C'est quoi l'innovation chez SNCF Connect & Tech? Available at: www.sncf.com/fr/innovation-developpement/innovation-recherche/innovation-chez-sncf-connect-tech (archived at https://perma.cc/V6AK-S2ZF)

16 Vairet, F. (2023) Interview – Christophe Fanichet (SNCF Voyageurs): 'Personne n'aurait pu imaginer de tells chiffres de frequentation sur les trains', Les Echos Start, 24 March. Available at: https://start.lesechos.fr/au-quotidien/voyage-expatriation/christophe-fanichet-sncf-voyageurs-personne-naurait-pu-imaginer-de-tels-chiffres-de-frequentation-sur-les-trains-1918707 (archived at https://perma.cc/7K2L-2ABK)

Smart ways to use capacity

8

- How future airports will process more people and improve their experience.
- How mass transit systems can integrate better with the urban environment to improve experience and transport more people – faster and more effectively.
- How smart traffic management systems work and why they often get tangled up in politics.
- How e-commerce logistics expands and drives the digitization of parcel shipment.

Once the symbol of a glamorous lifestyle, air travel – especially short- and medium-haul – has over the decades been commoditized in the minds of many passengers. As airports became more crowded, travellers found themselves part of a mass processing operation. After the terrorist attacks of 11 September 2001, heightened security measures were introduced, making the airport experience even less of a pleasure. Passengers typically have to arrive two or more hours before take-off and join a series of queues to check baggage, show their passport and go through security checks. This is often followed by a long wait for boarding, sometimes including an uncomfortable ride standing in a bus.

Many airports are now finding ways to be more efficient and offer a more agreeable experience. In 2016, Carrasco International Airport in Uruguay launched its 'Easy Airport' campaign to make the border crossing process quicker and easier. It then became the first fully digital airport in Latin America, with a curb-to-gate biometric journey in which passengers are identified by their physical characteristics at various checkpoints. 'Time is more important than ever,' says Diego Arrosa, CEO of Aeropuertos Uruguay. 'If I want to spend time in airports, it must be my choice, not because of the queues, the controls. We have to use biometrics, and we have to use AI to predict and to reduce the time we lose in terminals.'[1]

Air travel has become an essential part of the global economy and passenger numbers are only projected to increase. The global commercial aviation fleet is expected to expand by 33 per cent, to more than 36,000 aircraft by 2033, according to an Oliver Wyman analysis. ACI World predicts an average annual growth of 5.8 per cent in passenger traffic between 2022 and 2040, when more than 19 billion passengers will pass through world airports each year.

But the aviation industry needs to handle this increase while making less of an imprint on the environment – both local and global – and while improving the passenger experience. That means airports are trying to become smarter and more efficient and to find innovations that help increase non-aero revenues, a critical component of their financial viability. 'In aviation,' says James Cherry, former Chief Executive Officer of Montreal Airport, 'we are still scratching the surface of the value that digital services will provide in the future – to infrastructure such as airports, through digital customer service and security; to operators, through end-to-end planning and process digitalization; and to passengers, through a true online onboard experience.'

This response is an example of how the wider mobility industry is dealing with one of its greatest challenges for the twenty-first century: financial, political and geographical limits on new physical infrastructure. Though the solution to growing mobility demand might seem to be endless expansion of roads, car parks, rail track, airports and stations, they cost too much money, run into opposition or require more than the available space.

Metro lines are now very expensive to build in cities that have already been built up, as space underground is crammed with water, sewage and gas

"In aviation, we are still scratching the surface of the value that digital services will provide"
James Cherry

pipes, as well as cables for telecoms and power supply. As a result, many cities are now opting to build new tramlines, which were common in the first part of the twentieth century but in many cases abolished to make room for cars.

The British struggle over its HS2 high-speed line between London and the north of England shows how the cost of big infrastructure projects can turn them into political issues. The plan was announced in 2012 and the UK government in 2015 set a budget of more than £55 billion ($67 billion) for the whole project. But an official review in 2020 showed the cost had increased to around £106 billion for just a high-speed line connecting London and Birmingham. To build the line, the government needed to acquire land from property owners along the route. These costs tripled from just over £1 billion to £3.3 billion over the initial six-year period, according to the UK spending watchdog. Meanwhile, other costs soared as well. In 2021, the government scrapped a leg planned between Birmingham and Leeds. Then, in October 2023, amid more general concerns over the state of the UK economy, the government decided the route would only reach Birmingham. Moreover, it will be extended to central London only if enough private investment is secured. Otherwise, trains will stop in western suburbs of London and passengers travelling to the city centre will have to change.

Mobility projects also reach geographical limits – especially airports, which are often controversial due to the noise they create and their need for land near cities. Japan realized this after the expropriation of land to build Narita International Airport near Tokyo led to decades of protests, both before and after its opening in 1978. When planners wanted a better air connection for Osaka, the country's second city, they decided to build Kansai International Airport offshore. From the late 1980s, three mountains were excavated to build an artificial island, 4 km long and 2.5 km wide, reached from land by a 3 km bridge. The new airport opened in 1994.[2]

The overall challenge of the mobility industry, therefore, is to use facilities more efficiently – to get more people through stations and airports, more cars along the same stretch of road and trains along the same stretch of track, and to do all this using less energy (generating lower emissions) per person or vehicle or package of goods. In financial terms, to boost the return on investment of a mobility ecosystem, the overall system needs to deliver more mobility in passenger-km volumes (the numerator) at an optimized total cost (the denominator). Infrastructure has to become smarter rather than just bigger.

Railway stations need to allow more passengers to pass through per hour so they can access offices and shopping and then get home with ease – all the way from the station on foot if possible. And, where it has been installed, advanced signalling enables trains to run more safely and more frequently, even if they are run by different operators in an increasingly competitive environment.

On roads, autonomous vehicles can drive closer to each other more safely, meaning a greater number can pass without the need for bigger highways. Smarter highways will facilitate autonomous driving, while systems that charge for road use can induce better traffic flow, as in Singapore. Smart parking systems, which make more efficient use of urban space, have already been rolled out in much of Europe and are seen to have growth potential in the United States, according to a recent Oliver Wyman Forum survey of new mobility technology.

New airports are a continuation of efforts by the aviation industry – airports, aircraft manufacturers and airlines – to improve the passenger experience and the revenues generated from each customer. There have been three main waves over the past half century. In the mid- to late-1980s, the hub-and-spoke model of airport connections was established, while airlines developed yield-management capabilities to optimize revenues from each flight. The most-dominant carriers included American Airlines, United Airlines and Delta Airlines in North America, as well as Lufthansa, British Airways and Air France in Europe.

In the second period, starting in the 1990s, airlines grouped into alliances and invested in customer-value management. They aimed to understand and profit from high-value customers' travel wallets through loyalty programmes and other means to increase the stickiness of their relationship with these travellers, who delivered a large portion of their revenues and an even larger share of their profits. At the same time, they were coordinating schedules to reach more destinations with less aircraft. In parallel, low-cost carriers dominated the segment for travellers seeking cheap leisure flights for trips, often by using secondary airports with lower access costs.

More recently, flying has been changed by the development of large, efficient, long-range aeroplanes, such as the Boeing 787 and Airbus A350. These have enabled a greater share of direct point-to-point flights, which no longer depend on the hub-and-spoke model.

Technology innovation in airports

Biometrics and digital identity management solutions are increasing the opportunities to rethink the internal design and layout of airports, making possible on-the-move passenger processing, with no – or few – stopping points. In 2015, for example, Aruba Airport introduced a 'Happy Flow' system using facial recognition. First, a biometric photo of a passenger is taken and this is then linked to their passport. They then need only stand in front of a camera at most touchpoints – currently excluding security screening – for the system to verify their identity.

Dubai International Airport has a pre-populated biometric database and uses artificial intelligence to instantly verify passengers via their unique facial features. The system allows passengers to pass through check-in, lounges, boarding and immigration. Previously only usable by residents and citizens, the biometrics programme was extended in 2023 to international travellers. Despite concerns that travellers might resist the changes, more are embracing digitization and the smooth, efficient progress it enables through an airport: 45 per cent of air travel passengers say they would be ready to drop paper passports for digital identities, and 73 per cent of passengers today state their willingness to share their biometric data to improve airport processes, up from 46 per cent in 2019.

Before long, touchless digital ID cards may replace paper passports and boarding passes. They could act as a single source of information that confirms identity, passport and visa details, as well as past and current travel information. Combined with biometric technology, this digital ID would let a passenger clear security and other checks uninterrupted at a walking pace. Baggage management options could include bag-drop points outside the airport and collection from and delivery to origin or destination using a third-party logistics service. Paper baggage tags could be replaced by electronic tracking that can be updated with a passenger's journey details and followed on a smartphone.

'By 2050, many processes within airports will be fully autonomous, increasing the speed and quality of activities – from security to immigration and boarding,' stated Rana Nawas, Partner in Oliver Wyman's Transportation & Services practice based in Dubai and leader of the firm's 2023 wide-ranging research on the airports industry.

There will likely be no more huge departure and baggage handling lobbies – such space-saving processes will be particularly important for city airports, where land is at a premium. Global hub airports will benefit especially from faster processing of passengers and baggage, as they handle high volumes. An early example is Changi Airport in Singapore, which has a fully autonomous terminal with automated processes for check-in, baggage drop, immigration and boarding – all using facial recognition technology. Dubai International Airport has installed smart gates using biometric facial recognition to speed people's passage through the airport, and baggage screening no longer requires the removal of electronic devices from carry-on bags. Royal Schiphol Group in the Netherlands has launched a major programme to create a fully autonomous airport by 2050. Other terminals and airports will follow and build upon this model.

The enormous potential of this technology will only be realized through collaboration between regulators and the industry on data sharing in a way that maintains safety and security. Many airport CEOs agree that the different rules and regulations in different jurisdictions create a complex environment that does not facilitate the exchange of data. However, if governments and regulators coordinate their efforts, there is a prospect of an internationally recognized digital identity for all passengers by 2050. A lot of this technology is 'already here', said Justin Erbacci, CEO of Los Angeles International Airport, in the Oliver Wyman study. 'It's just about combining it and getting more standardization across the globe, so that we don't need to have multiple types of technologies depending on the airport or the airline.'

Another possibility is to reimagine major hub airports to personalize journeys through them. Currently, passengers arrive by road or rail at a main terminal and proceed through a central processing area, but it might be more efficient to combine airport facilities with surface transport links. Passengers could then reach their gates via disaggregated smaller terminals, or even directly, via sealed trains or pods. 'Imagine a long train where you've got individual pods joined together,' says Dubai Airports CEO Paul Griffiths. 'Each one is designated to go to a specified terminal. That train takes you directly to your micro terminal where your New York flight is waiting. You

"By 2050, many processes within airports will be fully autonomous, increasing speed and quality"

Rana Nawas

could even have pods that decouple as you go along. You have the intimacy of a small airport, with the complexity and economies of scale of a large one, but the passenger doesn't need to see the huge scale of background processes.' Train manufacturers are anticipating such future needs by designing a new generation of airport people movers that offer this flexibility via next-generation train control systems and train consists with better adapted and autonomous movements.

Technology, data sharing and improved surface connectivity will also improve air cargo operations, as e-commerce grows and businesses demand faster delivery along their supply chains. Memphis International Airport is the world's second-busiest cargo airport after Hong Kong. It is home to the FedEx Express global hub and handles 47 per cent of global FedEx volume, as well as 69 per cent of US domestic volume. FedEx has installed robotic arms to streamline the repetitive sorting process for small packages and letters and they each sort between 1,000 and 1,400 packages per hour. Narita Airport, another air cargo hub, is suffering from labour shortages in areas such as ground handling. President and CEO Akihiko Tamura thinks digital solutions will improve human resource and work efficiency. 'The emergence of labour shortages is an opportunity to rethink conventional approaches to airport activities,' he says.

Connecting planes and trains

City airports are often constrained in terms of capacity, particularly for infrastructure development. They tend to serve major urban centres, providing connectivity and acting as a gateway for business, leisure and family travel. They are best viewed as part of the public transport system and one of their functions is as an intermodal point to other vehicle types. To be effective, they need to be extremely easy for passengers to use. And because of their locations near population centres, they must be sensitive to their impacts – such as noise and other types of pollution – on local communities.

City airports in Europe are relatively mature, but those in Asia and the Middle East will likely be the growth engines for regional travel in coming decades. One major trend that will have an impact on airports worldwide is the move away from personal vehicle transport and towards public transport. That means airports will need to coordinate with local transport operators, so that they are connected to wider networks. After a long-term study showed that 50 per cent of Geneva Airport's passengers were arriving at the airport by public transport, the airport decided in 2022 not to add more car parking spaces. Instead, it offers free tickets to the public transport system for arriving passengers, as do surrounding hotels. The airport plans to extend the offer to departing passengers too. The goal is to encourage people to shift further from using cars and to increase public transport use to 60 per cent by 2030. 'If we were to build more parking lots, they would be empty,' says André Schneider, Chief Executive Officer of Geneva Airport. 'We have the national railway system, which has its station within the airport, and we are a hub for buses, so are already well integrated and working to improve further. That's our main target. Hence, the need to integrate airports more within overall public transport systems.' The airport intends to decarbonize 90 per cent of its vehicle fleet by 2030 by retrofitting diesel buses with electric engines. These will need charging stations, as will the private cars and ride-hailing services that continue to operate.

However, future airport connections might become individualized in other ways. It may become easy for an individual to order a bus, which they would take with four or five other people – something between a personal car and an official airport bus. Urban air mobility (UAM) and electric vertical take-off and landing aircraft (eVTOL) could also offer a fast alternative way to connect airports and surrounding cities. To make this possible, airports will need to build specialized infrastructure – for example, by repurposing airport parking lots, even though parking facilities are a key element of airports' profit model.

By around 2050, airports could be models of connected and integrated travel, featuring a variety of links – intercity and regional rail, as well as mass transit. These will be managed through integrated system-flow management concepts, which balance demand and capacity across all an airport's operations. Geneva Airport is already using airport collaborative decision-making (A-CDM), so that planes do not sit idle on the runway when their arrival gate is not ready. The airport envisages taking A-CDM a step further by integrating decision-making into the public transport system that serves the airport.

Airports are also an experience for travellers – one that plays a significant role in how visitors remember a destination. They are therefore looking for ways to reduce the time spent on arduous processing and to make the rest of the experience pleasant. One way is to replace physical lines with virtual queuing. Seattle-Tacoma International Airport (SEA) and Los Angeles International Airport (LAX) have trialled the system, while airlines including Delta have used a similar tool to notify passengers when their seat is boarding.

Travellers increasingly expect comfortable lounges, diverse food and beverage outlets and free Wi-Fi, but airports can go further. To improve the experience, airlines are requesting that lounges be upgraded with leisure options such as cinemas, pools and virtual-reality gaming. A further model could even aim to transform an airport zone into a destination rather than just a place to catch a plane: it would offer business and leisure activities, thus decoupling revenues from air transport and landing fees and therefore building commercial resilience.

Today, Asia leads the way in this diversification. More than 100 Chinese airports incorporate the principles, while Singapore's Changi Airport has an entertainment, retail, hotel and leisure complex called Jewel, with nature as its central theme. It houses the world's tallest indoor waterfall, the Rain Vortex, which is surrounded by an artificial terraced forest. In the Middle East, Riyadh Airport plans to become a so-called 'aerotropolis' with retail, residential and recreational facilities, and retail outlets. It is aiming to accommodate up to 120 million annual passengers by 2030 and 185 million by 2050.[3,4]

Airports are also exploring new ways of doing business via e-commerce, such as letting passengers order food and drink to be delivered in time for a flight and buy duty-free products online to be delivered at the destination. Airports are more than just runways and terminals, says Gert-Jan De Graaff, CEO of Brisbane Airport Corporation. They 'will further develop vibrant urban campuses that contain offices, hotel, retail offerings, but also entertainment and different modes of transport to the airport'.

Airports that serve as gateways to resorts, such as Carrasco International and Punta Cana in the Dominican Republic, aim to start the holiday experience at the airport. At Punta Cana, open-air terminals have roofs covered in palm fronds and there is even an outdoor swimming pool. Eventually, by leveraging the local culture and a sense of community warmth, airports will go beyond gateways and become a part of the destination itself.[5]

The world's best metro systems

In contrast to air travel, most public transport has not changed much over the past few decades: features that determine passenger comfort, such as seats, air conditioning and noise-reduction installations, vary little from one version to the next. One reason, according to André

Navarri, former President and Chief Operating Officer of Canada's Bombardier Transportation, is that it is usually run by public transport authorities, which focus on cost and short lead times when ordering new rolling stock products. They therefore tend to replicate prior orders, allowing for only minor innovation.

However, some metro systems in East Asia have been highly innovative in the way they integrate their stations with the cities they serve. Just like the forward-looking airports, they combine travel with shopping and entertainment facilities – and, in the case of urban transit, homes. Hong Kong's Mass Transit Railway (MTR) system covers 221 kilometres and people carry out around 5 million journeys each weekday – in a territory with a population of 7 million. In recent years, 99 per cent of trains have been on time – that is, with a delay of less than three minutes. The system is also relatively cheap to use and makes a profit.[6,7]

One remarkable thing about the MTR is the interchanges. Cross-platform interchanges allow a passenger to change from one train to another train on a different line simply by crossing an island platform between the two lines. Two intersecting lines, each with trains travelling in two directions, will have a total of eight possible interchange movements. If two island platforms are built in each of two adjacent stations, all possible movements between trains can be carried out cross-platform. Variations exist that cater for only the most common of the eight possible movements.

MTR stations are far more than just stations. Buildings sit over more than half of the system's 99 stations, amounting to millions of square metres of floor area with more millions of square metres planned. They contain retail space, where people can buy breakfast and pretty much anything else they need for the day. And they let people walk from station to office without going outside when it is raining. This model has its origin in the late 1960s and early 1970s, when Hong Kong wanted to solve traffic congestion and to create a fast commuter link between Kowloon peninsula and Hong Kong Island. The government saw the dense, efficient Tokyo and Seoul metro networks as examples to follow, so it set up a new company dedicated to the operation and maintenance of a metro rail system.

When the time came to build the network in the early 1970s, the global economy was suffering from the oil crisis. Moreover, construction costs were higher than estimated at first. Hong Kong was run according to liberal economic principles, with the government minimizing its involvement in the economy. The new Mass Transit Railway Corporation (MTRC) was set up as an independent company and not as a service provided by a governmental body. (That said, the government has control over the corporation and appoints its board and chair.) The MTRC was asked to run on 'prudent commercial principles', meaning it should find ways to earn sufficient revenues to repay its debts, meet its operating costs and, eventually, make profits.

To help the MTRC cope with the financing difficulties, the government granted it development rights above and around the stations. The Mass Transit Railway Corporation Ordinance of 1975 stated that the MTRC could 'acquire, hold and dispose of all kinds of property movable and immovable and in any manner which it thinks fit' and 'improve, develop or alter any property held by it'. That meant that, as well as operating, maintaining and investing in the metro network, the corporation could act as a developer. From the early 1980s, it developed vast commercial areas around metro stations with shopping malls, hotels and community facilities. It also managed its own residential estates and shopping malls.[8]

The designs of the developments have evolved over the decades, starting with simple residential towers and later embracing a wider range of facilities, so that they resemble self-contained towns. Early examples included the high-rise apartment blocks built in the 1980s over stations and cover relatively small sites. One of these, over Tin Hau Station on the Island Line, was completed in 1989 and has car parking and bus connections. However, these make the area less friendly to pedestrians and relatively little attention was paid to the station's surroundings.

Later projects were larger in scale. Tung Chung Station, on Lantau Island and close to the international airport that was opened in 1998, covers 21.7 hectares, an area nearly 40 times as large as that of the Tin Hau projects. It functions as an integrated, transit-oriented new town, including housing, shops, offices and a hotel. A network of elevated walkways let residents of the towers, which are more than 30 stories high, walk to the town centre and amenity podiums without having to negotiate car traffic.

Another example closer to the centre of Hong Kong shows that transit-centred development can be carried out in an upscale urban environment as well as in the form of greenfield projects. Kowloon Station, on the Airport Express line that links Hong Kong Island with the airport, was built on reclaimed land, with the last phase completed in 2010. It contains public open space, offices and residential towers, as well as five-star hotels and luxury boutiques. The results of the various developments can be seen in the MTRC's net income. Between 2000 and 2012, according to the World Bank, just 34 per cent of this came from railway and related operations, while 38 per cent came from property development. A further 15 per cent came from station commercial business and 13 per cent from rental and management business.

One reason for Hong Kong's emphasis on rail transit and the success of this model is the territory's scarce land and dense population. It has a hilly landscape, so less than a quarter of its land is usable for development. As a result, some areas are very densely populated: Kowloon, for example, has over 44,500 inhabitants per square kilometre. This makes rail, which is effective for carrying a large number of people to a dense city centre, a better mobility solution for Hong Kong than buses or cars. Moreover, the dense population means that real estate is highly valuable.

That said, some of these developments are several decades old and it will be a challenge to find the funds to update them. 'For railway authorities and property managers, there is a key question around the future needs to rejuvenate and upgrade the infrastructure over time, and how these future activities will be funded,' says TC Chew, President of Arup's Global Business Operations. 'Future upgrade costs are not always properly integrated in the public-private partnership's debt formula, hence future rounds of funding might be challenging 40 years down the road.'

Other countries in East Asia are investing heavily in mass transit, says Chew. 'Singapore has established a strong long-term masterplan for 300 km of interconnected light-rail and metro lines, which will be interweaved with the bus network. By 2030, the aim is that every citizen will be within 400 m walking distance of public transport. This is a powerful statement.'

"Future rounds of funding might be challenging 40 years down the road"
TC Chew

Riding and shopping in Japan

Japan is another example of success in combining mass transit rail with commercial and residential real estate. One reason was the conditions imposed when much of Japan's rail network was nationalized in the early twentieth century. The 1906 Railway Nationalization Law said that private railways could only build new lines that did not compete with government lines. That forced them to serve areas with relatively small populations and to look for ways to generate ridership and revenues from a limited customer base.

Their solution was to diversify. Japan's private railways typically divide their operations into four or so divisions. One is rail – mainly commuter but sometimes also intercity, resort access, airport access and freight. Another is transport – bus and taxi links to railway lines, intercity express buses and sightseeing buses. A third is real estate, both commercial and residential. And they also engage in other activities, including retail, restaurants and leisure facilities. Traffic volumes remained high. Japan's population is mostly concentrated in dense, walkable clusters on the country's few plains, which helps support mass transit networks. As a result, even when rail lost ground to buses and cars in all parts of Japan after World War II, this did not happen to the extent it did in the United States or even Europe.

As Japan's economy boomed from the 1960s, land became increasingly valuable and the railways found that their stations were sitting on prime real estate in city centres. Vast crowds of people passed through their stations every day on their way to and from work, so the companies opened malls above the stations crammed with shops and eateries, all integrated into the stations to ensure maximum footfall. One of the railways, Tobu, runs large

"By 2030, the aim in Singapore is that every citizen will be within 400m walking distance of public transport"
TC Chew

department stores, a zoo and a theme park called Tobu World Square, containing more than 100 1:25 scale models of famous buildings, such as the Statue of Liberty, the Taj Mahal and the Egyptian Pyramids. All are, of course, easily accessible by train.[9]

Tokyu Corporation – a contraction of Tokyo Express Electric Railway – is especially well known for its development-based land value-capture practices. Its oldest predecessor company was founded in 1908 and in the high-growth period from the 1960s to the 1980s, it developed so-called 'garden cities' along the extensions of its lines into prosperous Tokyo suburbs. These were designed to be self-sufficient, containing a variety of businesses, ranging from offices and supermarkets to schools and medical centres.

In the twenty-first century, Tokyu's development strategy has evolved along with demographic and business changes along its railways. Its office spaces targeted innovative industries and creative workers, distinguishing them from the offices in central Tokyo for more conventional white-collar businesses. To generate commercial synergies in station areas, Tokyu's new shopping facilities are aimed at younger consumers.

In recent years, real estate has accounted for about a third of Tokyu's net income, while a further quarter came from residential, business and leisure services. Even the formerly nationalized Japan Railway Companies have moved into real estate and retail since their 1987 privatization. Some years, JR East earned nearly a quarter of its corporate income from station space utilization and from its businesses in shopping centres and office buildings.

This use of capital on non-transport businesses is a rational strategic choice so long as the diversified operations are related, according to Kenichi Shoji, Kobe University professor of transport policy. Amusement parks and housing, for example, are destinations for rail travel, encouraging ridership. 'The diversification we are discussing here is not random but is aimed strictly at increasing rail ridership,' he wrote in a 2001 paper. 'This focused methodical long-term strategy has given these transport providers a reliable ridership base.' Unlike urban and suburban rail in Europe and North America, many Japanese operators have rail divisions that are profitable at operations level.[10]

The value of Swiss time

Sometimes, however, top-performing rail operations are mainly achieved simply through mastery of the train system. Swiss Federal Railways (SBB in

German and known as CFF in French and FFS in Italian) boasts one of the costliest timepieces in the world – and it's not a bejewelled watch made in Geneva. In 1944, Swiss electrical engineer and designer Hans Hilfiker designed a clock for the country's railways in simple Bauhaus style. Its red second hand is in the shape of a disc that station controllers used in the past to signal to train drivers that they could leave. This second hand is famous for its delayed jump: it pauses for about 1.5 seconds after it reaches 12, which serves as a reminder that trains always leave the station precisely on the minute. The clocks are ubiquitous in Swiss railway stations and can also be found in people's houses on kitchen walls and in watch format. The clock was lauded as an example of outstanding twentieth-century design by the Design Museum in London and the Museum of Modern Art in New York, both of which display originals.

The clock was considered so cool that Apple used it for the iOS6 mobile operating system it released in 2012 – without permission. At the time, the railway had said it was happy that Apple had adopted the clock, as it confirmed the status of its design. But it was also the owner of the clock's trademark and copyright and had licensed Swiss watchmaker Mondaine to use it in wall clocks, desk clocks and wrist watches since 1986. So SBB announced legal action, which was settled in 2012 for a sum reported to be CHF20 million ($21.5 million). The clock did not feature in later Apple operating systems.[11,12]

The clock is more than just a nice design, it is important to the culture of SBB because it symbolizes what the rail company does right: running trains on time – and its definition of 'on time' is arriving with no more than a three-minute delay, which compares with the five minutes of wiggle room that most railway companies allow themselves. Some 92.5 per cent of trains operated by the Swiss Federal Railways in 2022 were on time, according to the company. And of the 10 trains that were most frequently delayed in 2022, most originated in cities from neighbouring countries.[13]

A major role for punctuality is that it helps passengers make their connections. SBB's system was created in the 1980s by Benedikt Weibel, who later became chief executive of the company. His 'Rail 2000' vision was for a closely integrated system with high-frequency services. Speed was not such an interest, as it would lead to relatively little improvement in transit times in a relatively small end-to-end country. Part of the vision was that passengers would be able to catch a connecting train within 15 minutes.

Today, the SBB smartphone app is designed to make connections happen as smoothly as possible. It tells a passenger where to change trains and provides a notification when the train is getting close to the connecting station. It also says which platform the passenger should go to, how busy each carriage is in the connecting train and where to stand on the platform for each carriage. In 2022, 98.7 per cent of passengers caught their connections.[14,15]

Swiss railways have around 5,700 km of track, making it one of the densest networks in the world. SBB and other operators run even more trains per kilometre of track per day than Japan and nearly four times as many as France. Switzerland is also a major transit country for both road and rail. The key north–south Rhine-Alpine (RALP) Core Network Corridor (CNC) passes through the country and the Gotthard Tunnel alone handles some 36 million gross tons of mixed-mode rail cargo traffic every year.

'Switzerland is a laboratory for a large, interconnected urban and peri-urban network in which long-, medium- and short-haul transport operations are closely managed within a coordinated schedule,' says my colleague Joris D'Incà, Partner in Oliver Wyman's Transportation and Services practice and market leader for Switzerland.

There are plenty of signs that Swiss rail could get even better. Part of its strength comes from the enthusiastic adoption of new technology, which is needed to manage increasingly dense traffic. Central nodes such as Zurich may have a train passing through every minute or so and any interruption causes a delay. Therefore, the points (switches) are changed every six months to ensure reliability, and SBB spends more than other countries on preventive infrastructure maintenance compared to corrective maintenance, which may create operations disruptions.

....

"Switzerland is a laboratory for a large, interconnected urban and peri-urban network"

Joris D'Incà

....

Switzerland is also an early adopter of advanced signalling systems. The European Union has been promoting the adoption of ERTMS, the European Rail Traffic Management System. This is a standard for the command-and-control systems – at present, partly installed trackside and partly onboard – that maintains safety on railways, by enforcing trains' compliance with speed restrictions and signal status. The system promises to improve safety and increase the capacity of existing rail lines: by reducing the headway between trains, it can lead to a 30 per cent increase in capacity on currently existing infrastructure. As it is a Europe-wide standard, infrastructure managers will be able to purchase compatible equipment anywhere in Europe and all rolling stock suppliers will be able to bid for any opportunity. That will make the equipment market more open and competitive.[16]

Although not a member of the European Union, Switzerland is a leader in ERTMS deployment. In 2000, SBB's signalling system was complex and signalling infrastructure ageing, so it made a strategic commitment to deploy ERTMS. It has been implementing it throughout its network since 2011. This now has more than 3,000 km of track fitted with Level 1 signalling, which uses track-to-train communications, and more than 500 km of track with Level 2, which has continuous communications between the train and a radio block centre. This has boosted capacity significantly. On the line between Mattstetten and Rothrist, for example, an estimated 242 trains pass every day and headways have been reduced to 110 seconds while train speeds have increased to 200 kph.[17]

In 2007 SBB remarked that 'ETCS (European Train Control System, a central component of the ERTMS) is a hugely expensive game', but that it was needed in order to compete with road transport. At an industry gathering in London in 2018, SBB managers provided feedback on their introduction of ETCS. Passenger numbers were up 28 per cent since 2009, train movements had risen 16 per cent and track usage had improved 9 per cent. That had been carried out while reducing energy consumption by 4 per cent and train running costs by 25 per cent. 'Operational experience is highly satisfactory,' SBB managers reported on the signalling system and 'the high requirements on safety, reliability and availability are fully fulfilled'.

New ideas to make traffic flow

For many people, the most visible – and aggravating – sign of the pressure on mobility infrastructure today is the traffic gridlock in many cities. In a few years, cars with some level of autonomy might relieve some of the pressure. In a 2008 experiment, 22 drivers were instructed to drive single file round a circular track while maintaining the same speed – and, therefore, the same gap between cars. They couldn't. Within about 40 seconds, some of the cars had been brought to a halt. They started moving again, but others came to a halt, and this process continued in a series of waves. This is basically what happens when in a 'phantom' traffic jam with no obvious cause. It shows that human drivers are not very good at the kind of consistent driving skills needed to get cars through cities or along motorways.

A similar experiment was carried out in 2017, with a crucial difference. Of around 20 cars on the track, one could switch into self-driving mode. Before it did this, the cars went through a series of stop-and-go waves, like in the 2008 experiment. But when it went autonomous, the waves dissipated and the traffic kept flowing round the track. (The self-driving car seemed to hold back, keeping a steady, moderate speed, even if this allowed a gap to open between it and the preceding car. The cars with unconstrained human drivers – as observed on pretty much every road in every part of the world – appeared anxious to catch up and close the gap with the car in front.) In one of the test runs, fuel consumption of the cars in the ring was reduced by more than 40 per cent and excessive braking events dropped from 8.5 per vehicle-kilometre to near zero. The experimenters concluded that traffic flow control would be possible in real-life traffic with less than 5 per cent of cars being made autonomous.[18,19,20,21]

Before cars like these become widespread, the most effective way to keep traffic fluid is road pricing. This too involves technology – as well as bold regulation, which may not always be popular.

London introduced a congestion charge for the city centre in 2003. At the time of writing, drivers have to pay a £15 daily charge to drive in the Congestion Charge zone between 7 am and 6 pm from Monday to Friday and between noon and 6 pm at the weekend and on public holidays. However, this flat fee provides little incentive to drive during off-peak hours. A higher charge for peak hours could be justified because driving at those times creates a cost for others in the form of increased congestion.[22,23]

Singapore has a more effective system, which adjusts fees according to the time of day. Starting in 1975, the city-state made motorists buy licences to enter the central business district, covering about 7 square kilometres, during peak hours in the morning and evening on workdays. A similar licence was needed to drive on Singapore's three expressways. The scheme reduced peak-hour traffic sharply and raised average speeds inside the restricted zone by a fifth. Some drivers switched to off-peak travel or now take buses or trains, and through-traffic declined.

In 1998, the system was upgraded to an electronic road pricing (ERP) scheme that uses stored-value smart cards and automated checks. The charging was done automatically by means of microwave communication between an electronic device in the car, into which the smart card is inserted, and an overhead gantry. Instead of traditional payment plazas, cars could keep travelling.[24]

The current system aims to set prices in a way that maintains a minimum average road speed, of around 45 kph. Every quarter, the Singapore Land Transport Authority (LTA) reviews traffic conditions on the roads where the ERP is in operation and it adjusts the rates where necessary to minimize congestion and maintain traffic speeds on the roads. The ERP system was scheduled to switch to a satellite-based format in 2023 and might eventually use this to charge motorists for the distances they travel.

The LTA says the system optimizes road usage. 'The pay-as-you-use principle of ERP makes motorists more aware of the true cost of driving,' it wrote in a statement. 'A motorist... may choose a different route, mode of transport, time of travel, or not travel at all. Those who choose to pay and stay on the road will enjoy a smoother ride.'[25,26]

Thanks to ERP and other features, Singapore regularly places near the top of the multi-year Oliver Wyman Forum's annual Urban Mobility Readiness Index. Its scheme – as well as those of London and Stockholm, which also has congestion pricing – has resulted in lower carbon emission, fewer collisions and cleaner air. From an economic point of view, too, road pricing is very logical. It uses prices to ration a scarce resource (space on roads) and it makes the consumers of such a good pay for it.

After they are seen to work, road-pricing schemes have gained in popularity. London's congestion charge faced opposition at first, but later surveys showed that just one-fifth of Londoners opposed the idea of an updated road-pricing scheme. Stockholm piloted its congestion zone for seven months in 2006, after which voters narrowly chose to make it permanent – 53 per cent for and 47 per cent against. By 2011, about 70 per cent of residents backed the scheme, polls showed.[27]

At first, however, most people simply don't like the idea of road pricing as it gives the impression of charging for something that appears to be a public good and to have been free up to now. The Netherlands hoped to run a 60,000-vehicle trial of road-pricing in 2011, on the way to a nationwide scheme. But opposition politicians and motoring organizations fought so hard that the plans were dropped.[28]

As of 2023, the Metropolitan Transportation Authority (MTA) of New York was planning to introduce a charge to drive in parts of Manhattan as early as spring 2024. Though the rates had not been decided at the time of writing, a report last year said the MTA was reviewing proposals to charge drivers up to $23 for a rush-hour trip and $17 during off-peak hours. This would apply when they enter Manhattan south of 60th Street, one of the world's busiest and most traffic-clogged commercial districts.

A discount for certain low-income drivers is envisaged and some of the fees would go towards communities that may experience more traffic because of congestion pricing, including $20 million for a programme to fight asthma and $10 million to install air filtration units in schools near highways. However, the bulk of the receipts, estimated at around $1 billion a year, will go to improving New York's mass transit.

The MTA estimates that New Yorkers lose, on average, 117 hours each year on account of congestion, which adds up to roughly $2,000 in lost productivity per person. Looked at another way, driving into Manhattan imposes delays on others, slowing down buses, taxis and delivery trucks. One estimate is that taking a private car into Manhattan during the morning rush hour and back out during the evening rush hour creates congestion costs per unit of well over $100.[29]

'It seems ridiculous to argue that anyone should have the right to do that much damage to other people's lives without paying considerably more than the current tolls' levied on the use of bridges and tunnels, wrote economist and *New York Times* columnist Paul Krugman. 'That would be like arguing that some people should have the right to dump trash on their neighbor's land because they don't feel like paying the fees for garbage pickup.'

Nevertheless, the proposal triggered a storm of protest. In particular, New Jersey sued the Federal Highway Administration in July for its 'decision to rubber-stamp' its approval of congestion pricing in June 2023. It cited concerns that the tolling programme will place unfair financial and environmental burdens on New Jersey residents. This is another example of the difficulty of transport policy in a country with a lively democracy and authority divided between different levels of government and regional and urban service priorities. In contrast, Singapore, a city-state, has not had a change in governing party in its history.

E-commerce: another new transport demand

If private cars aren't already jamming up cities enough, the recent e-commerce explosion might be expected to make city traffic even worse. However, technology and new concepts mean that, overall, it could actually reduce city journeys – and the resulting emissions. Online shopping has been booming. Global retail e-commerce sales amounted to $5.2 trillion in 2021, according to one estimate – nearly four times their value in 2014. They are forecast to grow to about $8.1 trillion by 2026.[30]

For logistics companies, business-to-consumer (B2C) e-commerce drives the growth in parcels volume but complicates delivery. When businesses ship their products to other businesses, they do this in relatively large lots. But consumer delivery implies smaller shipments. An online shopper can usually choose from among multiple delivery options – to home or a pickup point, express or standard – at significantly different prices. That implies multiple-stop delivery rounds. To complement home deliveries, parcel delivery companies have also developed new capabilities and facilities, such as networks of lockers and retail associates where they can drop off parcels for consumers to pick up themselves. 'In 2008, Geopost anticipated e-commerce logistics growth and the need for an integrated pan-European B2C express delivery strategy, so it created Europe's largest ground delivery network,' says Paul-Marie Chavanne, who was Chief Executive Officer at the time after having built Geopost almost from scratch. 'The related urban logistics proposition now aims to offer 100 per cent decarbonized delivery by 2035.'

"Geopost anticipated e-commerce logistics growth and the need for an integrated pan-European B2C express delivery strategy"

Paul-Marie Chavanne

The trend towards personalization will likely increase, as Generation Z account for an increasing share of overall consumption: nearly 60 per cent of Gen Z enjoy seeing and being offered personally relatable content on social media, according to 2023 Oliver Wyman Forum research dedicated to Gen Z.[31]

There are signs that the kind of products bought online will expand. China has in some ways leapfrogged Europe and North America to become a leader in online commerce. In particular, Chinese retailers and product makers have become expert in combining online shopping with offline. For instance, store experience is still very important to Chinese Gen-Z luxury shoppers: only 1 per cent of them say they would only buy luxury fashion items and accessories online, according to 2021 research by Oliver Wyman. On the other hand, they are increasingly happy to buy luxury watches and Louis Vuitton bags online. Of Gen-Z luxury spenders in China, 88 per cent said they bought luxury items both online and offline. In the past 12 months, 38 per cent of their luxury spending had been carried out online. Even among the over-25s, just 24 per cent said they shopped exclusively offline for luxury items.[32]

It seems only a question of time before high-end consumers in Western markets buy luxury products online. That will come with extra demands on the quality of delivery, which many consumer goods brands consider to be part of their value proposition: the higher the value of their products and consumer base, the higher the requirements for qualitative, reliable, branded and, increasingly, sustainable delivery.

This unprecedented personalization can make each shipment or trip complex to engineer and serve. A significant part of the value of the shipment lies in the coordination of choices and the price paid by the end-customer is split among the operators that implement the delivery. Moreover, many of these options – in particular multi-stop delivery of small parcels – are costly by nature. But shippers are under pressure to do it all for less money. Platforms and branded websites increasingly integrate transport costs within the product cost, so that they can offer customers 'free shipping'. In mass markets, this represents a real margin squeeze for the delivery operator.

Restructuring and consolidation

The result has been pressure on logistics and last-mile delivery providers to create efficiencies and reduce their operating costs. Not all operators have been able to cope, leading to significant consolidation, especially of parcel-delivery services. Geopost, which is wholly owned by France's La Poste Group, made multiple European acquisitions, notably BRT in Italy, SEUR in Spain and DPD (Deutsche Packet Dienst) across Europe.

GEODIS, the other French logistics leader, is also leveraging acquisitions at global scale to provide its customers more holistic coverage. In 2015 GEODIS acquired OHL, one of the world's leading third-party logistics companies, operating more than 120 value-added distribution centres in North America and providing integrated global supply chain management solutions. In 2022, the same GEODIS acquired American company Need It Now Delivers, which significantly expanded GEODIS's US presence in the areas of contract logistics and final-mile delivery and strengthened its end-to-end freight network domestically in the US and internationally. 'The logistics provider needs an integrated, end-to-end view of the customer's supply chain,' says Chief Executive Officer Marie-Christine Lombard. 'That's why we, at GEODIS, are continuing to focus on inorganic growth, especially in the United States.'

United Parcel Service (UPS) tried to buy struggling Dutch parcel company TNT in 2013 to boost its presence in Europe and emerging markets, but the European Commission blocked the attempt because of concerns that the transaction would diminish competition in select segments and markets and lead to higher prices. The General Court of the European Union later annulled that decision, but not before UPS rival FedEx had acquired TNT instead. UPS sued the EU antitrust regulator, seeking €1.74 billion (about $2 billion) in compensation, but this claim was rejected.[33,34]

Some traditional postal services recognized the need to move into premium parcel delivery in the 2000s, when FedEx and UPS dominated the space. Starting from largely domestic footprints in the United States, those companies have become multinational, multimodal networks serving ship-

"The logistics provider needs an integrated, end-to-end view of the customer's supply chain"
Marie-Christine Lombard

pers and receivers on a global basis with unified internationally recognized brands in Europe, North America and beyond.

One example is Canada Post, which was tied to public service requirements at the start of the twenty-first century, when volumes of mail, its core business, eroded sharply as communications switched from paper by mail to digital via email. Recognizing the potential growth from e-commerce and the digital transformation of logistics and mail, in 2011 the company hired Deepak Chopra as CEO from Pitney Bowes, a specialist in mail-related technology, ogistics and financial services. The crown corporation was tied to public service requirements and standards, which were extremely difficult to maintain economically: Canada has, on average, just four inhabitants per square kilometre, which makes it hugely costly to cover the entire country with a universal service level. Chopra and his leadership team decided to set parcels at the core of a new operating model, providing a full suite of services from online ordering to tracking. He built a leadership programme for the top 300 managers with Queen's University in Ontario. This aimed to make the management culture more commercial and experimental – better suited to growing a business in the digital age.

Canada Post persuaded the largest Canadian shippers and retailers that it could offer capacity and density within, from and to Canada that no other service in the country could match. In a matter of two years, Canada Post took a leading share of the country's e-commerce distribution market, providing the full suite of services end to end. This success helped it to boost its brand image, especially among the growing millennials consumer segment (born between 1981 and 1996), and it became one of Canada's top 10 brands. 'Launching a postal incumbent into e-commerce delivery required a massive transformation consisting of both substantive and symbolic structural changes and a shift in leadership mindset,' says Chopra. 'We turned our network operating model upside down and centred it on parcel flows rather than traditional mail traffic.'

"Launching a postal incumbent into e-commerce delivery required a massive transformation"
Deepak Chopra

How technology keeps parcels flowing

As they strive to meet the new demands of e-commerce, delivery firms must also meet another new set of requirements. Consumers in developed countries are becoming increasingly conscious of societal and environmental challenges and governments are responding. Low-emissions zones in many cities already have an impact on delivery vehicles and environmental regulations are expected to be tightened in coming years.

Some delivery companies are investing in urban logistics solutions that reduce emissions and fit with new expectations for quality of life, such as reducing noise and congestion and improving air quality. La Poste Group in France set up such a business unit in 2014 under the Urby brand, based on a concept which anticipates future regulations to reduce congestion and transport emissions. Urby builds logistics centres in the outskirts of a city, which receive incoming goods and then distribute them to stores and companies via zero- or low-emissions vehicles, such as small vans or cargo bikes. These vehicles also take goods and objects for recycling back to the logistics centre, so that they can be further transported. In addition, there are small urban logistics centres, which can help local businesses with their needs to store goods, collect recyclable items and deliver purchases to consumers. To date, Urby has set up operations in about 20 French cities. However, it is still largely viewed as an experiment (it was showcased in the French pavilion at Dubai Expo 2020) and its economic performance is undisclosed.[35]

Among the existing components of parcel delivery, every link in the logistics value chain is also impacted by climate change and sustainability requirements. Linehaul freight carriers will need to decarbonize their operations. A 2023 Oliver Wyman analysis of six European countries showed that home delivery of a single, 1 kg parcel through a country's most common postal system in two days or more generates an average of 1,075 g of CO_2e, a measure of the global-warming effect of greenhouse gases in terms of the equivalent quantity of carbon dioxide. It also showed that the best way to minimize emissions per parcel was not to reduce delivery speed but to optimize last-mile delivery and use the largest possible vehicles in the linehaul and maximize their loads.[36]

Warehousing contractors can reduce their environmental impact by building their facilities closer to the areas where consumers live, as well as setting up efficient, transparent links to e-commerce platforms. The location and size of their buildings – as well as others, such as delivery stations and pickup points – are the second most important factor influencing emissions. Buildings' impact can be even greater than that of transportation, especially in countries that depend heavily on fossil fuels to produce electric power, such as Germany and Italy.

For last-mile distributors, customer interface is essential to reduce missed deliveries and optimize the customer experience. One example is a digital predictive model for last-mile delivery, which forecasts a tight delivery time window and communicates to the person about to receive the parcel. Geopost, which operates under the DPD brand in many countries, uses a comprehensive last-mile delivery routing modelling and communication service called Predict. This forecasts delivery time to a window as narrow as two hours or less. It informs the receivers, who can ask for rescheduling or rerouting if they are not going to be available. In the United Kingdom, the initial deployment market, Predict enabled DPD to achieve a market-leading first-time-right rate. This leads to lower CO_2 emissions, minimizes the number of missed-delivery calls to the customer service department and significantly reduces the number of returns – in some cases by as much as 50 per cent. 'Supply chains, shippers and receivers demand precision more than speed today,' says Paul-Marie Chavanne. 'This lets them optimize inventory and reduce return rates. Digitalization is key to enabling this shift.'

Overall, the environmental impact of e-commerce appears to be positive, according to an Oliver Wyman study from 2021. While e-commerce needs delivery vans to circulate, these reduce car traffic by between four and nine times the amount of traffic they generate because fewer consumers go to the shops by car. And land use for e-commerce is lower than for physical retail when logistics, selling space and related parking space are included. Offline shopping results in between 1.5 and 2.9 times more greenhouse gas emissions than online shopping.[37]

"Supply chains, shippers and receivers demand precision more than speed today"

Paul-Marie Chavanne

KEY TAKEAWAYS

- To cater to denser populations and to cope with limited footprints and funding concerns, mobility systems need to transport more people without dramatic increases in the size or number of roads, railways, stations and airports.

- Digital technology solutions are being developed that meet many of the challenges and improve the cost, quality and experience of commuting and travel.

- Some East Asian railways have integrated city infrastructure and public transport. The operators have helped to construct and logically distribute towns around their mass transit hubs, letting people get around easily and funnelling consumers to shopping centres and other attractions.

- Smart – and paying – traffic systems may be the best way to keep cars flowing in cities. But they often meet public opposition. That is leading to a growing number of experiments and a variety of systems worldwide.

- The expansion of e-commerce logistics and digitized parcel shipments is revolutionizing retailing and streamlining the economics of B2C supply chains, while contributing to the sector's decarbonization.

Notes

1 Oliver Wyman Forum (2023) The evolution of airports, a flight path to 2050. Available at: www.oliverwymanforum.com/content/dam/oliver-wyman/ow-forum/mobility/2023/Evolution_of_Airports-Report.pdf (archived at https://perma.cc/X3QC-HKRB)

2 Key Aero (2018) The airport built from tree mountains'. Available at: www.key.aero/article/airport-built-three-mountains (archived at https://perma.cc/FF8T-V7DQ)

3 jewelchangiairport.com. (n.d.) Experience wonder at Jewel Changi Airport – Jewel Changi Airport. Available at: www.jewelchangiairport.com/en.html (archived at https://perma.cc/9XXT-7CRZ)

4 Lane, M. (2022) Plan revealed for Riyadh airport expansion to accommodate 185 million passengers by 2050, The Moodie Davitt Report, 28 November. Available at: www.moodiedavittreport.com/plan-revealed-for-riyadh-airport-expansion-to-accommodate-185-million-passengers-by-2050/ (archived at https://perma.cc/XE2T-TKHQ)

5 Alcivar, C. (2019) This outdoor swimming pool at Punta Cana Airport is worth the plunge, 6 April. Available at: www.vanemag.com/punta-cana-airport-outdoor-swimming-pool/ (archived at https://perma.cc/4WSA-DY4T)

6 Suzuki, H., Murakami, J., Hong, Y.-H. and Tamayose, B. (2015) Financing transit-oriented development with land values: Adapting land value capture in developing countries. The World Bank. doi: https://doi.org/10.1596/978-1-4648-0149-5 (archived at https://perma.cc/2G67-74FV)

7 Transport and Housing Bureau (2014) Follow-ups on the service suspension of Tseung Kwan O Line and part of Kwun Tong Line on 16 December 2013, and report on subsequent major incidents on East Rail Line and Light Rail. Available at: www.legco.gov.hk/yr13-14/english/panels/tp/tp_rdp/papers/tp_rdp0228cb1-980-5-e.pdf (archived at https://perma.cc/XTC5-BHBE)

8 Musil, C. (2020) Rail-plus-property development: A model for financing public transportation in developing cities in Southeast Asia?, Amsterdam University Press. Available at: www.academia.edu/43320687/_Rail-plus-Property_Development_A_Model_for_Financing_Public_Transportation_in_Developing_Cities_in_Southeast_Asia_Cl%C3%A9ment_Musil (archived at https://perma.cc/4AC8-UMR2)

9 Tobu World Square (n.d.) Guide map. Available at: https://en.tobuws.co.jp/park-guide/ (archived at https://perma.cc/Y2GR-7KJA)

10 Shoji, K. (2001) Lessons from Japanese experiences of roles of public and private sectors in urban transport, *Japan Railway & Transport Review*, 29, 12–18. Available at: www.ejrcf.or.jp/jrtr/jrtr29/pdf/f12_sho.pdf (archived at https://perma.cc/2V2P-C5QT)

11 SwissInfo (2013) Apple drops Swiss Railways clock. Available at: www.swissinfo.ch/eng/end-of-an-icon_apple-drops-swiss-railways-clock/36883422 (archived at https://perma.cc/6H5T-UMKK)

12 House of Switzerland (n.d.) 10 good reasons to travel by train in Switzerland. Available at: https://houseofswitzerland.org/swissstories/society/10-good-reasons-travel-train-switzerland (archived at https://perma.cc/R6UJ-EREQ)

13 De Boer, J. (2023) The 10 most delayed trains in Switzerland in 2022 revealed, IAMEXPAT.CH, 31 January. Available at: www.iamexpat.ch/expat-info/swiss-expat-news/10-most-delayed-trains-switzerland-2022-revealed#:~:text=With%2093%2C7%20percent%20of,the%20country%20is%20famous%20for (archived at https://perma.cc/MH8H-A453)

14 Not Just Bikes (2022) Why Swiss trains are the best in Europe. YouTube. Available at: www.youtube.com/watch?v=muPcHs-E4qc (archived at https://perma.cc/6JRA-T3LB)

15 SwissInfo (2023) Swiss Federal Railways judges itself 'very punctual' in 2022. Available at: www.swissinfo.ch/eng/society/swiss-federal-railways-judged--very-punctual--in-2022/48247710#:~:text=Some%2092.5%25%20of%20trains%20operated,the%20company%20said%20on%20Tuesday (archived at https://perma.cc/V95J-3ZDG)

16 ERTMS (2021) Factsheet #28 – ERTMS Advantages. Available at: www.ertms.net/wp-content/uploads/2021/06/28.-ERTMS-Advantages-factsheet_final.pdf (archived at https://perma.cc/T7N2-RQKB)

17 ERTMS (2021) Factsheet #6 – ERTMS Deployment in Switzerland. Available at: www.ertms.net/wp-content/uploads/2021/06/6-ERTMS-Deployment-in-Switzerland.pdf (archived at https://perma.cc/3EB2-UHET)

18 O'Neill, S. (2021) Alexandre Bayen is a driving force behind mixed-autonomy traffic, Amazon Science, 23 August. Available at: www.amazon.science/research-awards/success-stories/alexandre-bayen-is-a-driving-force-behind-mixed-autonomy-traffic (archived at https://perma.cc/H649-MJPU)

19 Lunawat, D. (2019) How do driverless trains work?, ScienceABC, 6 May. Available at: www.scienceabc.com/innovation/driverless-trains-work.html (archived at https://perma.cc/WZ93-QQ5M)

20 www.youtube.com. (n.d.) Traffic jam without bottleneck – experimental evidence. Available at: www.youtube.com/watch?v=7wm-pZp_mi0 (archived at https://perma.cc/73YJ-WKXL)

21 www.youtube.com. (n.d.) Self-driving cars experiment demonstrates dramatic improvements in traffic flow. Available at: www.youtube.com/watch?v=2mBjYZTeaTc&t=9s (archived at https://perma.cc/38W5-CRHA)

22 *The Economist* (2018) The right way to handle congestion. Available at: www.economist.com/leaders/2018/08/25/the-right-way-to-handle-congestion (archived at https://perma.cc/Q8UE-LFQH)

23 Richardson, M. (1993) Singapore Notebook: Big Brother works to thin out Singapore's traffic jams, *The New York Times*, 19 April. Available at: www.nytimes.com/1993/04/19/business/worldbusiness/IHT-singapore-notebook-big-brother-works-to-thin-out.html (archived at https://perma.cc/VJ7N-HXNX)

24 *The Economist* (1997) Singapore's plan. Available at: www.economist.com/special/1997/12/04/singapores-plan (archived at https://perma.cc/3XDJ-HRY2)

25 Singapore Ministry of Transport (2022) How ERP works as a speed booster. Available at: www.mot.gov.sg/what-we-do/motoring-road-network-and-infrastructure/Electronic-Road-Pricing/Details/how-erp-works-as-a-speed-booster (archived at https://perma.cc/89HD-UHR9)

26 Tan, C. (2020) New ERP system to start in 2023 but no distance-based charging yet; replacement of IU from second half of 2021, *The Straits Times*, 8 September. Available at: www.straitstimes.com/singapore/transport/new-erp-system-to-start-2023-but-no-distance-based-charging-just-yet (archived at https://perma.cc/4XQG-UJZR)

27 Bellafente, G. (2023) Congestion pricing is coming. It doesn't have to be painful, *The New York Times*, 8 September. Available at: www.nytimes.com/2023/09/08/nyregion/congestion-pricing-.html (archived at https://perma.cc/4DBP-TFDG)

28 *The Economist* (2017) How and why road-pricing will happen. Available at: www.economist.com/international/2017/08/03/how-and-why-road-pricing-will-happen (archived at https://perma.cc/5R69-8ZDD)

29 Larangeira, G. (2022) Opinion: The congestion pricing toll really should be $80, StreetsBlogNYC, 27 January. Available at: https://nyc.streetsblog.org/2022/01/27/opinion-the-congestion-pricing-toll-really-should-be-80 (archived at https://perma.cc/T9QL-3Z4D)

30 Chevalier, S. (2022) Global retail e-commerce market size 2014–2026. Statista. Available at: www.statista.com/statistics/379046/worldwide-retail-e-commerce-sales/ (archived at https://perma.cc/6ZXP-ZYZH)

31 Oliver Wyman Forum (2023) What business needs to know about the generation changing everything. Available at: www.oliverwymanforum.com/content/dam/oliver-wyman/ow-forum/template-scripts/a-gen-z/pdf/A-Gen-Z-Report.pdf (archived at https://perma.cc/2ULU-A2AQ)

32 Wouters, I. and Sham, K. (2021) The new faces of Chinese luxury shoppers, Oliver Wyman. Available at: www.oliverwyman.com/content/dam/oliver-wyman/v2/publications/2021/dec/the-new-faces-of-chinese-luxury-shoppers.pdf (archived at https://perma.cc/3Q27-Z73L)

33 Bray, C. (2018) UPS seeks more than $2 billion in damages over TNT bid, *The New York Times – Deal Book*, 26 February. Available at: www.nytimes.com/2018/02/26/business/dealbook/ups-tnt-eu.html (archived at https://perma.cc/H3BQ-CX4Y)

34 Yun Chee, F. (2022) UPS loses $2 billion claim for EU veto on TNT bid, Reuters, 23 February. Available at: www.reuters.com/business/eu-court-rejects-ups-2-billion-claim-eu-veto-tnt-bid-2022-02-23/ (archived at https://perma.cc/JR8G-KWS3)

35 La Poste Groupe (n.d.) Urby, spécialiste de la livraison de marchandises en centre-ville. Available at: www.lapostegroupe.com/fr/urby-le-specialiste-de-la-livraison-de-marchandises-en-centre-ville (archived at https://perma.cc/SR5D-NH5K)

36 Oliver Wyman (2023) Delivery Decarbonization Pathway. Available at: www.oliverwyman.com/content/dam/oliver-wyman/v2/publications/2023/may/Delivery%20Decarbonization%20Pathway-Long%20Report.pdf (archived at https://perma.cc/J4QM-HEJL)

37 Oliver Wyman (2021) Is e-commerce good for Europe? Available at: www.oliverwyman.com/content/dam/oliver-wyman/v2/publications/2021/apr/is-ecommerce-good-for-europe.pdf (archived at https://perma.cc/A8RC-6ASK)

Future visions 9

- The challenges and possibilities of mobility on the world's fastest growing continent.
- How to tackle the industry's toughest decarbonization challenge.
- Some disruptive new technologies that could revolutionize transport – or perhaps just remain niche activities.
- And to conclude, nine themes to capture possible scenarios for the future of mobility.

Where this book looks to the future, it does so mostly in areas where there are at least the beginnings of a roadmap. These areas are also where most of our panel of 30 leaders and experts have been operating. We may not know precisely how transport systems will be decarbonized – but we have a fair idea about some of the underlying technologies that will help. Digitally-enabled mobility-as-a-service is developing in various forms and directions – but we can already guess the kind of solutions and services that may be offered. It's not clear exactly what future cities and their transport systems will look like – but we can see plenty of technologies and solutions being developed that will likely enable more traffic and more passengers to flow without giant new infrastructure.

Other challenges and possibilities are less certain. Africa has major mobility challenges and opportunities, but the bottlenecks are more financial and political than technological. In the case of net-zero aircraft fuel, there are questions as to whether any technology can be developed at scale in time to make a difference. The technology for autonomous vehicles is moving forward, but we don't know how far it will go or by when. Urban air mobility will happen in some form – but its scale could range from limited specialist services to a common means of getting around.

To conclude this exploration of the transformations in mobility, I explore these challenges and possibilities and discuss nine themes that emerged from my conservations with mobility leaders and experts which will shape the future of mobility.

How to keep Africa moving

Lagos, Nigeria, already the most populous city in Africa with more than 15 million people in 2023, is forecast to become the biggest in the world later this century, with a population reaching more than 50 million, according to some estimates. What's unclear is how all those people are going to get around. After a decade of delays, Lagos's only metro line started operations in September 2023. The city also doesn't have a functioning bus system. Instead, nearly 100,000 informal 'danfos' – mostly aging vans bought used from richer countries – are the main form of public transport. They carry 20 or so passengers and compete for space on the roads with hawkers and informal street markets. The result is gridlock. It can take three hours to travel 15 km, according to some reports.[1]

Despite the challenges, millions continue to pour into Lagos from the rest of Nigeria, fleeing poverty or conflict. Nigeria's birthrate is one of the world's highest, so the city is also growing rapidly on its own. A 2020 study published in *The Lancet* forecast that Nigeria will become more populous than China by the end of the century.[2,3]

Lagos is an extreme example of a phenomenon in various parts of the world and especially in sub-Saharan Africa. Only half the world's urban population has convenient access to public transport, according to 2019 UN data from 610 cities in 95 countries. In sub-Saharan Africa, just 33 per cent of the urban population have access to public transport, compared with 75 per cent in Europe and North America. In sub-Saharan Africa, 3 per cent have access to high-capacity systems within 1 km, compared with 32 per cent in Europe and North America.[4,5,6]

As a consequence, unlike people in many other regions of the world, many Africans travel on foot or use motor vehicles collectively. In Dakar, for example, 70 per cent of all journeys are made on foot. This is the kind of practice that many Western cities are actively trying to encourage to reduce congestion, emissions and pollution. However, in most of Africa, this practice has come from poverty, not as a result of a deliberate climate policy. For the most part, walking in Africa is not a pleasant experience: 9 out of 10 roads on which pedestrians travel do not have safe and barrier-free footpaths. Using buses and other forms of motorized transit each day would cost the poorest 20 per cent of households in African cities an average of 30–50 per cent of their incomes. The shortage of affordable transport in Africa's sprawling cities limits people's range of movement and makes it difficult to secure formal employment. It's essential to improve city mobility in Africa.

Birthrates are expected to shrink rapidly in some parts of the world – East Asia, eastern and southern Europe – and level off in others, such as the United States. But most of Africa's population will continue to grow rapidly this century. As well as Nigeria, Ethiopia, the Democratic Republic of Congo and Tanzania are forecast to be among the 10 most populous countries by 2100. The continent is also urbanizing at unprecedented speed, already turning Cairo, Kinshasa and Lagos into megacities with more than 10 million inhabitants each. Others will follow soon and by 2040, Johannesburg, Luanda, Dar es Salaam, Nairobi and Abidjan are also expected to be megacities. In some projections by the University of Toronto's Global Cities Institute, Africa will account for at least 10 of the world's 20 most populous cities in 2100. Without solutions, the transport needs of these growing urban populations could exacerbate the problems of cities.[7]

The potential to leapfrog?

Many Western cities are suffering from their past development when they were designed for privately owned vehicles and high-emission transport systems. In much of North America, car dependent suburbs sprawl over vast areas which are not dense enough for effective public transport. In Europe, historic city centres were tightly concentrated around rivers, ports and other commercial hubs and they became congested after cars were let into their cramped streets. But Africa is still in the early stages of motorization. Of the nearly 1.45 billion vehicles on the road worldwide in 2022, just 26 million were in Africa. The continent therefore has the potential to jump straight to low- or zero-emissions transport and modes that do not take up as much space as individual cars.[8]

Telecommunications could be a precedent. African countries have little fixed-line telephone infrastructure, but Africans in many countries are well connected: they skipped the fixed-line stage and jumped straight into the mobile era. Mobile phones first arrived in Nigeria in 2001, when a model with basic functionality was a luxury only a few could afford. After two decades of exponential growth, the country had nearly 190 million mobile or SIM connections in January 2021, according to DataReportal. This enabled an explosion in mobile banking, enabling access to financial services without the need for banks to develop networks of physical branches.

Is it conceivable that Africa will also leapfrog, in some ways, more industrialized regions in transport? One contribution could come from the use of mobile phone data for evidence-based decision-making and planning. More than 80 per cent of Africa's urban areas have 4G network coverage and 41 per cent of Africans have an active mobile broadband connection. There are already examples of digital firms working in this space. In 2013, Digital Matatus, a Kenyan American research group, created the continent's first digital map of a minibus network, for the city of Nairobi. WhereIsMyTransport, founded in Cape Town in 2015, collects data from more than 50 cities in the Global South, including some in Africa, which transport planners can use to make investment decisions. DigitalTransport4Africa (DT4A) represents a large, diverse network of city governments, residents, universities, civic technology companies, local and other governments, and international development partners. Together, they are committed to building digital commons and applying the Digital Principles of Development to the goals of Sustainable Urban Mobility and Access across Urban Africa.

Why electrification is harder in Africa

Perhaps an important task is to electrify the African vehicle fleet to reduce transport-related emissions. Today, 80 per cent of urban residents in Africa do not own a motor vehicle, but motor traffic is growing faster than the population because of high transport demand and the lack of appealing alternatives.

This growth could add fuel to the climate crisis at just the wrong time. Between 1990 and 2017, Africa's CO_2 emissions rose 123 per cent, slower than in Asia but more than twice as fast as the global average. That trend would put the world's climate goals out of reach. Africans would be particularly vulnerable, as millions live in low-lying coastal regions, which would be threatened by rising sea levels. If global warming is to be kept below 2°C relative to preindustrial times, the goal of the 2015 Paris Agreement, Africa's CO_2 emissions too will have to peak soon and fall to net zero by the end of the century.

The transport sector will have an important role to play in the reduction of Africa's emissions, while also improving mobility. The electrification of mopeds could be relatively quick. Electric mopeds are more expensive than conventional models with combustion engines, but the lower energy, maintenance and repair costs of electric two-wheelers make up for that. The total cost of ownership (TCO) is lower than that of conventional two-wheelers after just five years.

However, the electrification of cars and trucks is likely to take longer. One reason is the large proportion of old, used vehicles sold: more than 60 per cent of those added to the fleet annually in Africa are imported used vehicles, though this varies from zero in South Africa, which bans these imports, to 97 per cent in Kenya. Because EVs are relatively new everywhere in the world, and they have only recently started to become a mass product, there are almost no used EVs available for sale. New EVs are not able to compete on price with old, low-cost internal combustion vehicles that are readily available. Electric cars and trucks will only be able to compete in Africa without incentives when large numbers of used four-wheel EVs land on the market at low prices, something unlikely before at least the mid-2030s. 'Africa can avoid the serious problems of mass motorization that Europe and North America have experienced, even as its rate of motorization grows and increasing numbers of people use motorized transport,' said a report by Agora Verkehrswende and the Deutsche Gesellschaft für Internationale Zusammenarbeit (GIZ). 'To do this, Africa must tackle a difficult challenge: ceasing its risky reliance on the import of end-of-life vehicles and developing value chains in its domestic industries.'[9]

Mopeds also present less of a recharging challenge. They have relatively small batteries, which can be charged on mini-grids, or swapped for a fully charged battery when an even faster turnaround is needed. However, four-wheeled vehicles that travel more than 100 km a day with limited stops would require costly fast-charging infrastructure to be installed, say along major roads or in commercial centres. An even more basic issue is access to electricity. In North Africa, almost everyone has this, even in rural areas. But only 5 per cent of the rural population of central African countries have electricity. Even where there is a power supply, it is often unreliable.

However, Africa has enormous potential to generate renewable electricity from the sun, and water as well as plenty of wind. In particular, Africa has 60 per cent of the world's best solar resources. Aside from a few countries, these natural resources have so far contributed almost nothing to the overall electricity supply. But that could soon change. In its Sustainable Africa Scenario, the International Energy Agency projects that the 260 gigawatts of power plant capacity currently installed on the African continent will nearly double from 2022 to 2030 – and that the bulk of the increase will be solar, wind and hydropower plants.[10]

Paratransit – from chaos to solution?

In the meantime, projects like the Lagos metro system stall for lack of funds. A network of five lines is envisioned, but so far only a section of one line, the Blue Line, has started to run. This was originally planned to be completed in

2011, but it was delayed because of funding shortages. That's a common problem in Africa, where tax revenue tends to be low.

For now, people get around through informal services, such as Lagos's danfos. Shared taxis in the form of minibuses have long been a major form of transport in many African cities and they have been joined recently by passenger cars, mopeds, rickshaws and bicycles. Collectively, the services are termed 'paratransit' – flexible transport services that mostly respond to demand instead of following fixed routes and schedules. The paratransit share in public transport is estimated to be 58 per cent in Cape Town, 86 per cent in Accra, 87 per cent in Nairobi and 80 per cent in Kampala. Around 100,000 people are employed in paratransit in Kampala and 500,000 in Lagos.

There are plenty of downsides to paratransit: poor working conditions for the drivers, a high risk of accidents and low levels of comfort, which make it hard for older people or those with limited mobility to use. Also, the services simply respond to urban growth rather than playing a role in shaping it. But they are a major way for people to get around most African cities and will continue to offer mobility options in rural areas. Despite the population explosion in its cities, Africa is the world's least urbanized continent, with 57 per cent of people living in rural areas. One billion people still live more than 2 km away from a usable road, according to the World Bank. Only one in three rural dwellers lives within 2 km of the nearest all-season road, making it hard for them to handle everyday challenges.[11]

A good way to improve mobility in African cities would be to regulate these informal services better. That could include fixed stops, better licensing systems and improvements to road and occupational safety standards. The report by Agora Verkehrswende and GIZ recommended several approaches. One is formalization: contracts between local governments and operators to define pricing and service conditions in a way that ensures profitability for the transport services, as well as convenience and reliability for passengers. A second is to use digital technologies to map routes and carry out online payments. Governments could also subsidize the informal transport sector so that paratransit operators can modernize and electrify their vehicles. In any case, action is needed fast.

Sustainable air fuels

Globally, aviation is struggling with a hugely challenging ambition where action is also needed. Like other modes of transport, it needs to reduce carbon emissions to net zero to meet its global climate goals. But unlike the others, there is no commercialized technology yet that can fully achieve this.

Aircraft manufacturers, airlines and airports have long been working to make their products and operations more efficient. But annual passenger numbers are forecast to double to around 10 billion by 2050 and these improvements will not be enough to contain emissions. Engineering and operational advances don't produce the efficiency gains they once did and today they reduce fuel consumption by only 1 per cent or 2 per cent a year. Without progress in new forms of propulsion, carbon emissions from aviation will increase 40 per cent or so by 2050.[12]

A number of technologies are being developed that might fix the problem, including hydrogen- and battery-powered planes (see Chapter 6). So far, however, these are mainly a prospect for shorter routes and most global carbon emissions today come from longer flights. Moreover, these machines are unlikely to be manufactured in volume before the second half of the 2030s, after which it would take several decades to replace the tens of thousands of existing fossil fuel-propelled aircraft. That would be too late to meet the goals of the Paris Agreement, which include the achievement of net-zero emissions by 2050.

The best hope – at least until 2050 and probably longer – for the industry is sustainable air fuels (SAFs), which emit up to 80 per cent less carbon dioxide than conventional jet fuel and are currently sometimes used in a blend with conventional fuel. These are defined by the International Air Transport Association (IATA) as fuels that can be continually and repeatedly resourced in a manner consistent with economic, social and environmental aims and that conserve an ecological balance by avoiding depletion of natural resources. In addition, they meet the technical and certification requirements for use in commercial aircraft: They are a 'drop-in fuel', meaning they can be easily incorporated into existing fuelling systems, and they require relatively minor changes to aircraft design or the supporting infrastructure in airports. Obviously, they must not depend on conventional fossil-sources, such as oil, coal and natural gas.

Current global aviation emissions are 1.8 gigatonnes of CO_2. According to one recent Oliver Wyman analysis, a pathway to net zero by 2050 might require 25 per cent of that to be reduced through improvements to aircraft and operations, a combined 13 per cent through electric and hydrogen propulsion, and 6 per cent through carbon-capture technologies. That would leave more than half (55 per cent) of the reduction to come from SAFs.

SAFs have the same basic chemical makeup as the fossil fuels that aircraft currently use and they release carbon dioxide into the air when they burn. But this should be around the same amount that is used up during the various stages of their manufacturing: when the fuels come from biomass, for example, burning them simply returns to the atmosphere CO_2 that was previously absorbed by plants. The fuels fall into two main categories: biofuels and synthetic electrofuels, or e-fuels.

Types of SAF

E-fuels are made from two main building blocks, hydrogen and carbon dioxide. But their manufacture is expensive today because the process is inefficient and still isn't done at commercial scale. Proof of concept is expected only in 2025 at the earliest and production would only follow later. They would require a massive amount of renewable electricity to make the hydrogen needed and require a high level of capital investment. Their projected share of total SAF supply by 2030 is just 1–2 per cent. However, they could have a large role in the longer term because they reduce carbon dioxide emissions more than other SAFs and they won't be limited by supply, unlike biofuels.

Biofuels come from a range of biological sources. One technology is gasification, a process that converts biomass- or fossil fuel-based carbonaceous materials into gases. Another is the conversion of alcohols to jet fuel based on catalytic steps. However, the technology is not mature in either of these two cases: commercial tests are still under development and there is no large-scale production. In both cases, the feedstock would consist of corn and sugar crops, agricultural and forestry residues, municipal solid waste and purposely grown cellulosic energy crops. Alcohol-to-jet fuels could face regulatory restrictions to prevent excessive diversion of food crops, while the gasification process has low yields.

For now, the most realistic SAF comes from HEFA: hydroprocessed esters and fatty acids. This fuel is projected to make up between 70 per cent and 90 per cent of SAFs in 2030. It uses feedstocks including waste, residue fats (such as vegetable oil, used cooking oil and animal fats) and purposely grown plants. The technology is mature: it has been shown to be safe and scalable, and it requires relatively little capital investment. This makes it the most realistic and least expensive current technology and it is the source of more than 95 per cent of commercial SAFs today. However, long-term growth will be limited by the supply of feedstock supply due to regulation related to food production. In contrast, the feedstocks for SAFs made through gasification and alcohol-to-jet are plentiful and less expensive than HEFA and could also prove critical to driving long-term scale in SAF.

Many aviation net-zero plans, like the one published by IATA, assume that SAFs will make up most of the industry's climate progress in the coming decades. Several test flights powered by 100 per cent SAFs have taken off. However, alternative fuels made up less than 0.2 per cent of the global jet fuel supply in 2022, so there is a lot of progress needed to supply alternative fuels that are helpful for the climate.[13]

Where will SAF come from?

Governments and regulators have started to act, as illustrated by the Biden administration's 2021 challenge to supply at least 3 billion gallons of SAF per year by 2030 and have enough SAF by 2050 to meet all aviation fuel demand. In 2023, the European Union agreed binding targets for airlines in Europe to increase their use of sustainable aviation fuels, in an attempt to kickstart demand for green fuels. Fuel suppliers must ensure that 2 per cent of fuel made available at EU airports is SAF in 2025, rising to 6 per cent in 2030, 20 per cent in 2035 and 70 per cent in 2050. The proportion of these SAFs that are e-fuels will have to increase too. According to the agreement, 1.2 per cent of fuels must be synthetic fuels from 2030, rising to 35 per cent in 2050. Airlines will receive about €2 billion in funding from the EU carbon market to help them switch to SAFs.[14,15]

Another boost for demand will come from commitments from the many Western European and US airlines that have come to understand the pivotal role SAF has to play moving forward. They are encouraging SAF production with pledges of 10 per cent usage by 2030. Those commitments, while not binding, exceed the proposed blending targets called for by the European Commission and IATA. But SAF producers still worry that airlines will not follow through because the aviation biofuel runs two to three times the price of conventional jet fuel and fuel is a significant portion of an airline's cost structure: for airlines worldwide, fuel constituted 19 per cent of total expenditure in 2021.

Demand is expected to reach about 19 megatonnes by 2030, but that far exceeds even the most aggressive production scenario forecasts for 2030, which are around 16 megatonnes. Global supply is projected to reach 4.9 megatonnes in 2025. That means that, by 2030, despite dozens of new production facilities and billions of dollars invested in SAF production, there won't be enough of it to stop the rise in global aviation emissions – let alone reduce it. According to one calculation, the best-case scenario for SAF supply in 2030 would represent only about 5 per cent of jet fuel consumption globally, which in turn would translate into a rise in airline emissions given the steady growth in air travel worldwide.

For at least the next decade, flying is likely to increase its share of global transport emissions, as passenger numbers rise and as other modes continue to gradually reduce their carbon footprints. Some governments and businesses are trying to encourage people to fly less, for example by stopping short, domestic flights when high-speed trains are available or by capping the growth of passenger volumes at major airports. A growing number of young people, especially among Gen Z, now refuse to fly on principle. And some airports are deprioritizing private jets or imposing extra taxes on them. Regardless, aviation's carbon footprint is likely to grow representing a major challenge for the industry in the future.

Autonomous vehicles

After decades of anticipation and billions of miles of data collection, autonomous vehicles are nearly – but not quite – a mass product. And that has been the case for several years now. For a glimpse of how far the technology has come and why it's not fully ready, we can look towards San Francisco, one the world's leading centres for autonomous R&D.

Google-owned Waymo and General Motors-owned Cruise tested their self-driving cars in the city for several years before rolling out a small fleet of cars without drivers in 2020. The companies were then allowed to operate between 10 pm and 6 am, at a maximum speed of 30 mph (48 kph). In August 2023, a California commission voted to allow two self-driving car companies to begin commercial operations around the clock. Waymo will also be allowed to drive at up to 60 mph (96 kph).

But even in one of the most tech-friendly, forward-thinking places on Earth, the vote was contested. It drew more than 200 public commenters and went over seven hours. Several representatives from blind communities said they had had difficulty hailing Uber and Lyft vehicles because drivers will deny passengers and refuse to ferry a service dog, something they said would not happen with autonomous vehicles. Disability advocates, including the Blinded Veterans Association, the Epilepsy Foundation of Northern California and the Curry Senior Center, signed an open letter calling for approval to expand the two services. 'They increase access to transportation for members of the communities we represent,' the letter read. 'Far too many people still find it far too hard to get where they need to go safely.'

However, city officials have repeatedly complained about the vehicles. The San Francisco fire department chief warned against the expansion because the driverless cars had already interfered with emergency situations 40 times. There had already been almost 70 self-driving vehicle collisions in 2023, according to the California Department of Motor Vehicles. The cars, said the fire chief, were 'not ready for prime time'.

Then, two months after the vote, California's department of motor vehicles suspended Cruise's permits to operate self-driving cars on the state's public roads, effective immediately. The agency said in October that Cruise's vehicles posed a danger to the public and that the company had misrepresented key facts about them.[16,17]

The state of the technology

This kind of debate over the plus points and drawbacks of current autonomous vehicles is one of the reasons they will likely continue to be almost ready for another few years to come. Many new cars now come equipped with systems that help maintain control. Thanks to cameras and sensors, they enable a 360-degree view around a car, twice as much as humans have. They can thus guide the vehicle or prompt the driver to take action to maintain distance from the car in front or to stay in a lane. But drivers still have to be in charge of the car at all times. These are classed as Level 1 (assisted) and Level 2 (partial automation) systems.

From around 2025, Level 3 (conditional automation) cars will be able to cope even if the driver does not monitor the system at all times – though the driver will still have to be in a position to resume control when needed. High automation (Level 4) could be available from 2030: the system will manage all situations automatically in a defined use case, during which the driver would not be required. From 2035 or so, Level 5 – full automation – might be possible: no driver would be required.

The greatest benefit claimed for higher-level automation will be improved road safety. US government data identifies driver behaviour or error as a factor in 94 per cent of crashes, with much of the devastation caused by impaired driving – that is, driving under the influence of drugs or alcohol, while tired, or while distracted by something such as a smartphone. Lower-level driverless systems will help impaired drivers avoid crashes, while the highest level should eliminate driver error entirely.[18]

Autonomous vehicles also promise a means to get around for people with reduced mobility and older adults, letting them live better lives. They should also make shared-mobility services cheaper and more convenient: a car could come round to pick up a passenger and there would be less concern as to whether a car is available nearby. They could thus help people without cars in areas without public transport or provide first- and last-mile connections, adding capacity, availability and flexibility to mass transit.

In addition, the technology is likely to reduce congestion. The cars are programmed to maintain a safe and consistent distance between vehicles, which can help to reduce the number of stop-and-go waves that produce road congestion for no apparent reason. Researchers at the University of Texas predict that tightly spaced platoons of AVs could reduce congestion-related delays by 60 per cent on highways.

Environmental gains will include space and energy savings. Fewer traffic jams and less unnecessary braking and acceleration will save fuel. And fully autonomous vehicles may be able to travel more closely together, reducing air drag. A highway platoon of automated vehicles could reduce fuel consumption by 10 per cent, according to one estimate.

By operating closer together, the cars will need less road space, meaning less need to construct new highways or new lanes on existing roads. If vehicles are used to increase carsharing, overall mobility needs could be served by a smaller number of cars, reducing the demand for parking, which currently takes up valuable urban land. Even when people continued to own their personal car, they could let it park itself in a remote garage and hail it when they wanted a ride, effectively treating it as a personal taxi service.

Finally – and this is the stated dream of many commuters, business travellers and holidaymakers – drivers could spend their journey working, sleeping or watching a movie instead of having to keep their eyes on the road. That represents a huge saving in time: in 2022, drivers in the United States drove 2.8 trillion miles (4.5 trillion km) in a total of 227 billion trips – spending 93 billion hours driving, according to the AAA (American Automobile Association).[19]

Autonomous driving is one of the most relevant applications of artificial intelligence to mobility and vast amounts of data have already been gathered. By 2020, Tesla drivers had driven more than 3 billion miles on Autopilot. Yet researchers are still working on some core technology hurdles.[20]

Mcity, the University of Michigan's public-private research partnership devoted to future mobility, has a test facility with more than 16 acres

(6.5 hectares) of roads and traffic infrastructure to simulate urban and suburban streets, and 5G-connected sensors to collect driving data. There, autonomous vehicles are put through increasingly difficult scenarios to test their decision-making abilities.[21]

One challenge is the 'curse of dimensionality', says Henry Liu, the Director of Mcity. The systems need to negotiate differences in weather conditions, in road infrastructure, such as traffic lights or signs indicating directions, and in the behaviour of various road users, such as pedestrians and cyclists. The centre also generates scenarios to see how the car reacts to them. That could be when a traffic light turns amber and there's a pedestrian crossing the road, but another vehicle is in front, blocking the car's line of sight. 'This is more like a road test for human drivers,' Liu said in an interview with the Oliver Wyman Forum.

The second challenge is the 'curse of rarity', Liu says. 'Autonomous vehicles can handle 99.99 per cent of use cases. But once you get to the 0.001 per cent, AVs may not be able to handle it because they haven't seen the scenarios yet. The machine learning model isn't trained for it.'

The other key challenges are public acceptance and government support, which are closely linked and vary in different countries and cultures. A 2022 survey of four large automotive markets, Germany, China, the United States and Japan, revealed significant differences in attitudes. In Germany and the US, more than one in two respondents rejected the use of fully autonomous cars. But in Asia, survey participants were far more open to the technology. In China, only 10 per cent of all respondents were against its use and in Japan 22 per cent. In both those countries, one in two respondents could even imagine buying a fully autonomous vehicle, indicating a high potential level of adoption.[22]

Acceptance and perception of risk

Another study sought to explain why people might be more or less willing to accept autonomous vehicles. This showed that people are likely to accept them if they have high expectations of their benefits and a relatively low perception of their risks. The study's authors concluded that the most significant way in which makers and operators of autonomous systems could boost acceptance would be to raise or maintain expectations of them among the public.

They should also engage more positively with the public to combat negative perceptions on media platforms, for example through demonstration projects. In addition, they should actively address the fears that autonomous vehicles instil in pedestrians, perhaps by limiting maximum speed settings on city streets or by designing the fronts of vehicles to minimize injuries to people in the case of a collision.[23]

These are areas in which China appears to have a first-mover advantage. The country is already launching demonstrations through waves of pilot schemes, especially in zones around Beijing and Shanghai. From September 2023, the Beijing suburb of Yizhuang, home to corporations such as JD.com, is officially letting local robo-taxi operators – primarily Baidu and startup Pony.ai – charge fares for fully autonomous taxis, with no human staff inside. Previously, commercial public-facing robo-taxis were required to have an employee to sit inside with the passenger.

More approvals for robo-taxi operations in the city were coming, said Ning Zhang, Vice President at Pony.ai and head of its Beijing research and development centre. Citing conversations with Beijing's mayor, Zhang said that by the end of 2023, the city aims to expand robo-taxi testing areas to Daxing International Airport and around one train station. 'We have very high confidence ... maybe only in three years, our full driverless vehicles are going to be running over the whole Beijing city,' he told US TV channel CNBC.[24,25]

China shows some sharp differences with much of the rest of the world in governance and the relative importance of individual choice. In Europe, the management and protection of data spark debate, but the Chinese government already collects data on smartphone use. Western governments must follow democratic processes and procedures when setting up pilot zones or infrastructure for driverless cars. But China, similar to the way it builds metro systems or high-speed rail lines, relocates and compensates people more swiftly. Ethical decisions in China tend to focus on benefits for the greatest number, making it easier to decide how to program an on-board computer to deal with situations such as safety-related dilemmas.[26]

As with the roll-out of electric vehicles, China seems to be moving faster in autonomous vehicles. The regulatory system appears to work quickly at different levels of government. To develop autonomous-driving laws and regulations, the central government sets an agenda for local governments, which gets implemented through pilots. Moreover, the rapid growth of Chinese cities demands urgent mobility solutions, as transport affects quality of life, the productivity of workers, and the movement of goods and services. This has been the motivation behind the vast expansion of public transport, such as metro systems and high-speed rail. But autonomous vehicles could make an even bigger impact in the future.

Vertical take-off and landing aircraft

Once cars became a mass product, people soon wanted something more. They wanted ways to beat the traffic, complete a journey faster and be free from the confines of roads. Partial solutions emerged to some of these, such as SUVs, which allow people to drive over rough terrain. But the ultimate dream has been a flying car. Over the past century, designs have included cars with wings stuck on top and small aircrafts fitted with road wheels.

None was a commercial success and 'Where's my flying car?' became a joke about technology's inability to realize futuristic visions. In 2013, PayPal co-founder Peter Thiel famously expressed his disappointment that the key technological achievements of the twenty-first century were things like social media. He cited the old rule about the length of a Twitter message: 'We were promised flying cars, and instead we got 140 characters.'[27,28]

Actually, flying cars look like they're finally here – or at least a decent substitute. Inspired by drone technology, electric vertical take-off and landing (eVTOL) vehicles are being piloted by dozens of companies around the world and are expected to deliver packages and cargo, act as urban and intercity taxis, and be used by emergency and other public services.

eVTOLs are light commercial aircraft powered by batteries that take off and land vertically but are simpler, more manoeuvrable and more efficient than helicopters. In cruising mode, many fly forward like aeroplanes, but they are designed to fly at a lower altitude than commercial aircraft. Some propulsion systems are a bit like those used in drones: the aircraft are wingless and there are multiple rotors; they have a top speed of about 90 kph and a maximum range of about 50 km. Winged models are more efficient while cruising: they often combine propellers that lift and propel the aircraft forward with wings for faster flight speeds; they can reach up to 300 kph and have ranges of up to 300 km.[29]

Current versions being piloted include drones for package delivery and air taxis with payloads ranging from a single person (100 kg) to nine people plus baggage (1,000 kg). In 2023, for example, Germany-based Volocopter carried out a series of air taxi test flights in Neom, the new urban area being built in northwest Saudi Arabia. These eVTOLs look a bit like helicopters with multiple rotors. Airbus, Europe's largest aerospace company, has a unit called CityAirbus, which has developed a four-seat eVTOL prototype with wings. Called NextGen, it has an 80 km operational range and a cruise speed of 120 kph.[30,31]

The European Union Aviation Safety Agency (EASA) says eVTOLs used to transport goods will most likely be remotely piloted. However, it expects those that transport people to initially have pilots – though this is likely to change as the technology develops. 'Maybe in 10 years from now, we expect to see the human pilots on board air taxis being gradually replaced with remote pilots on the ground,' it says. 'And in a further evolution we may see air taxis operating autonomously, without any human intervention during flight.'[32]

Will public service lead to public acceptance?

Because eVTOLs will come in a variety of forms and be able to fly autonomously or be controlled remotely, a number of different types could be coordinated in a single operation. For example, if an accident occurs in a congested city, emergency services could immediately launch a fleet of drones. Some would carry equipment to help people on the scene carry out first aid and assess the condition of people with injuries. Others would transport and help set up temporary signs to regulate the traffic. Medical services would then analyse information relayed back to them and, if necessary, dispatch a flying ambulance with paramedics.

This kind of public service application will be crucial in persuading the public to accept the new flying machines criss-crossing their cities. A 2021 study for EASA showed that EU citizens expressed a positive attitude towards and interest in urban air mobility. They saw it as a new and attractive means of mobility, and a majority were ready to try it out. However, a determining factor for acceptance was the notion of general or public interest – that is, the machines should have use cases that benefit the community, such as medical or emergency transport and the connection of remote areas.

The single most significant factor that will ultimately determine the widespread adoption of eVTOLs is human safety. When encouraged to reflect upon the concrete consequences of potential urban air mobility (UAM) operations in their city, EU citizens indicated that they want to limit their own exposure to safety, noise, security and environmental impact. However, the study also showed that citizens trust the current aviation safety levels and would be reassured if these levels were applied to UAM.[33]

eVTOLs will therefore need extensive regulatory oversight, in particular the establishment of robust certification, testing and regulatory standards. Since they may be flying in large numbers above populated areas, the rules will have to include measures to address the concerns of urban residents about noise, visual pollution and privacy. Product manufacturers will then need to design and develop the aircraft according to these standards and inform the public about their safety. Air traffic management agencies – EASA and the US Federal Aviation Administration (FAA) – are developing standards for innovative air traffic control systems to manage high-density drone and eVTOL traffic.

Other factors that will determine how fast eVTOLs are adopted include advances in sustainable energy sources. Currently, the energy comes from batteries, which have made advances over the past decade thanks to the electric-car industry. But future energy sources developed for traditional aeroplanes could also have a role. Another important technology is 5G communications, as large volumes of eVTOLs would need real-time communications to avoid collisions in busy city skies.

Forecasts of the global market for eVTOLs by 2030 vary widely, from somewhere over $10 billion to several hundred billion dollars. It seems pretty likely that eVTOLs will at least play a role in cargo and package delivery (for remote areas), provide help for authorities to carry out emergency and medical operations, and serve as high-end air taxis; one such service is being contemplated for Paris CDG Airport for the Paris 2024 Olympic Games, with a partnership between the Paris region, RATP Ile de France commuter operator and Volocopter. It's also conceivable that they could become a popular means of transport, thereby increasing the radius over which people can function in daily life, as mass transit systems and then cars did in the past. To reduce the price of using the machines and maintain order in the skies, eVTOLs might mainly be managed by service providers and not be sold to consumers. They wouldn't quite be the flying cars as first imagined, but as carsharing may gradually take over from private car ownership, perhaps there wouldn't be much difference.[34]

The future of mobility

As a last question in my conversations with the panel of 30 leaders and experts, I consistently asked about their visions of the future of mobility, in the next 15–20 years. The vast majority are convinced that mobility will remain a fundamental human need, so the mobility sector will continue to grow in aggregate. As Alex Bayen notes, much of the work in future mobility will be to integrate various modes and services into cohesive systems. As Xavier Huillard puts it: 'Mobility is an essential need for human beings, and this is pretty stable in space and time. This has been well established by anthropologists.'

Building on this prediction, nine themes emerge to summarize the panel's views on the future of mobility.

Theme 1: New paradigms for major cities

Urban centres will be greener and the densest areas at their cores will for the most part exclude individual cars. In some cities, mobility will be fully integrated into urban design and people will increasingly get around with vehicles such as bicycles and e-scooters that they power – at least partly – themselves. Small, low-emission vehicles will also play a role in logistics operations, where micro-mobility solutions will be a part of last-mile logistics, especially in megacities. Passenger and freight rail will be better coordinated in order to move more freight rail traffic overnight in cities. Emission-free mass transit systems will serve urban centres and passenger flow will be smoothed by dynamic pricing. Mobility systems will be much more integrated and will contribute to cities' quality of life. Business centres and residential areas will have to be reshaped, which will have an impact on real estate development. Car parks will continue to flourish with extended business scope by offering proximity as a service.

....

"Mobility is an essential need for human beings, and this is pretty stable in space and time"
Xavier Huillard

....

Theme 2: Electrified and automated technology

Electric cars and trucks will be widespread, though the source of electricity will vary by region, and the range accessible by electric vehicles will increase. New low-emission fuels will be available for non-electrified train lines.

Automation will continue to progress and autonomous trains might be available before 2030. Autonomous aircraft may be available by 2035, even if certification will take time. Full autonomy for cars will be difficult and might need up to another 50 years. Level-5 autonomy – where a vehicle can drive anywhere in road traffic and under all conditions without human intervention – might be available in specific sub-sections of road networks, but it will require system-level regulation. This level of autonomy will mean that a given level of infrastructure investment yields greater vehicle capacity, which in turn will affect the share of rail and road mobility, especially in urban areas.

Trucks, too, will increasingly be autonomous, sometimes using dedicated lanes, and some experts see even greater changes in freight transport than for passenger, as the ecosystem is driven by technology and economics. Fleets of interconnected electric trucks and delivery drones (for low-volume, remote deliveries only) might be connected to 3D printing facilities, improving reliability in logistics and reducing the inventories and working capital needed. Diversified freight will tend towards smaller, lighter vehicles that travel fast and increase overall velocity and flexibility. This will put pressure on rail freight and governments might have to regulate to protect rail's share of the freight market.

Increased computer power, AI and 5G communications will be critical enablers of this increase in automation, and improvements to vehicle-human interfaces will enable further automation, reducing costs and boosting safety. Aircraft cockpits will also undergo fundamental change, aviation executives suggest.

Theme 3: Future modes of transport

The mobility business leaders I interviewed were divided on urban air mobility. Well regulated, it might become part of the design of some urban areas, such as new greenfield cities. But in existing cities, especially in their centres, UAM will likely remain limited to premium consumers and some public services such as emergency transport, and it is unlikely to evolve into a form of mass transit. Some experts see a future for very high-altitude travel, but hypersonic aircraft are no longer seen as economically viable. Maglev-type technology could become viable as a niche infrastructure in selected regions.

Theme 4: Highways and rail track: the backbone of mobility

Rail and trunk roads have the ability to handle high volumes of traffic, so they are expected to remain the backbone of the land mobility systems. As people travel more sustainably, some shorter-distance air travel will be replaced by high-speed rail, depending on journey distance and door-to-door transit time. However, high-speed rail will remain limited to high-density routes and elsewhere it is cheaper to establish air connections. Intermodal hubs will therefore need to be built out, so that outlying destinations are connected to the high-speed backbone.

More meaningful rail links will be built to serve airports, increasing efficiency and improving traveller experience. But, as they develop, these links may have a significant impact on airports' economic model, given the revenues and profits airport managers generate today from car parking.

Theme 5: The growth in sharing

As the propensity to own individual cars declines and digital technology supports the development of asset-sharing communities, carsharing will continue to expand, serving all distances and purposes, from regional commuting to long-distance travel. The sharing providers will consolidate regionally into a handful of scaled service organizations with large communities of members. But this migration will take longer than a lot of people think and the public sector may need to intervene to steer and accelerate asset sharing in some modes. As a result, fleet management services will become a critical core competency.

Theme 6: China, the trend setter

China is at the leading edge in quite a lot of areas of future mobility: it is the lab in which new technologies and services are being experimented on at full scale. Now the country has built the world's largest electrified high-speed rail network, Chinese automakers are pushing production of electric fast and on a global scale, expanding their capabilities worldwide. China is also innovating in freight and logistics, including capacity-sharing platforms and freight exchanges – that is, digital platforms for the country-wide movement of goods. And China is using artificial intelligence and robotics in warehouses at industrial scale, as well as augmented reality to improve productivity and precision.

Theme 7: A world of coalitions and adapted governance

Mobility coalitions will unite trunk network incumbents and providers of new services. They will coordinate different modes and will combine start-ups with current mobility behemoths such as major automakers and aerospace manufacturers. These alliances will blur the boundaries between public and individual transport and they will enable bundled, personalized services that are difficult to achieve today. The coalitions will also have to include public authorities to ensure that public transport is fully integrated into the ecosystem. The goals of those coalitions are to access new capabilities and create ample customer benefits, so they have a good chance of being welcomed by anti-trust regulatory bodies.

New partnership models will develop, involving technology providers, operators, data managers and fleet managers. Infrastructure will adapt to this new context and develop smart concepts that optimize capacity, allowing real estate to be redeployed for uses that benefit society and the economy such as housing and business.

For the coalitions to be sustained, transport governance will need to adapt and transcend the usual political alternations. Another task for governments is to prepare for another pandemic, which a number of executives think is highly likely in the future. The growth of interconnected multimodal mobility may risk spreading a virus faster.

Theme 8: Mobility on demand in a multimodal environment

Mobility-on-demand will provide personalized door-to-door transport enabled by digital applications and mobility will be consumed in a fundamentally different way. Consumers' thinking will be summed up as 'I will go where I want how I want. Thanks to my digital assistant, I will plan and execute my trip on my own'. Supply will continue to be fragmented and trust will be an increasingly powerful currency for operators and service providers.

Individuals' ownership of assets will decline. Mobility services will be made available on demand via flexible apps that combine multiple modes and providers and are directly connected to consumers' electronic diaries. It will be much easier to use transport networks, which will have seamless connections. Travellers will have full control over their trips and itineraries and the mobility experience will be far better than at present: it will become pleasant and rewarding.

Market power will lie with cross-sector platforms that let travellers navigate their trips and pay for them with integrated payment systems. They will capture traveller data to increase the scope of their services and data will become a critical asset to own, control and leverage. Value along the mobility value chain will migrate towards data holders and managers.

In the delivery of consumer goods, e-merchants will be best positioned to steer the logistics value chain. They will steer a new balance between offline and online sales, partly depending on the type of goods sold and consumers' tastes. Digital applications will make logistics services and the flow of goods fluid and visible from end to end.

Logistics providers will use advanced forecasting systems to place inventory close to end-consumers and provide fast and seamless last-mile distribution. Goods manufacturers and other companies may, as a result, outsource more of their freight logistics and inventory management. The global logistics business will be dominated by a small number of global companies with strong digital capabilities.

Theme 9: A decarbonized mobility value chain

The modal mix will continue its trend towards a greener value chain and mobility will eventually be fully decarbonized, driven both by regulations and market demand. It will be essential to work with a fully developed green mentality, as the young generation has a strong collective consciousness of the need to combat climate change. Financing needs to be better directed to facilitate transitions in infrastructure and energy sources and some existing infrastructures will be decommissioned. Freight providers will have to demonstrate the decarbonization of their supply chains to both customers and suppliers.

Mobility will be more frugal. All waste will be recycled, a major shift for equipment manufacturers. Carbon offsets will be repriced to better fit the true price of greenhouse gas emissions. Infrastructure innovations will contribute to decarbonization. For example, roads will be made of material that absorbs solar energy and stores it for future use.

It will be vital to create a carbon-free mindset in mobility in order to avoid popular backlash, especially among new generations, and also if carbon taxes are introduced for transport. Decarbonization – or, at least, a roadmap towards it – will be a condition to attract young talent to work in the mobility industry. In rail, hydrogen in some regions may replace diesel in a matter of 10 years to power locomotives on lines that have not been electrified. Railways will need to organize the logistics of this shift. The airline industry will need to try to meet the environmental challenge in a cost-effective way. If low-emission propulsion systems are not developed, air travel might witness an erosion in its modal share. Airline operators may decide to deploy rail instead of air services for some short- and medium-haul markets.

Conclusion

Growth in demand for mobility will not cease as long as humans are around – and nor will the changes in how this demand is satisfied. The progress of the past three decades will be followed by as many changes over the next three, if not more. The new generation of mobility leaders can rely in many ways on the foundations set by their predecessors, who have shown ingenuity and passion for human and economic development. The challenges the new generation have to tackle now – and the opportunities that await them – will shape the future of the industry.

KEY TAKEAWAYS

- Many fast-growing cities in sub-Saharan Africa have huge problems with congestion and a lack of public transport. However, the region also has the potential to leapfrog industrialized countries by skipping car ownership and adopting shared, electrified transport modes.
- Aviation faces a tougher challenge than other modes in achieving net zero emissions. Some potential solutions are being developed, but they will all take much longer than the electrification of land-based transport.
- High-tech advances promise a future of autonomous road vehicles and flying taxis. But the technology is tricky to operate on a mass scale. Moreover, public acceptance will be a challenge.
- There are several specific attractive use cases for vertical take-off and landing (eVTOL) equipped mobility, but full urban air mobility will likely be restricted to specific regions and local ecosystems.
- Nine key themes capture the panels' views on the future of Mobility.

Notes

1   Bearak, M., Moriarty, D. and Ledur, J. (2021) Africa's rising cities – How Africa will become the center of the world's urban future, *The Washington Post*, 19 November. Available at: www.washingtonpost.com/world/interactive/2021/africa-cities/ (archived at https://perma.cc/BD2F-BH96)

2   Vollset, S.E. et al (2020) Fertility, mortality, migration, and population scenarios for 195 countries and territories from 2017 to 2100: A forecasting analysis for the Global Burden of Disease Study, *The Lancet*, 396(10258), 1285–1306. doi: https://doi.org/10.1016/S0140-6736(20)30677-2 (archived at https://perma.cc/FXB8-TQYA)

3   Hoornweg, D. and Pope, K. (2014) Socioeconomic pathways and regional distribution of the world's 101 largest cities', Global Cities Institute, Working Paper No. 04. Available at: https://media.wix.com/ugd/672989_62cfa13ec4ba47788f78ad660489a2fa.pdf (archived at https://perma.cc/DZR5-U83G)

4   United Nations (n.d.) Statistics division – make cities and human settlements inclusive, safe, resilient and sustainable. Available at: https://unstats.un.org/sdgs/report/2020/goal-11/ (archived at https://perma.cc/2KRY-CMHX)

5   World Bank Group Transport (n.d.) Transport – the essential connector. Available at: https://thedocs.worldbank.org/en/doc/157201585683713721-0190022020/original/WBTransportNarrative.pdf (archived at https://perma.cc/6BVE-ZLVU)

6   Agora Verkehrswende and GIZ (2023) Leapfrogging to sustainable transport in Africa. Twelve insights into the Continent's sector transformation. Available at: https://changing-transport.org/wp-content/uploads/2023_Leapfrogging-to-Sustainable-Transport-in-Africa_EN.pdf (archived at https://perma.cc/37RH-UV7P)

7   Hoornweg, D. and Pope, K. (2014) Socioeconomic pathways and regional distribution of the world's 101 largest cities', Global Cities Institute, Working Paper No. 04. Available at: https://media.wix.com/ugd/672989_62cfa13ec4ba47788f78ad660489a2fa.pdf (archived at https://perma.cc/9R26-5YGD)

8   Bonnici, D. (2022) How many cars are there in the world?, *WhichCar?*, 23 April. Available at: www.whichcar.com.au/news/how-many-cars-are-there-in-the-world (archived at https://perma.cc/C8LJ-XCJA)

9   United Nations Environment Programme (2022) Used vehicles and the environment. A global overview of used light duty vehicles: Flow, scale and regulation. Available at: https://wedocs.unep.org/bitstream/handle/20.500.11822/34175/UVE.pdf?sequence=1&isAllowed=y (archived at https://perma.cc/559F-V5HE)

10 En:former (2022) IEA explores pathways to Africa's sustainable energy system. Available at: www.en-former.com/en/iea-explores-pathways-to-africas-sustainable-energy-system/ (archived at https://perma.cc/JA6L-ZH5A)

11 United Nations (n.d.) Statistics division – make cities and human settlements inclusive, safe, resilient and sustainable. Available at: https://unstats.un.org/sdgs/report/2020/goal-11/ (archived at https://perma.cc/6KX4-XKLJ)

12 *The Economist* (2023) The aviation industry wants to be net zero – but not yet, 14 May. Available at: www.economist.com/business/2023/05/14/the-aviation-industry-wants-to-be-net-zero-but-not-yet (archived at https://perma.cc/CT7P-YLLT)

13 Crownhart, C. (2023) Everything you need to know about the wild world of alternative jet fuels, *MIT Technology Review*, 24 May. Available at: www.technologyreview.com/2023/05/24/1073568/all-about-alternative-jet-fuels-safs/ (archived at https://perma.cc/2W87-R6F3)

14 Shepardson, D. (2022) U.S. outlines roadmap to boost sustainable aviation fuel, Reuters, 23 September. Available at: www.reuters.com/business/energy/us-outlines-roadmap-boost-sustainable-aviation-fuel-use-2022-09-23/ (archived at https://perma.cc/8524-GE4A)

15 Abnett, K., Kar-Gupta, S. and Plucinska, J. (2023) EU agrees binding green fuel targets for aviation, Reuters, 26 April. Available at: www.reuters.com/business/sustainable-business/eu-council-european-parliament-reach-provisional-deal-decarbonising-aviation-2023-04-25/ (archived at https://perma.cc/5WQX-TJEX)

16 Bhuiyan, J. (2023) San Francisco to get round-the-clock robo taxis after controversial vote, *The Guardian*, 11 August. Available at: www.theguardian.com/us-news/2023/aug/10/san-francisco-self-driving-car-autonomous-regulation-google-gm (archived at https://perma.cc/5ZZN-FKSW)

17 Montgomery, B. (2023) Cruise driverless cars pulled off California roads after safety incidents, *The Guardian*, 24 October. Available at: www.theguardian.com/us-news/2023/oct/24/driverless-car-self-driving-california-cruise-gm (archived at https://perma.cc/4GGX-N8ZN)

18 Coalition for Future Mobility (2017) Highly automated technologies, often called self-driving cars, promise a range of potential benefits. Available at: https://coalitionforfuturemobility.com/benefits-of-self-driving-vehicles/ (archived at https://perma.cc/MR8C-4CNQ)

19 Gross, A. (2023) American Driving Survey, NewsRoom.aaa, 13 September. Available at: https://newsroom.aaa.com/2023/09/american-driving-survey/#:~:text=Key%20Findings&text=Projecting%20these%20results%20nationwide%2C%20drivers,2.8%20trillion%20miles%20in%202022 (archived at https://perma.cc/27HJ-QXF3)

20 Lamber, F. (2020) Tesla drops a bunch of new Autopilot data, 3 billion miles and more, Electrek, 22 April. Available at: https://electrek.co/2020/04/22/tesla-autopilot-data-3-billion-miles/ (archived at https://perma.cc/8JVP-C2P6)

21 Nienhaus, A. and Wilkinson, A. (2022) Autonomous vehicles and the curse of rarity, Oliver Wyman Forum, 13 September. Available at: www.oliverwymanforum.com/mobility/2022/sep/autonomous-vehicles-and-the-curse-of-rarity.html (archived at https://perma.cc/UT4H-3FNZ)

22 Business Wire (2023) Acceptance and use cases for autonomous vehicles differ greatly among major automotive markets. Available at: www.businesswire.com/news/home/20230523005518/en/Acceptance-and-Use-Cases-for-Autonomous-Vehicles-Differ-Greatly-Among-Major-Automotive-Markets-%E2%80%93-Global-Car-User-Survey-by-Asahi-Kasei (archived at https://perma.cc/9VAM-QXUG)

23 Taniguchi, A., Enoch, M., Theofilatos, A. and Ieromonachou, P. (2022) Understanding acceptance of autonomous vehicles in Japan, UK, and Germany. *Urban, Planning and Transport Research*, 10(1), 514–535. doi: https://doi.org/10.1080/21650020.2022.2135590 (archived at https://perma.cc/7FHC-SLLR)

24 Cheng, E. (2023) China's capital is letting the public take fully driverless robotaxis – and has bigger rollout plans, startup Pony.ai says, CNBC, 19 September. Available at: www.cnbc.com/2023/09/19/chinas-capital-city-beijing-has-big-plans-for-robotaxis-ponyai-says.html (archived at https://perma.cc/FTT2-3JAJ)

25 Wenderoth, M. (2018) Why this country (not the USA) will be first to adopt driverless cars, *Forbes*, 31 May. Available at: www.forbes.com/sites/michaelcwenderoth/2018/05/31/why-this-country-not-the-usa-will-be-first-to-adopt-driverless-cars/?sh=3bc91e07769a (archived at https://perma.cc/67XN-ES9S)

26 Wenderoth, M. (2018) Why this country (not the USA) will be first to adopt driverless cars, *Forbes*, 31 May. Available at: www.forbes.com/sites/michaelcwenderoth/2018/05/31/why-this-country-not-the-usa-will-be-first-to-adopt-driverless-cars/?sh=3bc91e07769a (archived at https://perma.cc/7HG6-BLMN)

27 The VC Factory (n.d.) 'We wanted flying cars, instead we got 140 characters' – Peter Thiel. Available at: https://thevcfactory.com/we-wanted-flying-cars-instead-we-got-140-characters-peter-thiel/ (archived at https://perma.cc/B4DY-9MZD)

28 The Atlantic (n.d.) Don't go west, young entrepreneur. Available at: www.theatlantic.com/sponsored/allstate/dont-go-west-young-entrepreneur/292/ (archived at https://perma.cc/QTU3-QHZA)

29 Capgemini Engineering (2022) Enroute to urban air mobility. Available at: https://prod.ucwe.capgemini.com/wp-content/uploads/2021/12/Enroute-to-urban-air-mobility-Whitepaper_-23-March-2022.pdf (archived at https://perma.cc/B7JV-PZMP)

30 Volocopter (2023) NEOM and Volocopter: First electric air taxi flight in Saudi Arabia. Available at: www.volocopter.com/en/newsroom/volocopter-flies-in-neom (archived at https://perma.cc/9U8A-8P8G)

31 Airbus (n.d.) CityAirbus Next Gen. Available at: www.airbus.com/en/innovation/low-carbon-aviation/urban-air-mobility/cityairbus-nextgen (archived at https://perma.cc/AG6J-CGZS)

32 EASA (n.d.) Frequently asked questions on UAM. Available at: www.easa.europa.eu/sites/default/files/dfu/uam_-_faqs.pdf (archived at https://perma.cc/QKL9-5DC5)

33 EASA (2021) Study on the societal acceptance of urban air mobility in Europe. Available at: www.easa.europa.eu/en/downloads/127760/en (archived at https://perma.cc/823F-72FB)

34 Wenderoth, M. (2018) Why this country (not the USA) will be first to adopt driverless cars, *Forbes*, 31 May. Available at: www.forbes.com/sites/michaelcwenderoth/2018/05/31/why-this-country-not-the-usa-will-be-first-to-adopt-driverless-cars/?sh=3bc91e07769a (archived at https://perma.cc/S4CE-3VMG)

APPENDIX

About the interviewees

Bernard Amory

To me, Bernard, a charming gentleman, is the reference international antitrust lawyer whom I have worked with a lot on EC competition reviews.

Bernard Amory has held the position of Co-Head of the Global Competition & Antitrust practice at Jones Day in Belgium since 2018. Between 2011 and 2018, he was the Partner in charge of the Brussels office at Jones Day. His professional achievements include being named Lawyer of the Year for Regulatory Communications by Who's Who Legal from 2005 to 2010. He studied law at Université de Namur, Université Catholique de Louvain and the University of Exeter. He has over 30 years' experience on legal matters in the mobility and technology sectors.

Alexandre Bayen

Alex is an academic leader who has created, in collaboration with Oliver Wyman, an innovative tool, the 'City Readiness Index', which provides practical benchmarks to global mobility experts and executives.

Alexandre Bayen is a Professor of Electrical Engineering and Computer Science at the University of California, Berkeley, where he also serves as Associate Provost. In addition, he has served as a Senior Advisor at Oliver Wyman since 2016. His past roles at UC Berkeley include serving as the Director of the Institute of Transportation Studies from 2014 to 2020 and as the Director of Aerospace Program Development from 2020 to 2021. Alexandre Bayen completed a BS at École Polytechnique (France) and obtained an MS and PhD in Aeronautics and Astronautics from Stanford University, in 1999 and 2003 respectively. He has more than 20 years' experience as a global expert in the mobility sector.

Fabrice Brégier

Fabrice's leadership has always been grounded in a profound knowledge of the aerospace and defence ecosystems as well as his expertise in operations management and enterprise transformation.

Fabrice Brégier is the Chairman of Palantir France, a position he has held since 2018, and the Chairman of SCOR since 2023. Prior to this, he led Airbus as President and CEO from 2012 to 2018, after serving as COO from 2006 to 2012. Earlier in his career, he held various leadership positions, including Chairman and CEO of Eurocopter and CEO of MBDA. He studied engineering at École Polytechnique and École des Mines de Paris. He has over 30 years' experience in the mobility sector.

Olivier Brousse

Olivier and I first met in Washington DC in 2004 when he was leading Veolia Transportation North America. I have fond memories of the origins of the growth trajectory in the Americas of this global public transport giant.

Olivier Brousse is the Group CEO of IDverde, a position he has held since 2021. His past roles included Senior Executive Vice President of Strategy & Innovation at Veolia from 2020 to 2021, CEO of John Laing Plc from 2014 to 2020 and CEO of SAUR in France from 2008 until 2014. Earlier in his career he held several executive roles in Veolia Transportation and other enterprises in France, the UK and the US. Olivier Brousse studied engineering at École Polytechnique and École Nationale des Ponts et Chaussées. He has more than 25 years' experience in the mobility sector.

Gwendoline Cazenave

Gwendoline's career growth trajectory in the transportation sector is impressive and I have no doubt it will reach new heights in the future. For now, she leads one of the travel sector's most iconic brands.

Gwendoline Cazenave is the CEO of Eurostar Group, a position she has held since 2022. She also holds non-executive roles at the Union Financière de France, Tallano Technologies and Irish Rail. Her previous roles include Partner at Oliver Wyman from 2020 to 2022 and various key positions at SNCF Group in Business, Operations, Strategy and Finance from 1994 to 2020. She has led a number of initiatives within gender equality and social and environmental responsibility in her past and current positions. She completed her education in Business at NEOMA Business School and McGill University. She has more than 20 years' experience in the mobility sector.

Paul-Marie Chavanne

I admire Paul-Marie for his vision and leadership. He led the development of Geopost, one of the world's leading road express companies, while maintaining within his organization a strong culture of autonomy and entrepreneurship.

Paul-Marie Chavanne is Non-Executive Chairman of the Executive Board at Egis, a role he has held since 2020. His previous roles include Chairman and CEO of Geopost from 2001 to 2020 and Executive Vice President at Citroën from 1992 to 1997. He started his career as Division Head and Vice President for the Treasury Department at the Ministry of Finance in France. Paul-Marie Chavanne completed his education in engineering at École Centrale Paris and administration and finance at École Nationale d'Administration (ENA). He has over 25 years' experience in the mobility sector.

James Cherry

A prominent figure in the Montreal and Canadian business community, Jim has bravely shaped the future of Montreal's airport by refocusing all operations on the Montreal-Trudeau platform and the relentless attraction of new air carriers into and via the expanding airport.

James Cherry serves as a Senior Aviation Advisor to Arup Worldwide and as a Corporate Director at Cogeco, positions he has held since 2017 and 2016 respectively. He was a board member at the Canada Infrastructure Bank from 2017 to 2021, at Logistec Inc from 2011 to 2021 and was President and CEO of ADM Aéroports de Montréal from 2001 to 2016. James Cherry completed his education in accounting and finance at McGill University. He has over 35 years' experience in the mobility sector.

Tai Chong Chew

TC is a truly global mass transit and rail executive. He can easily share his experience from Singapore, Hong-Kong, mainland China, but also London or Toronto in the same line of thoughts. He has been covering these markets for more than 30 years.

Tai Chong Chew is the President of Global Business Operations at Arup, a position he has held since 2018. Prior to this he led Samsung C&T's international business operation from 2015 to 2017. His previous roles include Projects Director at MTR from 2009 to 2014, Head of Mass Transit at Bombardier Transportation from 2008 to 2009, President of London Underground Project Division at Bombardier Transportation from 2003 to 2008 and senior positions at Land Transport Authority (LTA) Singapore. Tai Chong is a chartered engineer and Fellow of several key institutions, including the Royal Academy of Engineering, the Institution of Civil Engineers, the Hong Kong Academy of Engineering Sciences and the Hong Kong Institute of Directors.

Deepak Chopra

I met and served with Deepak at Canada Post Corporation. I have witnessed his visionary leadership and the way he propelled the crown corporation towards the future of digital and e-commerce logistics.

Mike Cooper

Mike's testimony was particularly interesting for the purpose of the book as, a little like me, he has worked across multiple transport modes, including air, rail, parcels delivery and bus.

Deepak Chopra serves on the boards of the Descartes Systems Group, the North West Company, Sun Life Financial and Celestica. His previous roles include President and CEO of Canada Post Corporation from 2011 to 2018 and President and CEO of the Canada and Latin America region for Pitney Bowes from 2006 to 2010. Earlier in his career he also served as President of the Asia-Pacific and Middle East region and CFO for the EMEA region at Pitney Bowes. Deepak Chopra is a Fellow of the Chartered Professional Accountants of Canada. He completed his education in Business Management at the University of Delhi. He has over 25 years' experience in the mobility sector.

Mike Cooper is the CEO of Arriva, a position he has held since October 2020. His previous roles include CEO of Eurostar from 2018 to 2020, CEO of Yodel Delivery Network (one of the UK's largest delivery service carriers from 2015 to 2018) and various senior management roles at Arriva from 2005 to 2015 (including Managing Director of the UK Bus division and Deputy Group CEO and Managing Director of Mainland Europe). From 1997 to 2005, Mike Cooper held various senior positions in airline and tour operating companies, including Managing Director, Portland Direct, part of the Thomson Travel Group, now TUI, from 1997 to 2000, and Chief Commercial Officer at easyJet from 2000 to 2005. He completed his education in Economics at Newcastle University and Business Administration at Cranfield School of Management. He has over 30 years' experience in the mobility sector.

Barbara Dalibard

Barbara is a visionary leader, loved by her teams. She is a forceful advocate of sustainability as well as diversity in the workplace and has put her philosophy into action by actively developing women leaders under her leadership.

Barbara Dalibard has been President of the Supervisory Board at Michelin since 2021. Her past roles included CEO of SITA from 2016 to 2021 and CEO at Voyages SNCF from 2010 to 2016. Earlier in her career she held various positions at France Télécom and was CEO of Orange Business Services. Barbara Dalibard completed her education in mathematics at École Normale Supérieure and in Engineering at ENST (Telecom Paris). She has over 12 years' experience in the mobility sector.

Alexandre de Juniac

Alexandre was generous enough to share in great detail his leadership experience in navigating the Covid crisis at the helm of IATA. His story was full of emotion as well as pride for getting the job done in salvaging the industry during one of its most turbulent moments.

Alexandre de Juniac is a Senior Advisor in the Transportation & Services practice at Oliver Wyman, a position he took up in 2023, and a Senior Advisor at Morgan Stanley. His past roles included President of Europcar from 2021 to 2022 and Director General and CEO of the International Air Transport Association (IATA) from 2016 to 2021. Prior to this, he held several executive roles, including CEO of Air France – KLM, and senior executive positions at Thales, Thomson-CSF and other organizations, including the French Ministry of Finance where he was Chief of Staff between 2009 and 2011. Alexandre de Juniac completed his education in engineering at École Polytechnique and in administration at École Nationale d'Administration (ENA). He has over 25 years' experience in the mobility sector.

Joris d'Incà

Joris and I first worked together in the early 2000s during a rail integrator's post-merger integration. We've followed each other ever since. His long-time passion for all transport modes is shown with his bold development of the firm in the Swiss market.

Joris D'Incà has been a Partner at Oliver Wyman since 2001. He has been Global Head of the Logistics Sector since 2016 and Market Leader of Switzerland since 2015. Joris D'Incà has a master's degree in cience from ETH Zurich. He has over 30 years' experience in the mobility sector.

Josef Doppelbauer

Josef carries a combination of deep telecoms and transport experience. He has been able to bring the highly relevant experience of telecoms into the railway industry, from a technology, process and regulatory standpoint. I was pleased to chat with Josef in French, as he studied in Paris for some time.

Josef Doppelbauer is Executive Director at the European Union Agency for Railways, a role he has held since 2015. His past roles included Chairman of the European Rail Research Advisory Committee from 2012 to 2014 and CTO of Bombardier Transportation from 2008 to 2014. Earlier in his career he held various roles at Alcatel Transport Automation Solutions where he was CTO from 2001 and 2002 and Technical Director for Austria from 1997 to 2001. Josef Doppelbauer pursued his education in physics at Johannes Kepler University. He has more than 25 years' experience in the mobility sector.

Rupert Duchesne

Rupert is one of those Oliver Wyman Partners who has become a successful industry executive in the airline and then the loyalty sector. Rupert's business leadership and innovative mindset have been instrumental in bringing customer value management to the forefront of the travel sector's strategic agenda.

Rupert Duchesne is an Independent Director and Corporate Advisor serving clients in the sustainability, property development, transportation/aerospace and financial services sectors. He has served on many public and private sector boards. His previous roles include Group CEO of Aimia from 2005 to 2017 and various executive roles at Air Canada, including Chief Integration Officer during the Air Canada–Canadian Airlines merger, and CEO of Aeroplan, Air Canada's loyalty programme. Rupert Duchesne completed his education in pharmacology at the University of Leeds and business administration at Manchester Business School. He is a member of the Order of Canada. He has over 30 years' experience in the mobility sector.

Jean-Pierre Farandou

Across his career working on French railways, reaching the helm of the SNCF Group, Jean-Pierre has been an avid advocate of the rail trans–portation mode and now strongly promotes the leading contribution of rail to the transition of the mobility sector towards decarbonization.

Jean-Pierre Farandou has been Chairman and CEO of SNCF since 2019. His previous roles include Executive Chairman of the Keolis Group from 2012 to 2019, President of SNCF Proximités from 2006 to 2012 and various managerial roles in SNCF and Thalys International. Jean-Pierre Farandou studied engineering at École des Mines de Paris. He has over 40 years' experience in the mobility sector.

Xavier Huillard

A charismatic leader at one of the largest and most successful enterprises in concessions, energy and construction, Xavier always combines his strategic and business vision with thoughtful perspectives on societal trends and the evolution of humanity.

Marc Ivaldi

A veteran in transportation economics and econometrics, Marc brings unique perspectives on the sector's competitive dynamics and the impact of deregulation.

Xavier Huillard holds several positions, including Chairman and CEO of Vinci since 2010, Chairman of Vinci Concessions SAS since 2016 and Independent Director of the Executive Board of Air Liquide since 2017. Earlier in his career he had multiple executive roles within Vinci and various positions in Eiffage and SoGEA. Xavier Huillard studied engineering at École Polytechnique and École Nationale des Ponts et Chaussées. He has over 40 years' experience in the infrastructure and mobility sectors.

Marc Ivaldi is a Professor of Economics at École des Hautes Etudes en Sciences Sociales and Toulouse School of Economics. He is President of the Association Française d'Économie des Transports, Conference Director of the World Conference on Transport Research Toulouse 2026 and Head of Econometrics and Programming at NERA Consulting, roles he has held since 2022 and 2016 respectively. His past roles included President of the International Transportation Economics Association from 2018 to 2022 and Programme Director in Industrial Organization at the French Centre for Economic and Policy Research between 2003 and 2014. Marc Ivaldi studied economics at Université Toulouse I and the University of Pennsylvania. He has more than 40 years' experience in the mobility sector.

Patrick Jeantet

Patrick has had an eclectic career across multiple sectors of mobility, including engineering and construction, airports, mass transit and rail infrastructure, both in Europe and overseas, which allows him to bring broad insights across the mobility value chain.

Patrick Jeantet has served on the board of SPIE since 2020 and is a Senior Advisor for Vauban Infrastructure Partners. He was CEO and Deputy Chairman at SNCF Reseau from 2016 to 2020, Managing Director at Aéroports De Paris (ADP) from 2013 to 2016 and Managing Director France at Keolis Group from 2011 to 2013. He also held various executive positions at Keolis. Patrick Jeantet studied engineering at École Polytechnique and École Nationale des Ponts et Chaussées. He has over 35 years' experience in the mobility sector.

Mark Joseph

Mark is a thoughtful leader who brings a unique mix of leadership and entrepreneurial spirit. After taking his family transport business to new heights and joining a public transport behemoth, his next career phase included serving on the boards or as a senior advisor for a multitude of mobility businesses and start-ups.

Mark Joseph is CEO of Mobitas Advisors, a company he founded in 2019. He previously held roles such as Global Chief Commercial Officer at Transdev from 2017 to 2019, Vice Chairman and CEO North America at Transdev from 2006 to 2017, and President and CEO of Veolia Transportation from 2001 to 2006. Before 2001, he had various positions, including President and CEO of Yellow Transportation of Baltimore. Mark Joseph holds degrees in business and political science from American University. He has over 35 years' experience in the mobility sector.

Andrew Lezala

I thoroughly enjoyed working with Andrew and his management team in the UK in the mid-2000s, integrating Bombardier and Adtranz rail services businesses to build a reference after-sales services business across the industry.

Andrew Lezala is CEO of Lezala Consulting, a company he founded in 2019. Since 2016 he has been the Managing Director and CEO of Metro Trains Australia and the CEO of Metro Trains Melbourne since 2009. From 2001 to 2004, Andrew led Bombardier Transportation's global services division, the world's leading after-sales rail service provider. Andrew Lezala studied engineering at the University of Leicester. He has over 30 years' experience in the mobility sector.

Marie-Christine Lombard

Marie-Christine is a thoughtful and high-energy leader, who directed the GEODIS turnaround and is now growing its business forcefully, both organically and through M&A. She earns the respect of all via her passion for logistics services value proposition and her determination to build a global, successful and sustainable business.

Marie-Christine Lombard is CEO of GEODIS, a role she has held since 2013. Her past roles included Executive Director at GEODIS from 2012 to 2013, CEO of TNT from 2010 to 2012, and various managerial roles at TNT, Jet Services Group and Paribas. Marie-Christine Lombard completed her education in business management at École Supérieure des Sciences Économiques et Commerciales (ESSEC Business School). She has over 30 years' experience in the mobility sector.

Pierre Lortie

Pierre is a visionary leader who has worked across the aerospace and rail industries. He pioneered the regional jet aircraft product which became a blockbuster in Europe and North America, and subsequently merged two world-leading rail integrators.

Pierre Lortie is a Senior Business Advisor at Dentons Canada, a role he has held since 2004. His previous roles included Chairman of the Montréal Demerger Transition Committee from 2004 to 2005, President and COO of Bombardier Transportation from 2000 to 2003, and various leadership positions at Bombardier International, Bombardier Aerospace and Bombardier Capital. Prior to this, he was also President of the Montreal Stock Exchange. Between 1999 and 2004 he was the Representative of the Prime Minister of Canada at the APEC Business Advisory Council. Pierre Lortie completed his education in engineering at the University of Laval, economics at the University of Leuven and business administration at the University of Chicago. He has over 30 years' experience in the mobility sector.

Jean-Pierre Loubinoux

I first met Jean-Pierre when he was leading French Railways Ltd, part of SNCF in London. Jean-Pierre was instrumental in the development in 1994 of the distribution and sales network in the UK for newly launched cross-Channel rail operator Eurostar.

Since 2020, Jean-Pierre Loubinoux has held the role of Honorary CEO at the International Union of Railways (UIC). His past roles included Director General of UIC from 2009 to 2020, Chairman and CEO of SNCF International from 2001 to 2009, various positions at SNCF, including CEO of French Railways Ltd, and chairman of the Association of French Rail Engineers. Jean-Pierre Loubinoux completed his education in engineering at École Centrale de Paris. He has over 45 years' experience in the mobility sector. He is also President of the 'Cercle des Nouveaux Mondes', as well as a recognized poet and painter.

Frédéric Mazzella

Frédéric is a thoughtful entrepreneur and leader who has vastly scaled the concept of carpooling by building a worldwide community of trust which now counts 100 million members in more than 20 countries.

Frédéric Mazzella is the Founder and President of BlaBlaCar and Captain Cause. BlaBlaCar is the worldwide leader in carpooling. Captain Cause is a new platform that disrupts corporate commitment towards socially and environmentally impactful projects. Frédéric Mazzella is also the co-president entrepreneur of France Digitale, the largest association of start-ups in Europe and host of the weekly show and podcast 'Les Pionniers' on BFM Business channel, where he interviews pioneers in all domains. Frédéric Mazzella holds a master's degree in physics from the École Normale Supérieure (ENS Ulm Paris), a master's degree in computer science from Stanford University and an MBA from INSEAD. He is also the author of the book *Mission BlaBlaCar – Les coulisses de la création d'un phénomène* (Eyrolles, 2022).

Jean-Marie Metzler

Known as the 'pope' of TGV, Jean-Marie launched the very first high-speed rail technology in Europe in the early 1980s, which completely reconfigured the European mobility landscape, leading to four decades of uninterrupted growth.

Jean-Marie Metzler is an Independent Advisor for Transport and Information Systems, a position he has held since 2008. His previous roles were as Strategic Advisor to the President at SNCF International from 2005 to 2007, General Manager Division Opérateurs at Neuf Cegetel from 2003 to 2004, CEO at Telecom Development from 1997 to 2002, and Executive Vice President Grandes Lignes at SNCF from 1987 to 1994. Jean-Marie Metzler studied engineering at École Polytechnique and École Nationale des Ponts et Chaussées. He has over 40 years' experience in the mobility sector.

André Navarri

André is an authority in the rail industry, having led both Alstom and Bombardier Transportation during his career. He has been the mentor of two generations of rail designers, builders and advisors and can pride himself, among many other things, on the introduction of very high-speed rail in China in the late 2000s.

André Navarri is CEO of Avane Consulting, a role he has held since 2014. He is also Chairman of the Board at SATEBA. His past roles included Strategic Advisor to the President and CEO at Bombardier from 2013 to 2014, President and COO at Bombardier from 2004 to 2013, and various leadership roles at Alcatel-Lucent, Valeo and Alstom Transport. André Navarri completed his education in engineering at École Centrale Paris. He has more than 35 years' experience in the mobility sector.

Rana Nawas

Rana's forward-looking research on the future of airports is comprehensive and truly insightful.

Rana Nawas has been an Abu Dhabi-based Partner in Oliver Wyman's Transportation and Services practice since 2022. Prior to joining Oliver Wyman, Rana spent over a decade from 2004 to 2017 at the world's largest aircraft lessor, GE Capital Aviation Services, where she developed deep expertise in the Middle East and African aviation industry. After GE, Rana was Chief Revenue Officer for a logistics software company, helping to solve real-world infrastructure problems from 2021 to 2022. In 2017, Rana created a podcast called *When Women Win*, in which female role models share their inspirational stories and practical tools for success. It has audiences in 183 countries, is a media partner of UN Women, is aired on all Emirates Airlines flights and has been featured on CNN. Rana Nawas has a bachelor's degree in engineering and a master's in superconductivity, from the University of Oxford. She has over 22 years' experience in the mobility sector.

Guillaume Pepy

An inspiring leader with a huge strategic and commercial mindset, Guillaume has transformed SNCF Group into a growing digital mobility leader. Less discussed is his forceful enterprise transformation towards a more diverse and inclusive workforce.

Guillaume Pepy has been Chairman of Orpea since 2022 and President of Initiative France since 2020. He had various executive roles at SNCF from 1993 to 2019, including Chairman and CEO between 2008 and 2019. He also held several roles in the French government from 1987 to 1993, including Head of Cabinet of the Ministry of Labour. Guillaume Pepy studied political science at Sciences Po Paris and administration at École Nationale d'Administration (ENA). He has over 25 years' experience in the mobility sector.

Hugh Randall

I can't thank Hugh enough for bringing me into Oliver Wyman and its Transportation practice back in 1996. Hugh has been a mentor to me ever since and I have enjoyed his thoughtfulness and friendship. I have always admired his constant ability to entertain strategic conversations with industry executives on a very broad range of topics.

Hugh Randall is Senior Advisor at Oliver Wyman, a role he has held since 2006. His previous roles included Global Head of the Transportation practice at Oliver Wyman from 1992 to 2005, Senior Vice President and Managing Director at CSX/Sea-Land Logistics from 1985 to 1991, and various roles at Ryder/PIE Nationwide, Consolidated Rail Corporation and other companies. Hugh Randall studied accounting and administration at Antioch College and business administration at Harvard Graduate School of Business. He has over 40 years' experience in the mobility sector.

Sumati Sharma

In addition to her expertise in aviation as a long-time industry executive, Sumati brings a real passion for diversity and inclusion in the workplace and in the aviation and aerospace sector.

Sumati Sharma is a Partner at Oliver Wyman's Aviation practice in London, specializing in large-scale cost reduction and strategic transformation. Prior to joining Oliver Wyman, she became a Chartered Accountant with EY and then worked for Virgin Atlantic for 16 years. She took on a variety of roles at Virgin across finance, strategy, commercial and HR, covering both the airline and the tour operator. Sumati Sharma is the Founder and Board Co-Chair for the Women in Aviation and Aerospace Charter. With more than 250 companies now listed as signatories and supported by the UK government, the Charter is committed to creating a more balanced industry for women. Sumati Sharma holds a bachelor's degree in accounting and manufacturing engineering from the University of Strathclyde, Scotland, and the Chartered Accountancy fellowship from ICAS, Scotland. She completed the Senior Executive Programme at London Business School in 2022. She has over 20 years' experience in the mobility sector.

Adrian Slywotzky

Adrian is a global authority in business strategy and business design. His forward-looking mindset and inventiveness have inspired me throughout my career and I will always remember his induction speech in New York to welcome me to the global Oliver Wyman partnership.

Adrian Slywotzky is a renowned management consultant and business book author. He has published many top-selling business books, including *Demand: Creating what people love before they know they want it* (2011) and *The Profit Zone: How strategic business design will lead you to tomorrow's profits* (1998). He has been a consultant since 1979 and is now Partner Emeritus at Oliver Wyman. Adrian Slywotzky studied law at Harvard Law School and business administration at Harvard Business School.

Guillaume Thibault

My Oliver Wyman partner Guillaume is the inspiring leader of Oliver Wyman's Global Mobility Forum. He leads our research on mega-trends and co-designed the City Mobility Readiness Index.

Guillaume Thibault's work focuses on strategy, business and offer design in the travel, transport and services sector. He has been a Partner at Oliver Wyman since 2004 and has been the leader of the Oliver Wyman Mobility Forum since 2018. In 2008 he published a book titled *Quelle stratégie industrielle pour la France face à la mondialisation* while he was teaching at Cergy-Pontoise University. Guillaume Thibault completed his education in business at École Supérieure des Sciences Économiques et Commerciales (ESSEC Business School) and in political science at Sciences Po Paris. He has over 20 years' experience in the mobility sector.

Laurent Troger

Through a trusted and long-term relationship, Laurent has allowed me to learn about a hugely broad set of topics relevant to the mobility sector and the rail industry.

Laurent Troger is President of Altrius, a role he has held since 2019. His previous roles included President and COO of Bombardier Transportation from 2015 to 2019, various positions in Bombardier Transportation including CTO, COO and President of different divisions from 2004 to 2015, and Senior Vice President at Alstom Transport from 1989 to 2004. Laurent Troger studied at École Nationale Supérieure de Techniques Avancées (ENSTA Paris) and in management at INSEAD. He has over 30 years' experience in the mobility sector.

Andrew Watterson

A former Partner at Oliver Wyman, Andrew is a true expert when it comes to aviation across strategy, commercial and operations. I worked extensively with Andrew around irregular operations risk management and his depth of knowledge on this topic was truly second to none and ground-breaking. I am thrilled to see Andrew thrive at Southwest.

Andrew Watterson is Chief Operating Officer of Southwest Airlines, a position he has held since 2022. He held various executive roles at Southwest Airlines from 2013 to 2022, was Vice President of Planning and Revenue Management at Hawaiian Airlines from 2011 to 2013, and had roles at Oliver Wyman and Ernst & Young Management Consulting. Andrew Watterson completed his education in business administration at Washington University St Louis and in operations management at Vanderbilt University. He has over 20 years' experience in the mobility sector.

INDEX

Printed in the USA
CPSIA information can be obtained
at www.ICGtesting.com
JSHW061915160524
63288JS00019B/248